JOHN KNOX

IOANNES CNOXVS.

Portrait of John Knox from Beza's *Ikones*. 1580.

John Knox

THE HERO OF THE SCOTTISH REFORMATION

BY

HENRY COWAN, D.D.

AMS PRESS
NEW YORK

Reprinted from the edition of 1905, New York
First AMS EDITION published 1970
Manufactured in the United States of America

International Standard Book Number: 0-404-01788-6

Library of Congress Catalog Card Number: 70-133817

AMS PRESS, INC.
NEW YORK, N.Y. 10003

TO THE RIGHT HONOURABLE JAMES ALEXANDER
CAMPBELL, P.C., M.P., LL.D.

I Dedicate This Volume

in grateful remembrance of many words of wise counsel and
many acts of thoughtful kindness received from him during
thirty years of friendship;

and

as a sincere tribute to his private worth and public life-work,
as a high-minded and honourable statesman, a loyal and
devoted churchman, an effective writer and speaker on
religious and ecclesiastical subjects, a liberal benefactor of
the universities which he has long represented in Parliament,
and a generous friend of missionary and philanthropic
enterprise.

Henry Cowan.

PREFACE

TO have omitted John Knox from a series of *Heroes of the Reformation* would have been an unpardonable exclusion; and the year accepted by British and American Churches (whether rightly or wrongly) for the Quater-centenary commemoration of his birth, appeared to be the most appropriate time for the issue of this volume. The author acknowledges his indebtedness to earlier labourers in the same field; and his sources are given in the accompanying list. In that list (apart, of course, from what was written during or soon after the Reformer's own century), three works are of special value. *The Life of Knox*, by Rev. Dr. McCrie, published nearly a century ago, signally revived the interest not only of Scotland but of Christendom in the Reformer, and vindicated his name from many unjust imputations. Ten years ago, Professor Hume Brown gave to the world two substantial and scholarly volumes which contain almost all of importance that is known about Knox, including much that was unknown to Dr. McCrie. Most valuable of all is the monumental edition of *Knox's Works*, with learned introductions, notes, and appendices, by the late David Laing, LL.D. (1846–1864). Through this *magnum opus* the reader is able to form an independent judgment, from original sources, of the Reformer's character, history, and influence. The aim of the present writer has been, in the limited space at his disposal, to describe those portions of the career of Knox which are most likely to be of general interest; to place his life-work in its historical setting; to facilitate for students the consultation of original authorities; and to present a picture of the Reformer which, without concealing his infirmities, would help to vindicate his right to enrolment alike among the foremost heroes of the Reformation, and among the greatest and noblest of Scotsmen. In the revision of proofs, the writer's esteemed colleague, Professor Nicol, along with the editor himself, has been most helpful. To Mr. Pittendrigh Macgillivray, R.S.A., and to others, the author and publishers are indebted for permission to reproduce several illustrations. Kind friends in various scenes of Knox's ministry have contributed many photographs. The scholarly minister of Guthrie has rendered efficient service in the preparation of the Index. It is a disputed question how far one is justified, when quoting Knox, in modernising the spelling. To retain uniformly the original form of the words is not only inconvenient for many readers, but is sometimes even misleading; as when the Reformer writes of certain "pure" men, meaning not innocent but poor. The author, accordingly, has modified the spelling in most cases, retaining occasionally, however, archaic forms where such retention appeared to add to the significance.

H. C.

ABERDEEN, April, 1905.

NOTE

THE author and publishers of this work are indebted to Mr. T. Lupton, Solicitor, Stirling, for a photograph of the pulpit from which Knox preached in that town ; to the Rev. P. R. Landreth, of Perth, for photographs of the interior of St. John's Church; to the Rev. G. W. Mackenzie, English Chaplain at Frankfort, for a copy of the ancient print of the Church of the White Ladies ; and to Mr. J. McQuillen, of Newcastle, for a photograph of St. Nicholas' Church of that city, as it existed early in the eighteenth century. Permission has also been obtained to reproduce the following : (1) from Messrs. Cassell & Co., several illustrations in *Old and New Edinburgh*, viz., Edinburgh Castle (before 1573), Holyrood, St. Giles' and its former pulpit, and the supposed study in " John Knox's House " ; (2) from Messrs. Valentine & Sons, the castles of Berwick and St. Andrews, the ruins of St. Andrews Cathedral, the former pulpit of the Town Church, Greyfriars' Church, Stirling, and the Knox Memorial Stone and Tree in Giffordgate ; (3) from Mr. Alex. Inglis and Mr. A. J. Hay, Edinburgh, John Knox's House (external view) ; (4) from Mr. A. Downie, St. Andrews, the Parish Church of that city, as in the eighteenth century ; (5) from Mr. C. Bruce, Haddington, the Parish Church of that town ; and from Messrs. F. Frith & Co., Reigate, St. John's, Perth (outside view). The Librarian of Edinburgh University kindly allowed a photograph to be taken of a passage in the MS. of Knox's *Historie* in his custody.

CONTENTS

INTRODUCTORY SURVEY

INFLUENCES ALIENATING SCOTLAND FROM ROME PRIOR TO THE TIME OF JOHN KNOX

CHAPTER I

BIRTH AND EDUCATION OF KNOX—EARLY RELIGIOUS ENVIRONMENT AND ECCLESIASTICAL POSITION
1513 (OR 1505)–1543

CHAPTER II

THE REFORMATION IN SCOTLAND BETWEEN 1543
AND 1546: PARTICIPATION OF KNOX IN THE
MOVEMENT

1543–1546

CHAPTER III

KNOX AT ST. ANDREWS—HIS CALL TO THE REFORMED
MINISTRY—HIS CAPTURE BY THE FRENCH AND
EXPERIENCE IN THE GALLEYS

1546–1549

Contents

CHAPTER IV

JOHN KNOX IN ENGLAND—THE PIONEER OF PURI-
TANISM

1549–1554

CHAPTER V

KNOX ON THE CONTINENT OF EUROPE—A LEADER AND
PASTOR OF BRITISH PROTESTANT EXILES—
LITERARY ACTIVITY

1554–1559

Contents

CHAPTER VIII

FINAL RETURN OF KNOX TO SCOTLAND—THE CLOSING CONFLICT AND THE ESTABLISHMENT OF THE REFORMATION

1559–1560

Contents

Contents

CHAPTER XI

KNOX AND THE PROTESTANT STATESMEN OF SCOTLAND
—PRINCIPLE VERSUS EXPEDIENCY
1561–1565

CHAPTER XII

KNOX DURING THE PERIOD OF THE TEMPORARY DE-
PRESSION AND EVENTUAL RATIFICATION OF
PROTESTANTISM
1565–1568

CHAPTER XIII

LAST YEARS OF KNOX'S LIFE—POLITICAL, ECCLESIAS-
TICAL, AND PERSONAL TROUBLES—RESIDENCE
AT ST. ANDREWS

1568–1572

Contents

CHAPTER XIV

KNOX'S LAST DAYS—HIS DEATH—CHARACTER AND INFLUENCE

1572

ILLUSTRATIONS

ALPHABETICAL LIST OF BOOKS
REFERRED TO IN THIS WORK

COMPILED BY THE EDITOR

Acts of Parliament of Scotland [1124–1707], *The.* London, 1844 *sqq.* 12 vols.

ADAMNAN: *Vita S. Columbæ.* See *Historians of Scotland.*

AILRED: *Life of Saint Ninian.* See *Historians of Scotland.*

ALESIUS, ALEXANDER: *Primus liber Psalmorum . . . expositus.* Leipzig, 1554.

ANONYMOUS (JAMES LAWSON?) *Eximii viri Johannis Knoxii vera extremiæ vitæ et obitus historia.* See Thomas Smeton. Translated in Laing, *Works of John Knox*, vi., 649–660.

AYLMER, JOHN: *An harborowe for faithfull and trewe subjectes against the late bloune Blaste concerning the governmit of Wemen. Wherein be confuted all such reasons as a straunger of late made in that behalfe, with a briefe exhortation to obedience.* Strassburg, 1559.

BAILLIE, ALEXANDER: *True Information.* Edinburgh, 1628.

BAIN, JOSEPH: *Calendar of Documents relating to Scotland.* Edinburgh, 1881.

BALNAVES, HENRY: *A briefe sommarie of the work by Balnaves on Justification.* In Laing, *W. of K.*, iii., 13–28. *The Confession of Faith, conteining how the troubled man should seeke refuge at his God thereto led by faith: with the declaration of the article of justification at length. The order of good workes, which are the fruites of faith: And how the faithful, and justified man, should walke and live, in the perfite and true Christian religion, according to his vocation.* Edinburgh, 1584. In Laing, *W. of K.*, iii., 431–542.

BANNATYNE, GEORGE: *Ancient Scottish Poems*. Edinburgh, 1770.

BANNATYNE, RICHARD: *Memoriales of Transactions in Scotland*, 1569–73. Ed. R. Pitcairn. Edinburgh: Bannatyne Club, 1836.

BEDE: *Ecclesiastical History*. English trans., in Bohn's Antiquarian Library.

BELLESHEIM, ALPHONS: *History of the Catholic Church of Scotland*. Edinburgh, 1887–90. 4 vols.

BEZA, THEODORE: *Volumen Tractationum Theologicarum*. Geneva, 1570–82. 3 vols.

BEZA, THEODORE: *Epistolarum Theologicarum liber unus*, Geneva. 1573.

BEZA, THEODORE: *Icones, id est veræ imagines virorum doctrina simul et pietate illustrium, quorum præcipuè ministerio partim bonarum literarum studia sunt restituta, partim vera Religio in variis orbis Christiani regionibus, nostra patrúmque memoria fuit instaurata: additis eorundem vitæ & operæ descriptionibus, quibus adiectæ sunt nonnullæ picturæ quas* EMBLEMATA *vocant*. Genevæ, apud Ioannem Laonium M.D.LXXX.

Book of Common Order (*The*); *or, the form of prayers and ministration of the sacraments, etc., approved and received by the Church of Scotland*. Edinburgh, 1564 (In Laing, *W. of K.*, vi., 274–333).

Book of Discipline See *Buke*.

BOWER, WALTER: *Scotichronicon*. See *Historians of Scotland* (under John of Fordun).

BRIGGS, CHARLES AUGUSTUS: *American Presbyterianism. Its origin and history. Together with an appendix of letters and documents, many of which have recently been discovered*. New York, 1885.

BROWN, PETER HUME: *John Knox: A Biography*. London, 1895. 2 vols.

BUCHANAN, DAVID: "Life and Death of John Knox" (prefaced to his edition of John Knox's *Historie of the Reformatioun . . . of Scotland*. Edinburgh, 1644. 2d ed., 1645).

BUCHANAN, GEORGE: *The History of Scotland*. Glasgow, Edinburgh, London, 1855. 6 vols.

Buke (The) of Discipline. Edinburgh, 1560. In Laing, *W. of K.*, ii., 183–259.

BURNE, NICOL: *The Disputation concerning the controversit headdis of religion, holdin in the realme of Scotland, the zeir of God ane thousand fyue hundreth fourscoir zeiris. Betwix the prætendit ministeris of the deformed Kirk in Scotland, and Nicol Burne, Professor of Philosophie in S. Leonardis College,* &c. Paris, 1581.

BURNET, GILBERT: *The History of the Reformation of the Church of England.* Ed. N. Pocock, Oxford, 1865. 7 vols.

BURNS, WILLIAM : *The Scottish War of Independence.* Glasgow, 1874. 2 vols.

BURTON, JOHN HILL: *History of Scotland.* Edinburgh, 1867–70. 7 vols.

CALDERWOOD, DAVID: *The True History of the Church of Scotland.* Ed. T. Thomson. Edinburgh: Wodrow Society, 1842–49. 8 vols.

CALVIN, JOHN: *Opera.* Ed. Baum, Cunitz, Reuss, Erichson, Berlin, 1900. 59 vols.

CARLYLE, THOMAS: *On Heroes, Hero-worship and the Heroic in History.* London, 1840. Many editions.

CARLYLE, THOMAS: *Inaugural Address at Edinburgh,* April 2d, 1866 ("On the choice of books"). Edinburgh, 1866.

CHALMERS, GEORGE: *Caledonia.* London, 1807–24. 3 vols.

COCHET, JEAN BENOÎT DÉSIRÉ: *Répertoire Archéologique du Département de la Seine, Inférieure.* Paris, 1871.

Confessioun (The) of Faith professit and belevit be the Protestantis within the realme of Scotland. Edinburgh, 1561. In Laing, *W. of K.*, ii., 93–154.

Contra Collatorem. See PROSPER.

COOK, GEORGE: *History of the Reformation in Scotland.* Edinburgh, 1881. 3 vols.

COWAN, HENRY: *The Influence of the Scottish Church in Christendom.* London, 1896.

CRAMOND, WILLIAM: *The Truth about George Wishart.* Montrose, 1898.

CUNNINGHAM, JOHN: *The Church History of Scotland.* Edinburgh, 1859. 2 vols. 2d. ed., 1882.

DEMPSTER, THOMAS: *Historia ecclesiastica gentis Scotorum.* Ed. D. Irving. Edinburgh: Bannatyne Club, 1829.

DESMARQUETS, M.: *Mémoires chronologiques . . . de Dieppe.* Dieppe, 1785.

Diurnal of Remarkable Occurrents (A) *. . . since the Death of King James IV., till . . .* 1575. Ed. T. Thomson. Edinburgh: Bannatyne Club, 1833.

DRYSDALE, A. H.: *History of the Presbyterians in England, their Rise, Decline, and Revival.* London, 1889.

DUNBAR, WILLIAM: " Visitation of St. Francis "; " Friar of Berwick "; " Flyting." See *The Poems of William Dunbar.* Edinburgh: Scottish Text Society, 1884.

DUVAL, GUILLAUME ET JEAN: *Histoire de la Réformation à Dieppe*, 1557–1657. Ed. Emile Lesens. Rouen, 1878–79. 2 vols.

FLEMING, DAVID HAY: *Mary Queen of Scots from her Birth to her Flight into England.* London, 1897.

FORBES, ALEXANDER PENROSE: *Saint Ninian and Saint Kentigern.* See *Historians of Scotland.*

FORBES, PATRICK: *A Full View of the Public Transactions in the Reign of Queen Elizabeth.* London, 1740–41. 2 vols.

FORDUN, JOHN OF: *Chronicle of the Scottish Nation.* See *Historians of Scotland.*

FOXE, JOHN: *Acts and Monuments.* Ed. George Townsend. London, 1843–49. 8 vols.

FROUDE, JAMES ANTHONY: *History of England.* London, 1856–70. 12 vols. (Many editions).

GAIRDNER, JAMES: *The English Church in the Sixteenth Century, from the Accession of Henry VIII. to the Death of Mary.* London, 1903.

GREGORY I., POPE: *Epistles.* Eng. trans. of selected epistles by James Barmby, in Nicene and Post-Nicene Fathers. 2d series, vol. xiii. The Epistles on Image Worship in Marseilles are ix., 105 (p. 23) and xi., 13 (p. 53).

GRUB, GEORGE: *An Ecclesiastical History of Scotland, from the Introduction of Christianity to the Present Time.* Edinburgh, 1861. 4 vols.

GUIBERT, MICHEL CLAUDE: *Mémoires pour servir à l' Histoire de la Ville de Dieppe.* Dieppe, 1878. 2 vols.

Books Referred To xxvii

HADDAN, ARTHUR WEST, and STUBBS, WILLIAM. Ed. of Henry Spelman's *Councils and Ecclesiastical Documents.* Oxford, 1869–78. 4 vols.

HAILES, DAVID DALRYMPLE: *Annals of Scotland.* 3d ed. Edinburgh, 1819. 3 vols.

HAMILTON, ARCHIBALD: *De confusione Calvinianæ sectæ apud Scotos Ecclesiæ nomen ridicule usurpantis dialogus.* Paris, 1577.

HAMILTON, ARCHIBALD: *Calvinianæ Confusionis demonstratio, contra maledicam ministrorum Scotiæ responsionem, in duos divisa libros. Quorum prior: proprietatum veræ Ecclesiæ evictionim: posterior, earundem in hypothesi ad res subjectas applicatarum, contentionem continet.* Paris, 1581.

Hamilton Papers, The. Letters and Papers illustrating the political relations of England and Scotland in the XVI. Century. Formerly in the possession of the Duke of Hamilton, now in the British Museum. Ed. Joseph Bain. Edinburgh, 1890–92. 2 vols.

HARDY, SAMUEL: *Histoire de l' Église Protestante de Dieppe.* Paris, 1897.

HENRY, PAUL: *Das Leben Johann Calvins.* Hamburg, 1835–44. 3 vols. Eng. trans. by Henry Stebbins, London, 1851. 2 vols.

HERKLESS, JOHN: *Cardinal Beaton.* London, 1891.

Historians (The), of Scotland. Edinburgh, 1871–80. 10 vols. Vols. i., iv., John of Fordun's *Chronicle of the Scottish Nation.* Ed. W. F. Skene, 1871, 1874. Vols. ii, iii., ix., Andrew of Wyntoun, *Metrical Chronicle.* Ed. D. Laing, 1872, 1879. Vol. v., *Lives of Saint Ninian* [by Ailred] and *of Saint Kentigern* [by Jocelyne]. Ed. A. P. Forbes, 1874. Vol. vi., *Life of Saint Columba,* written by Adamnan. Ed. W. Reeves, 1874. Vols. vii., x., *The Book of Pluscarden,* being unpublished continuation of Fordun's *Chronicle,* by M. Buchanan. Ed. Felix Skene, 1877, 1880. Vol. viii., Thomas Innes, *Critical Essay on the Ancient Inhabitants of Scotland.* Ed. George Grub, 1879.

"History of the Estate of Scotland from 1558–1560." In *Wodrow Miscellany.* See Laing, David.

HODGE, CHARLES: *The Constitutional History of the Presby-*

terian Church in the United States of America. Part I., 1705–1741. Part II., 1741–1788. Philadelphia, 1839–40. 2 vols.

HURAUT, ÉTIENNE: *John Knox et ses relations avec les églises reformées du Continent.* Cahors, 1902.

JOCELYNE: *Life of Saint Kentigern.* See *Historians of Scotland.*

KEITH, ROBERT: *The History of the Affairs of Church and State in Scotland from the beginning of the Reformation to 1568.* Edinburgh, 1734. Reprinted by the Spottiswoode Society, Edinburgh, 1844–50. 3 vols.

KERR, SAMUEL: *Where John Knox was Born.* Edinburgh, 1860.

KNOX, JOHN: *History of the Reformation.* Ed. David Laing. See Laing, *Works of Knox.* Quoted uniformly as Knox, *H. of R.*

LABANOFF (Lobanov-Rostovsky, Alexsander Ivanovich), Prince: *Lettres inédites de Marie Stuart.* Paris, 1839.

LAING, DAVID: *The Works of John Knox.* Edinburgh: Wodrow Society, 1846–64. 6 vols. (Quoted uniformly as Laing, *W. of K.*).

LAING, DAVID: *The Miscellany of the Wodrow Society, containing Tracts and Original Letters Chiefly Relating to the Ecclesiastical Affairs of Scotland during the Sixteenth and Seventeenth Centuries.* Edinburgh: Wodrow Society, 1844.

LAING, JAMES: *De vita et moribus atque rebus gestis hereticorum nostri temporis.* Paris, 1581.

LANG, ANDREW: *History of Scotland.* Edinburgh, 1900–1904. 3 vols.

LAW, THOMAS GRAVES: *New Testament in Scots.* London, 1901.

LEE, JOHN: *Lectures on the History of the Church of Scotland from the Reformation to the Revolution Settlement.* Ed. William Lee. Edinburgh, 1860. 2 vols.

LEES, JAMES CAMERON: *St. Giles', Edinburgh. Church College and Cathedral from the earliest times to the present day.* Edinburgh, 1889.

LESLEY, JOHN: *History of Scotland, 1436–1561.* Edinburgh, 1830.

(LESLIE): *The historie of Scotland, wrytten first in Latin . . . translated into Scottish.* Edinburgh: Scottish Text Society, 1885–95. 2 vols.

Livre des Anglois à Genève. Ed. J. S. Burn. London, 1831. Ed. also by A. F. Mitchell (see below). Also by H. B. Hacket in the "Bibliotheca Sacra." (Andover, Mass.) Vol. for 1862.

LORIMER, PETER: *Precursors of Knox; or, Memoirs of Patrick Hamilton. . . . Alexander Alane or Alesius, . . . and Sir David Lindsay, of the Mount.* Edinburgh, 1857. 2d ed., 1860.

LORIMER, PETER: *The Scottish Reformation.* London and Glasgow, 1860.

LORIMER, PETER: *John Knox and the Church of England.* London, 1875.

LOUDEN, DAVID: *The History of Morham.* Haddington, 1889.

LUTHER, MARTIN: *Briefwechsel.* Best ed. E. L. Enders. Frankfurt-am-Main, 1884 *sqq.* Luther's letters will be found translated into modern German in vols. xxia and *b.*, of the Walch edition of Luther's writings, published by the Concordia Publishing House. St. Louis, Mo., 1903–5.

LYNDSAY, SIR DAVID: *The Poetical Works.* (Contains his "Complaynt of the Papyngo," "Ane Pleasant Satyre of the Thrie Estaites in commendation of vertue and vituperation of vice," and "The Tragedie of the Cardinall.") Ed. George Chalmers, London, 1806, 3 vols.; David Laing, Edinburgh, 1871, 3 vols.; Early English Text Society, London, 1863, *sqq.*

McCRIE, THOMAS: *The Life of John Knox.* Edinburgh, 1812. Many editions, best by Thomas McCrie, the younger. Edinburgh, 1855.

McCRIE, THOMAS: *Life of Andrew Melville.* 2d ed. Edinburgh, 1824. 2 vols.

McCRIE, THOMAS (the younger): *Sketches of Scottish Church History.* Edinburgh, 1841, n. e., 1875.

MAJOR, JOHN: *A History of Greater Britain, as well England as Scotland.* Trans. by A. Constable. Edinburgh: Scottish Historical Society, 1892.

MAJOR, JOHN: *Quartus sententiarum* [of Peter Lombard]. Paris, 1509, n. e., 1519.

MAJOR, JOHN: Commentary on Matthew (*in quatuor Evangelia expositiones*). Paris, 1529.

MARSDEN, JOHN BUXTON: *The History of the Early Puritans from the Reformation to the opening of the Civil War in 1642.* London, 1850.

MARTEILHE, JEAN: *Autobiography.* Trans. from the French. London: R. T. S., 1866 (later editions).

MARTINE, GEORGE: *Reliquiae Divi Andreæ; or, The State of the . . . See of St. Andrews.* St. Andrews, 1797.

MATHIESON, W. L.: *Politics and Religion: A Study in Scottish History from Reformation to Revolution.* Edinburgh, 1902. 2 vols.

MATTHEW PARIS: *Historia Anglorum.* Eng. trans. *English history, 1235–1273.* In Bohn's Antiquarian Library.

MELANCHTHON, PHILIP: *Opera* in "Corpus Reformatorum," i. Halle, 1834.

MELVILLE, JAMES: *Memoirs of his own Life; 1549–93.* Ed. T. Thomson. Edinburgh: Bannatyne Club, 1827.

MILLER, DAVID: *The Lamp of Lothian; or, The History of Haddington.* Haddington, 1844.

MILLER, ROBERT: *John Knox and the Town Council of Edinburgh.* Edinburgh, 1898.

MILLIGAN, GEORGE: *The English Bible. A Sketch of its History.* Edinburgh, 1895.

MITCHELL, ALEXANDER FERRIER: *The Scottish Reformation.* London, 1900.

MONCRIEFF, JAMES: *The Influence of Knox and the Scottish Reformation on England.* London (Y. M. C. A. Lectures), 1860.

MONIPENNIE, JOHN: *The abridgement or summarie of the Scots Chronicles.* Edinburgh, 1633. 2d ed., 1650.

Munimenta Alme Universitatis Glasguensis. Glasgow: Maitland Club, 1854. 4 vols.

MURRAY (afterwards AUST), Hon. S. (Mrs.): *A Companion and Useful Guide to the Beauties of Scotland &c.* London, 1779–1803. 2 vols.

NAU, CHARLES: *The History of Mary Stewart, from the*

Murder of Riccio until her Flight into England. Edinburgh, 1883.

National MSS. of Scotland, Facsimiles of. Southampton, 1867–71. 3 parts.

PERRY, GEORGE GRESLEY: *History of the Reformation in England.* London, 1886.

PETRIE, ALEXANDER: *A Compendious History of the Catholick Church from . . . 600 to 1600.* Hague, 1662.

PINKERTON, JOHN: *History of Scotland.* Edinburgh, 1797. 2 vols.

PITSCOTTIE (properly Robert Lindsay of Pitscottie): *The History and Chronicles of Scotland.* Ed. A. J. G. Mackay. Edinburgh: Scottish Text Society, 1899.

Pluscarden, Book of. See *Historians of Scotland.*

Proceedings of the Society of Antiquaries of Scotland. See *Transactions.*

PROSPER, of Aquitaine: *Chronicon.* In Migne, *Pat. Lat.* LI.

PROSPER, of Aquitaine: *Liber contra Collatorem* (against Cassian's *Collationes Patrum*). *Ibid.*

Registre des Bourgeois, of Geneva. Preserved in Geneva.

Registrum Episcopatus Glasguensis, Munimenta Ecclesie Metropolitane Glasguensis a sede restaurata seculo ineunte XII. ad reformatam religionem. Ed. C. Innes. Edinburgh: Bannatyne Club, 1843. 2 vols.

ROBERTSON, JOSEPH: *Statuta (Concilia Scotiæ Ecclesiæ Scoticanæ statuta* — 1225–1559.) Ed. Joseph Robertson. Edinburgh: Bannatyne Club, 1866.

ROGERS, CHARLES: *Life of George Wishart.* Edinburgh, 1876.

ROGERS, CHARLES: *Genealogical Memoirs of John Knox and of the Family of Knox.* London: Grampian Club, 1879.

ROW, JOHN: *The History of the Kirk of Scotland,* 1558–1639. Edinburgh, Wodrow Society, 1842.

RUTHVEN, PATRICK: *A Relation of the Death of David Rizzio.* London, 1699.

SADLER PAPERS (*The State Papers and Letters of Sir Ralph Sadler.* Ed. Arthur Clifford. Edinburgh, 1809. 2 vols.).

SCHAFF, PHILIP: *History of the Christian Church.* Vol. vii. *The Swiss Reformation.* New York, 1892.

SKELTON, JOHN: *Maitland of Lethington and the Scotland of Mary Stuart*. Edinburgh, 1887. 2 vols.

SKENE, WILLIAM FORBES: *Celtic Scotland*. Edinburgh, 1876–80. 3 vols.

SMETON, THOMAS: *Ad virulentum Archibaldi Hamiltonii Apostatæ dialogum, de confusione Calvinianæ Sectæ apud Scotos . . . orthodoxa respondia . . . Adjecta est vera historia extremæ vitæ et obitus Johannis Knoxii*. Edinburgh, 1579.

SMITH, WM., and CHEETHAM, SAMUEL: *Dictionary of Christian Antiquities*. London: John Murray, 1875–80. 2 vols.

Spalding Club (The new) *Miscellany*. Aberdeen, 1890.

SPOTTISWOODE, JOHN: *History of the Church of Scotland*. Edinburgh: Spottiswoode Society, 1847–51. 3 vols.

STALKER, JAMES: *John Knox, his Ideas and Ideals*. London and New York, 1904.

STARK, JOHN: *The Picture of Edinburgh*. Edinburgh, 1806. Sixth edition, 1834.

State Papers published under the authority of His Majesty's Commission. London, 1830 *sqq.*

STEBBING, HENRY: *Life of Calvin*. See Henry, Paul.

STEPHEN, THOMAS: *The History of the Church of Scotland, from the Reformation to the Present Time*. London, 1843–45. 4 vols.

STEVENSON, ROBERT LOUIS: *Familiar Studies of Men and Books*. London, 1882.

STORY, ROBERT HERBERT: *The Church of Scotland, Past and Present*. London, 1890–91. 5 vols.

STRYPE, JOHN: *Ecclesiastical Memorials*. London, 1721. 3 vols. (The Clarendon Press ed. of his works, Oxford, 1812–24. 19 vols.)

TEULET, JEAN BAPTISTE ALEXANDRE THÉODORE: *Papiers d'État relatifs à l'histoire de l'Écosse au XVIe siècle*. Edinburgh: Bannatyne Club, 1851–60. 3 vols.

THEINER, AUGUSTUS: *Vetera Monumenta Hibernorum et Scotorum historiam illustrantia*. Rome, 1864.

THOMPSON, ROBERT ELLIS: *A History of the Presbyterian Churches in the United States*. New York, 1895.

Transactions (or *Proceedings*) *of the Society of Antiquaries of Scotland.* Edinburgh, 1792 *sqq.*

TURGOTUS: *Vita Margaretæ.* Eng. trans. by William Forbes-Leith: *Life of Saint Margaret, Queen of Scotland.* 3d ed. Edinburgh, 1896.

TYTLER, PATRICK FRASER: *England under the Reigns of Edward VI. and Mary.* London, 1839. 2 vols.

TYTLER, PATRICK FRASER: *History of Scotland.* Edinburgh, 1850. n. e., London, 1877. 4 vols.

VITET, LOUIS: *Histoire des anciennes villes de France. Haute Normandie.* Dieppe. Paris, 1833.

WARREN, FREDERICK EDWARD: *Liturgy and Ritual of the Celtic Church.* Oxford, 1881.

WEBSTER, RICHARD: *A History of the Presbyterian Church in America, from its Origin until the Year 1760. With Biographical Sketches of its Early Ministers.* Philadelphia, 1858.

WINZET, NINIAN: *Certane tractatis for reformation of doctryne and maneris in Scotland,* 1562–3. Ed. J. K. Hewison. Edinburgh: Scottish Text Society, 1888–90.   2 vols.

Wodrow Miscellany. See Laing, David.

WYNTOUN: *Cronykil.* See *Historians of Scotland.*

JOHN KNOX

INTRODUCTORY SURVEY

INFLUENCES ALIENATING SCOTLAND FROM ROME PRIOR TO THE TIME OF JOHN KNOX

JOHN KNOX, by universal acknowledgment, is the hero of the Scottish Reformation. In the final revolt of Scotland against Rome, as well as in the establishment, organisation, and consolidation of the Reformed Church, his influence was paramount and his service unique. Not only, however, does an important share in the accomplishment of the work belong to his immediate predecessors, as well as coadjutors, in the sixteenth century; but the way was prepared by a series of events and a chain of influences extending over many generations.

I. The foundations of the Christian Church in what is now called Scotland were laid, for the most part, independently of the Roman See. The direct connection with Rome of Ninian of Whithorn in Galloway—the earliest conspicuous figure of North British Christendom—rests mainly on the meagre testimony of the Venerable Bede who wrote in 731, three centuries after Ninian's death. He states that Ninian was "a most reverend bishop and holy man of the British nation, who had been regularly instructed at Rome in the faith and in the mysteries of the truth," [1] but he says not a word about Ninian having been sent on a mission by Rome, or of Rome exercising any ecclesiastical authority over or through him. Palladius was undoubtedly sent forth, as his contemporary, Prosper of Acquitaine, testifies, by Cœlestius, Bishop of Rome, in 431 A.D., to be "first bishop of the Scots who believe in Christ" [2]; and a brief missionary ministry among the Scots of Ireland is universally attributed to him; but it is disputed whether what is now called Scotland received more than his venerated bones. [3] Even if the story of his arrival in the Mearns (Kin-

---

[1] Bede, *Hist. Eccl.*, iii., 4. Ailred's account (in the twelfth century) of Ninian being sent forth by the Bishop of Rome as an apostle to North Britain is too late to be trustworthy. (*Life of S. Ninian*, chap. ii.)

[2] Prosper, *Chron.*, under 431; *Cont. Collat.*, ch. xxi.

[3] The late Dr. W. F. Skene, the chief modern authority regarding Celtic Scotland, considers it "probable" that only the relics of Palladius were brought to the Mearns by his disciple, Ternan; on the ground (1) that in an Irish composition belonging to the ninth century, Palladius is represented as suffering martyrdom in Ireland, and (2) that in another ancient document, Ternan is identified with Palladius (Skene, *Celtic Scotland*, ii., 27–30). Andrew Lang concurs with Skene (*Hist. of Sc.*, i., 20).

cardineshire) be accepted,[1] his influence was local
and limited: the later records of an extensive
ecclesiastical organisation created by him in Scotland are unhistorical.[2]   Kentigern entered on his
missionary career in the valley of the Clyde about
the middle of the sixth century, not only without
any Roman commission, but—if the disinterested
testimony of his biographer in the twelfth century can be trusted—after consecration at Glasgow
administered by a single bishop, and therefore,
from the Roman standpoint, irregular.[3]

Still more significant is the entrance of Kentigern's great contemporary, Columba, on his memorable ministry as Abbot of Iona and Apostle
of Caledonia, neither on Roman impulse nor under

---

[1] Haddan and Stubbs (*Counc. and Eccl. Doc.*, vol. ii., part
ii., 291) regard the "balance of evidence" as in favour of
this view.

[2] Skene, ii., 31, 32, 197. The exaggerated representation
of Palladius's work in Scotland depends mainly on the
authority of Fordun, *Scotichr.*, iii., 8, 9 (fourteenth century).

[3] Jocelyne, *Life of S. Kent.*, xi.   Jocelyne wrote this biography on the basis of documents and traditions found in
Glasgow. He must have discovered strong evidence of the
non-Roman character of Kentigern's consecration; otherwise he would hardly, as a Roman monk, have given promin-
ence to the irregularity. On the other hand, his account of
Kentigern's seven journeys to Rome and of a pontifical confirmation of his irregular episcopate cannot be accepted as
historical: the tradition is apparently the outcome of later
belief in the necessity of such ratification. See Grub, *Eccl.
Hist. of Scot.*, i., 40; Forbes, *S. Ninian and S. Kent.*, p.
355.

papal patronage.[1] Ecclesiastical independence
was a characteristic of the Columban Church.
In the period which immediately followed the
death of its founder in 597, this Church, rather
than accept certain Roman usages (particularly
regarding the exact time of observing Easter)
inconsistent with Celtic tradition, withdrew
in 664 from its great work of Anglo-Saxon
evangelisation inaugurated at Lindisfarne, thirty
years before, by Aidan, a monk of Iona.[2] There
is no trace in Scotland, for several centuries after
Columba's time of what Protestants regard as
"Mary-worship," or of the superstitious veneration of images; although these errors, during this
period, became prevalent in Roman Christendom.[3]
The government of the early Scottish Church

[1] Adamnan, *Life of S. Col.*, 2nd Pref.; i., 7; iii., 4; Bede,
Hist. Eccl., iii., 4.

[2] Bede, iii., 3, 5, 21–26. The significance of this proceeding
is not nullified by the Church's *voluntary* adoption (in the
eighth century) of the Roman mode of fixing the date of
Easter.

[3] For illustrations of the Virgin in Christian art as an
object of ultra-veneration so early as the sixth century, see
Smith, *Dict. Chr. Ant.*, ii., 1154. This excessive veneration
was fostered through the designation "Theotokos"—Mother
of God—(sanctioned by the Council of Chalcedon in 451), as
well as through the festival of the Virgin's "Assumption,"
instituted in the sixth century. During the pontificate of
Gregory I. (590–604), a bishop of Marseilles represented
"image-worship" as rife in his diocese (Greg., *Epis.*, xi., 13).
In 787, the ultra-veneration of images already established as a
usage, was sanctioned by the Seventh Œcumenical Council,
which was acknowledged by Rome.

was vested not in bishops, but in abbots, and a bishop, while admitted to functional precedence in the celebration of Holy Communion and in the Ordination service, was under the jurisdiction of an abbot of Iona who was simply a presbyter.[1] Down to the age of Queen Margaret, moreover, in the eleventh century, the Church retained a non-Roman liturgy which to Catholic churchmen of the time appeared to be a "ritus barbarus"[2]; the Benedictine rule which mainly regulated Roman and monastic life was ignored[3]; and the territorial subdivisions of parish and diocese, established elsewhere, were in Scotland unknown.[4]

II. The spiritual decay of the Celtic Church of Scotland in the tenth and eleventh centuries paved the way for the Romanising as well as (in many respects) reforming influence of the Saxon

[1] Bede, iii., 4; Adam., *L. of S. Col.*, i., 29, 35.

[2] So it is called by Turgot, Queen Margaret's confessor and biographer, *Vita Marg.*, ii., 16. Probably, however, it was an ancient form of service, having affinity with the Gallic, Spanish, and Eastern liturgies. See Warren, *Celtic Ritual*, pp. 164, 165, who illustrates such affinity from the liturgical fragment (ninth century) in the *Book of Deer*.

[3] This rule appears to have been introduced into Scotland in 1097, when King Edgar restored Coldingham Monastery as a Benedictine "house." See Grub, *Eccl. Hist. of Sc.*, i., 205.

[4] Ednam, in Roxburghshire, is believed to be the earliest-founded parish in Scotland (1100 A.D.). See deed of foundation in *National MSS. of Scot.*, Part I., 8. The division into dioceses began about 1107 under King Alexander I., who created the Sees of Moray and Dunkeld out of the national bishopric of St. Andrews. His brother and successor, David I., practically completed the diocesan organisation.

Queen Margaret and her sons (1067–1153 A.D.).
Yet even after the Church had become Roman
in constitution and in usage, much of the Celtic
spirit of independence survived.   Amid occasional
controversy, indeed, with the Archbishops of York,
who claimed jurisdiction over bishops in Scotland,[1] the Scottish Church readily appropriated
the designation, conferred in 1188 by Pope
Clement III., of "Filia specialis" of the Roman
See.[2]   But otherwise subjection to Rome was
conspicuously minimised, and sometimes deliberately withheld[3].   In the latter part of the twelfth
century, King William the Lion and a bishop
of St. Andrews defied a papal excommunication
and interdict.[4]   In the following century Kings
Alexander II. and III., with the support of the
leading clergy, resisted the intrusion of papal
legates who offered advice which was not wanted,
and claimed (in the name of maintenance) money
which could ill be spared.[5]   In 1274, King and
clergy "with one voice and one heart" refused a

---

[1] *Book of Pluscarden*, vi., 30, 31.

[2] Jos. Robertson, *Statuta Eccl. Scot.*, i., p. xxxix.

[3] "The Scots were never tractable children of Rome."—
Andrew Lang, *Hist. of Sc.*, i., 227.

[4] *Scotichr.* (Bower), vi., 36, 37.

[5] Alexander II. is said to have met the legate of Pope
Gregory IX. at York in 1237, and to have warned him that
if he came to Scotland it would be at the risk of his life!
(Matthew Paris, *Chronica*, iii., 414).   Alexander III., in 1265,
"after consultation with the clergy of the realm," refused
the "visitation" of a legate (*Scotichr.*, x., 22).

papal demand for crusade-tithes[1]. During the
Wars of Scottish Independence, opposition to
papal interference and disregard of Roman jurisdiction were yet more notable. When Pope Boni-
face VIII., in 1302, denounced the patriotic
hierarchy of Scotland who had sympathised with
Wallace as "abettors of disturbance and discord," [2] the practical reply was a more definite
espousal of the national cause by the leading
clergy. In 1304, Lamberton, the Bishop of St.
Andrews, entered into a patriotic covenant with
Robert Bruce.[3] The Bishop of Moray, with special
reference to the periodical demands of the Roman
See for help against the Moslems, declared that
it was as "meritorious to rise in arms against the
King of England as to engage in a crusade for
the recovery of the Holy Land." [4] In 1306, when
a papal excommunication was about to be pronounced at Rome upon Bruce after the slaughter
of the Comyn in the Greyfriars' Church of Dum-
fries, Wishart, Bishop of Glasgow, along with
other clergy, crowned the delinquent at Scone.[5]
Three years later a General Council of the Scottish
Church at Dundee issued "to all the faithful in

[1] Fordun, *Annals*, chap. lix.

[2] Theiner, *Monumenta*, p. 171; Bellesheim, *Cath. Ch. of
Sc.* (Blair's transl.), ii., 11.

[3] Hailes, *Annals*, i., 309.

[4] William Burns, *Scottish War of Indep.*, ii., 188.

[5] Hailes, ii., 2; Bellesh., ii., 12. The papal interdict which
followed the excommunication was ignored (Burns, ii., 192).

Christ" a manifesto in which they render due
fealty to Bruce as "King of Scotland," declaring
that "with him the faithful of the kingdom will
live and die." [1]

Papal absolutions occasionally met with no
more respect in Scotland than papal bans. In
1329, a man charged with murder, whom the
Pope had absolved, was nevertheless condemned
and executed. [2] Defiance of Rome in the sphere
of discipline was accompanied by resistance to
Roman intrusion and extortion in the dispensa-
tion of ecclesiastical patronage. In 1322, Pope
John XXII. presented an Italian to a Glasgow
benefice. King Robert Bruce, with the aid of the
bishop of the diocese, set aside the presentation,
and a Scot received the charge. [3] Early in the
fifteenth century James I. and his Parliament
withstood the usurpation of Scottish church patronage by Rome; as well as the papal abuse by
which benefices were virtually sold under the pre-
text of confirmation fees being exacted. [4] The
support which the King received in this matter
from the hierarchy moved Pope Eugenius IV., in
1436, to denounce certain Scottish bishops as
"Pilates rather than prelates." [5] Manifestly,

---

[1] *National MSS. of Sc.*, Part II., No. XVII.

[2] *Scotichr.*, xiii., 18; Hailes, *Annals*, ii., 149.

[3] *Reg. Epis. Glasg.*, i., 230.

[4] *Acts of Parl. of Sc.*, pp. 6, 16 (year 1424); Rankine, in
Story's *Church of Sc.*, ii., 291–292.

[5] Robertson, *Statuta*, i., p. lxxxv.; Theiner, 373.

during this period of Roman jurisdiction the " Filia specialis" of the Roman See gave ample evidence of her determination not to be hampered by maternal leading-strings.

III. Scotland owes much to her Roman clergy —beautiful cathedrals and abbeys; a goodly educational heritage, and not a few bright examples of devotion: but, before the close of the fourteenth century, Scottish resistance to papal aggression had begun to be supplemented by resentment at clerical demoralisation. In the latter part of that century Christendom had been scandalised by the mutual anathemas of rival pontiffs during the period of Papal schism; and in 1410 this scandal was exceeded by the appointment of a pope—John XXIII.—whose flagrant immorality excited universal disgust. Turpitude in the Roman See could not but be widely reproduced among the clergy, and in Scotland there were special causes of declension. During the long conflict with England, church dignitaries often neglected their spiritual functions in order to engage in warfare,[1] and set the example, under pressure, of repeated breach of their oaths of allegiance.[2] The social disorganisation, moreover, which

---

[1] The practice of a portion of the clergy may be gathered from the fact that a synod, held during this period at St. Andrews, considered it necessary to forbid priests to carry about long knives called "hangers," or to celebrate mass in a short secular tunic. (Robertson, *Statuta*, ii., 66, 67.)

[2] Burton, *Hist. of Sc.*, ii., 258; Burns, ii., 170–171.

resulted from protracted political troubles, undermined clerical discipline. This is illustrated by the leniency with which a Scottish ecclesiastical statute of the fourteenth century dealt with priestly concubinage. After a first, and again after a second warning the transgressor was to be punished with a moderate fine; only after the neglect of a third warning was suspension to be pronounced.[1]

King James I., although hampered as a church reformer by his need of help from the clergy against a turbulent nobility, gave voice in 1425 to the growing national discontent in a remarkable letter of admonition to the heads of monasteries. He declares that the degeneracy of the times is due largely to the covetousness and carnality of the religious orders; exhorts those whom he addresses to "manifest a holy strictness"; and warns them that "where the helm of discipline is neglected, nothing remains but the shipwreck of religion."[2] Bishop Wardlaw also, who held the See of St. Andrews under James I., signalised his episcopate by his "repression of many disorders which had crept in among the clergy."[3] His successor, Bishop Kennedy, was equally earnest in

[1] Robertson, *Statuta*, ii., 65.

[2] *Scotichr.*, xvi., 32.

[3] Geo. Martine, *Reliquiæ Div. Andr.*, pp. 230–232 (composed in 1683; but an old MS. is quoted). Dempster (*Hist. Eccl.*, ii., 660) states that in his time (seventeenth century) a work of Wardlaw was extant, entitled *Reformation of the Clergy*.

his endeavour to remove ecclesiastical abuses, and with this view visited each parish in his diocese four times a year.[1]   Before the close of the fifteenth century, however, the evil apparently had become too deep-seated for cure without drastic treatment.   In 1459, James II. petitioned the Pope to suppress a monastery of Red Friars in Ayrshire on account of their flagrant and abominable immorality.[2]   A synodal Statute of St. Andrews during the primacy of Bishop Forman (1515–1521) admits that even the lenient laws against clerical licentiousness had not in the past been enforced.[3]   How, indeed, could such statutes be effectively administered by ecclesiastical dignitaries who themselves were often heinous transgressors?[4]

To this gross abuse, which could not but alienate from the Church a large proportion of the virtuous, there was added another scandal which moved the contempt of the intelligent—clerical ignorance.   The story related by Foxe regarding Bishop Crighton of Dunkeld (consecrated in 1527), whose learning was confined to his breviary and pontifical, and who thanked God that he "never knew what the Old and New Testaments were," is probably legendary; but the very fact of its

---

[1] Lesley, *Hist. of Sc.*, p. 37 (Vernac. ed.); Spottisw., ii., 33; Buchan., *Hist. of Sc.*, xii., 23; Pitscottie, *Hist. of Sc.*, p. 110.

[2] Theiner, 421–422.

[3] Robertson, *Statuta*, i., p. cclxxii.

[4] *Ibid.*, ii., 283.

being handed down as a proverbial testimony is significant.[1] The troubles of the time are expressly ascribed by an ecclesiastical council in 1549 to the " crass ignorance," along with " moral corruption," prevalent among " clergy of all ranks." [2] A suggestive side-light is thrown on the wide-spread incapacity of the priesthood in the age preceding the Reformation by the warning which accompanied the publication of Archbishop Hamilton's Catechism in 1552.

"Let rectors, vicars, curates take care to prepare themselves by daily repetition of the portion (of the Catechism) to be read on the next occasion, in order that they may not expose themselves to the mockery of their hearers, by stammering or stumbling." [3]

While the virtuous and the intelligent were thus estranged from the Church by the immorality and ignorance of the ministry, a third scandal excited the animosity even of the worldly-minded and the ill-living—clerical covetousness. At the

---

[1] Foxe, *Acts and Monuments*, v., 622 (Townsend's ed.). He states that out of the incident a proverb arose in Scotland, "Ye are like the Bishop of Dunkeld that knew neither old nor new law." *Cf.* Lyndsay, *Satyre of the Three Estaites*, l. 2920–2922, where the "Spirituality" is represented (about 1535 A. D.) as acknowledging:

"I read never the New Testament nor Auld:
Nor ever think to do so by the Rood:
I hear Friars say that reading does no good."

[2] Robertson, *Statuta*, ii., 81.
[3] *Ibid.*, 138.

close of the fifteenth century, about one-half of
the wealth of the kingdom is believed to have
been in ecclesiastical hands,[1] and an impoverished
or self-seeking nobility and gentry were thus
tempted to become spoilers of the Church. Yet
clerical greed continued to manifest itself in multiplied pluralities and ecclesiastical exactions. It
was common for a bishop to supplement his ample
episcopal income with the revenue of one or more
rich abbacies. Even Bishop Kennedy was not
free from this abuse.[2] In preceding periods the
Church had been endowed by the munificence of
the living; she now enriched herself through
thinly veiled plunder of the dying and the dead.
The Provincial Council held at Perth in 1428 declared that bishops had the right to confirm all
wills and to appoint executors for intestates; that
one-third of what was left without a will should
be set apart mainly for funeral rites and subsequent masses; and that the service of the bishop
should be requited with a tax of twelve pence

---

[1] Pinkerton, *Hist. of Sc.*, ii., 415; Rankine, in Story's *Ch.
of Sc.*, ii., 426. The Spiritual Estate allowed the Church to
be burdened with one half of any special assessment.

[2] Major, *Hist. of Greater Brit.*, vi., 19. Dunbar, in his
World's Instability, refers to bishops who held seven benefices. Archbishop James Beaton held the Chancellorship and
the Abbacies of Dunfermline, Arbroath, and Kilwinning.
The scandal was often disguised under the practice of ap-
pointing to benefices *in commendam* (*i. e.*, in trust); the appointment being nominally temporary (to supply a vacancy),
but practically permanent.

in the pound.[1] Among extortions which pressed
hard on the peasantry was the carrying off by
the priest of the "upmost cloth" or bed-cover,
and also of what was called the "kirk-cow," as
clerical dues after a death [2]; while Candlemas
and Easter offerings, fees for baptism, marriage,
and other ceremonies, clerk-mail, teind-ale, and
other exactions, caused the priest to be regarded
as a "devourer of widows' houses" and a greedy
absorber of poor men's gains.[3]

Not a Protestant historian, but Lesley, the last
Roman Catholic Bishop of Ross, thus describes
the ecclesiastical demoralisation which he dates
from the death of Bishop Kennedy in 1474. The
"secular" clergy "fell from all devotion and godliness to the works of wickedness." "Foul disgrace infected monasteries and monks through all
Scotland." "Idleness, luxury, and all bodily indulgence crept into religious houses." "God's
service began to be neglected." "Through such
accumulated abuses the clergy incurred the hatred of the common people."[4] Not a Protestant

---

[1] Robertson, *Statuta*, ii., 78.

[2] The "kirk-cow" was so called from its being regarded as
a recompense to the priest for service. See Lyndsay (*Satyre
of the Three Estaites*, vv. 1971–2000), where the pauper is
represented as accounting for his "misery" through the vicar
taking one cow when his father died, a second at the death of
his mother, and the third and last after his wife's funeral.

[3] See *First Book of Disc.*, vi.; Major, *Greater Brit.*, iii., 11.

[4] Lesley, *Vernac. Hist. of Sc.*, 1436–1561, p. 40; and his
larger *Hist. of Sc.*, in Sc. Text Soc.'s ed., ii., 90–91.

controversialist, but the Romanist, Ninian Winzet, a contemporary and literary antagonist of Knox, candidly admits that the bishops and clergy in the age preceding the Reformation were "for the most part" so "ignorant or vicious, or both," as to be "unworthy the name of pastors."

"Were not the sacraments of Christ Jesus"—so he addresses the prelates of his church—"profaned by ignorant and wicked persons, neither able to persuade to godliness by learning nor by living: of the which number we confess the most part of us of the ecclesiastical state to have been unworthily admitted by you to the ministration thereof."

Such scandals he declares to be "the special ground of all impiety and division this day within ye, O Scotland!" [1]

IV. Indignation and disgust at ecclesiastical abuses were shared in Scotland, as elsewhere, by many who were quite satisfied with the Church's dogmas; but by the close of the fourteenth century the presence of revolt against Roman *doctrine* is discernible; for, in 1398, it was enacted that the King at his coronation should take an oath to put down heresy. [2]

Although Scottish jealousy of England had been developed and embittered by the Wars of Independence, the earliest notable impulse to Protestantism

---

[1] See *First Tractate* and *Last Blast of the Trumpet* (Ninian Winzet's Works, i., 5, 44).

[2] *Acts of Parl. of Sc.*, i., 573, 640.

in Scotland appears to have been received from the other side of the Border. During the period of John Wyclif's labours as "Doctor Evangelicus" in Oxford (1361–1380) a large number of Scotsmen studied at that university [1]; and some of these, it may be presumed, came more or less under his reforming influence. Within twenty-two years after Wyclif's death in 1384, his doctrine was openly propagated in the northern kingdom. In 1406, or somewhat earlier, James Resby,[2] one of those itinerant home missionaries — mostly priests [3]—whom the Reformer had organised in 1380 as evangelical rivals of the degenerate mendicants, arrived in Scotland; driven thither, perhaps, by persecution at home, or, more probably, impelled by missionary zeal. Resby is stated to have denied the authority of the reigning Pope, as well as of any pontiff not personally holy [4];

[1] There is evidence that in 1365 eighty-one Scots were students at Oxford. See T. M. Lindsay, in "Scot. Hist. Rev.," April, 1904, p. 267.

[2] The common misnaming of Resby as John (by Burton, Cunningham, Bellesheim, Andrew Lang, and others) appears to be derived from Spottiswoode(*Hist. of Ch. of Sc.*, p. 56, orig. ed.). In the margin, however, of that work the "heretic" is correctly called James, as in the *Scotichronicon*, by Resby's contemporary, Bower.

[3] Hence the name "poor priests" given to the class. Resby was literally a priest (*Scotichr.*, xv., 20).

[4] *Scotichr.*, xv., 20: *Papa de facto non Christi Vicarius.* The two Popes *de facto*, Benedict XIII. and Gregory XII., were at this time so much estranging their own adherents that preparations were being made for the Council of Pisa, which deposed both.

and also to have rejected compulsory confession and priestly absolution; while as a follower of Wyclif he may be assumed to have abjured transubstantiation, and to have maintained strenuously the supreme authority of Holy Writ.[1] Bower, who was Resby's bitter opponent, testifies to his popularity as a preacher and to the widespread sympathy which his views obtained. The most learned Scottish churchman of his time, Laurence of Lindores, who bore the title of "Inquisitor of Heresy," "refuted" Resby's errors; the civil and ecclesiastical authorities united in condemning him to the stake; but through this Wycliffite priest evangelical truth obtained a footing in Scotland which, notwithstanding severe persecution, was never afterwards lost.

Soon after Resby's martyrdom the University of St. Andrews was founded by Bishop Wardlaw, who had taken a leading part in the prosecution of the English preacher. It was expected that this new institution would be a bulwark of the Church's faith, as well as a training-college for her clergy. Yet, so early as the year 1416, it was found needful to demand from all Masters of Arts an oath against "the assault of the Lollards[2];

---

[1] The *Scotichronicon* refers generally to forty *conclusiones periculosissimæ* of Resby.

[2] McCrie, *Life of Melville*, p. 405, where a MS. record of the University is quoted.

and Wyntoun, writing about 1420, bears witness
to the prevalence of "heresy" at that time when
he speaks of Regent Albany as a man who

"All Lollard hated and heretic." [1]

In 1422 a "heretic" was burnt at Glasgow [2]: and
two years later the Scottish Parliament passed an
Act enjoining bishops to search for Lollards
through the "inquisitores," with a view to their
punishment by the secular power. [3]

To the diffusion of Wycliffite views in Scotland
was added ere long the propagation of kindred
Hussite heresy. [4] In 1433, [5] Paul Crawar, a physician from Prague and disciple of John Hus,
settled in St. Andrews and gathered many adherents. He taught them to renounce transubstantiation, purgatory, saint-"worship," and
priestly absolution, as well as to study for them-

---

[1] *Orig. Cronykil*, ix., 2773.

[2] Knox, *Hist. of Ref.*, i., 5 (Laing's ed.).

[3] *Acts of Par. of Sc.*, ii., 7; Robertson, *Statuta*, i., p. lxxix.

[4] Intercourse between England and Bohemia had become
considerable at this time, owing (1) to King Richard II.'s marriage, in 1382, to Anne of Bohemia, who embraced Wycliffite
views; (2) to Bohemian students (including Jerome of Prague,
the future martyr) being attracted to Oxford by the fame of
its teachers, and English students similarly to Prague. Oxford University provided a link between Bohemia and Scotland.

[5] So Bower, *Scotichr.*, xvi., 20; Knox (*H. of R.*, i., 6) gives
the date as 1431.

selves Holy Writ.[1] Again the now aged Laurence
of Lindores (who had become one of the original
professors at St. Andrews University) confronts
the heretic whose "expertness in biblical knowledge and quotation" Bower candidly acknowledges. Again, the civil power, now personally
administered by the restored King, endorses the
ecclesiastical condemnation. Crawar was burned
in 1433; but the ball of brass put into the martyr's mouth at the stake to intercept his dying
testimony, could not prevent the diffusion of the
truth which he had boldly propagated in the religious metropolis of Scotland.[2]

History is silent for sixty years after Crawar's
death regarding the progress of Reformed belief.[3]
Bishop Kennedy's reforming activity, outside the
sphere of doctrine, may have led to temporary
decline of sympathy with movements against
Rome of a more radical character. Notwithstanding hierarchical repression, however, or diminution
of popular support, the revolt against Roman dog-
ma must have continued; for in 1494 it reappears

[1] *Scotichr.*, *l. c.;* Bellesh., *Cath. Ch. of Sc.*, ii., 56, 57.
Crawar went beyond Hus and followed Wyclif in rejecting
transubstantiation. Bower's statement that Crawar's sect
denied the resurrection of the dead and held communistic
views is not confirmed by other authority.

[2] Knox, *H. of R.*, i., 6.

[3] Archbishop Graham, indeed, was deposed in 1478, partly
for "heresy" (Theiner, *Monum.*, 480–481), but this charge
seems to have referred to fanatical pretensions, which suggest
insanity (Bellesh., ii., 93).

on the surface of history. In that year thirty persons, belonging to different parts of Ayrshire, several being men and women of high social position, were summoned before the King and his Privy Council, at the instance of the Archbishop of Glasgow, to answer the charge of " Lollardism."[1] These thirty were probably prominent representatives of considerable communities: for Knox describes the district as " an ancient receptacle of the people of God." The strong hold over the country which Wycliffite views had obtained since Crawar's time is significantly indicated by the procedure at the Council. Not only was no penalty inflicted on the accused, but their spokesman, Adam Reid of Barskimming, was allowed to turn the tables on his archiepiscopal prosecutor, and to charge him and his fellow prelates with forgetting their divine commission, which was " to preach Christ's Evangel and not to play the proud prelates."

About the time of this notable trial a poem was written by Walter Kennedy, *In Praise of Aige*, containing these significant lines:

> "The Schip of Faith tempestuous wind and rain
> Dryvis in the sea of Lollerdry that blawis." [2]

---

[1] Knox, *H. of R.*, i., 12. An interesting relic of these Lollards of Ayrshire was published in 1901 by Dr. T. Graves Law, viz., a MS. of Wyclif's New Testament "turned into Scots by Mordoch Nisbet," of Loudoun, near Kilmarnock, whose "eyes were opened to see the vanity and evil of Popery, some time before the year 1500" (*N. T. in Scots*, p. x.).

[2] G. Bannatyne, *Ancient Scottish Poems*, p. 258.

No doubt even in that age there were men, like Bishop Elphinstone of Aberdeen, who adorned their ecclesiastical office by blameless life and beneficent service. But amid the discreditable ignorance, vitiated doctrine, licentious laxity, and disreputable greed of a large proportion of the "kirkmen" who at this period manned the vessel of "Holy Church," the shipwreck not only of Church, but of faith, appeared imminent. Yet the darkest hour is that which comes before the dawn; and in the earlier part of the sixteenth century came the dawn of a brighter day for Scotland and for Christendom.

CHAPTER I

BIRTH AND EDUCATION OF KNOX—EARLY RE-
LIGIOUS ENVIRONMENT AND ECCLESIASTICAL
POSITION

1513 (OR 1505)–1543

JOHN KNOX was born at or near Haddington
early in the sixteenth century, but the year
of his birth is uncertain, the month and day
are unknown, and pilgrims to his birthplace find
themselves confronted with diversity of opinion
as to its location.

I. Two contemporaries of the Reformer—Sir
Peter Young, by 1579 a citizen of Edinburgh, and
Theodore Beza of Geneva, a personal friend of
Knox—indicate by their statements regarding his
age at death that he was born at some time be-
tween the 24th November, 1513, and the 24th
November, 1515.[1] The traditional date, on the

---

[1] Young (who shared with George Buchanan the responsibility for the education of James VI.), in a letter to Beza,
dated November, 1579, writes that Knox died in his fifty-
ninth year (see Hume Brown, *Life of John Knox*, ii., 323).
Beza (*Icones Illust. Virorum*, Ee iii.) states that the Reformer
died "after having attained to the age of fifty-seven."

other hand, is 1505.   It rests almost entirely on
the authority of Archbishop Spottiswoode, who
wrote the *History* containing his testimony about
half a century after the Reformer's death.[1]   Some
apparent confirmation of Spottiswoode's statement is afforded by the fact that a John Knox
entered the University of Glasgow in October,
1522 [2], when John Major, under whom, according
to Beza, Knox studied, occupied a chair in that
seat of learning.   But the University Register

---

[1] Spottiswoode, *Hist. of the Ch.*, ii., 180 (edition 1850).
The same statement is made by David Buchanan in his *Life
and Death of John Knox* (pp. 1, 7), prefixed to his edition of
Knox's *History of the Reformation*.   Buchanan's work was
published in 1644, five years after Spottiswoode's death, but
eleven years before the latter's *History of the Church* was
given to the world.   The two testimonies, however, are not,
as is often assumed, independent of each other: for internal evidence suggests that Buchanan had access to Spottiswoode's unpublished MS. before writing his own account of
Knox.   For example: (a) both authors speak of Knox as
born in Gifford of " honest parentage "; (b) Buchanan's
statement that "under Master John Mair, a man very famous
for his learning," Knox became so proficient that he was
"advanced to Church orders before the time usually allowed,"
is an obvious repetition of Spottiswoode's assertion (ii., 180)
that "he [Knox] made such profit in his studies under that
famous Doctor, Mr. John Mair, as he was held worthy to
enter into orders before the years allowed "; (c) when Buchanan writes, "He betook himself to the reading of the
ancients, especially of Augustine," and "was exceedingly
solaced," he seems to echo Spottiswoode's testimony, "by
reading the ancients, especially the works of St. Austin, he
was brought to the knowledge of the truth."
[2] *Munimenta Univ. Glasg.*, ii., 147.

shews that in the sixteenth and seventeenth centuries about forty Knoxes (of whom eight are called John) were students at Glasgow [1]; and Beza (followed here by David Buchanan) states distinctly that Knox was under Major at the University of St. Andrews, where the latter held office from 1523–1525, and from 1531 to 1549–50.[2] Until the discovery, moreover, by Dr. McCrie, about a century ago, of the entry in the academic Register at Glasgow, Knox's alleged connection with the university there appears never to have been suggested by any writer. On the whole, while the date of the Reformer's birth remains a subject of controversy, it appears to be most probable, in accordance with our earliest authority on the point, that he was born at the

---

[1] *Munimenta Univ. Glasg.*, ii. and iii.

[2] Æneas Mackay, *Life of Major* (prefixed to translation of the latter's *Greater Britain*), pp. lxx., ciii., civ. The absence of Knox's name from the Matriculation Roll at St. Andrews is by no means conclusive against his having been a student of the university there. Dr. Hay Fleming has pointed out (in a letter to the "Scotsman" of date 27th May, 1904) that the matriculation records are manifestly defective. By the courtesy of Mr. Maitland Anderson, the scholarly University Librarian, who is preparing the academic Registers for publication, the present writer has been able to examine the portion of the records referring to the years 1511–1532. The existence of *lacunæ* is obvious. In 1529, for example, when Knox might very well have entered the university, if he was born in 1513, only three "incorporations" are recorded, as compared with about forty in the year preceding and in the year following.

Site of Knox's probable birthplace, in Giffordgate, Haddington. The tree was planted by the direction of Thomas Carlyle.

close of the year 1513, or in the course of 1514.[1]

II. In a hamlet called Giffordgate, adjacent to Haddington, within the bounds of the parish, and near the ancient parish church, although on the opposite bank of the Tyne, there stands a memorial oak tree planted by direction of Thomas Carlyle. A tablet beside the tree bears the inscription, "Near this stood the house in which was born John Knox." The local tradition, accepted by Carlyle, was referred to as old in 1785.[2] In its favour is the fact that, when Knox was admitted as a burgess of Geneva, he was registered as "a native of Haddington," [3] and that he is so designated by his contemporary detractor, Archibald Hamilton.[4] This site is also consistent with the description of the Reformer by Beza and Spottiswoode as a Gifford man [5]; for Giffordgate, which was part of the estate of the Giffords of East Lothian, is repeatedly referred to, in ancient local

---

[1] See Additional Note at the end of this chapter.

[2] By the Rev. Dr. George Barclay, at a meeting of the Society of Antiquaries of Scotland (see *Trans. of Soc. of Ant.*, i., 69). The genuineness of the site was afterwards vindicated by Mr. John Richardson (*Proceed. of the Soc. of Ant. of Scot.*, iii. 52–55,), and it has been accepted by Dr. David Laing (*Works of Knox*, vi., p. xviii.), Prof. A. F. Mitchell (*Scott. Ref.*, 79), Dr. Hay Fleming (*O. S. Mag.* 1889) and others.

[3] See *Registre des Bourgeois* of Geneva.

[4] *De Confusione Calv. Sectæ apud Scotos*, p. 64.

[5] Beza refers to Knox as "Giffordiensis" (*Icones*); Spottiswoode, as "born in Gifford" (*Hist. of Ch.*, ii., 180).

documents of the fifteenth century, not as a mere "gate" or roadway, but as a district of land.[1]

The question has not been decisively settled; for the testimony in favour of Giffordgate is not ancient enough to command universal acceptance.[2] Something may be said for the village of Gifford, four miles from Haddington—the site favoured by Dr. McCrie in his *Life of John Knox*. The adoption of this site as Knox's birthplace would account most satisfactorily for the language of Beza and Spottiswoode. But the absence of any village of that name in detailed maps and descriptions of the seventeenth century[3] is an objection which can hardly be surmounted, unless evidence come to light of a more ancient Gifford hamlet which, in the interval between the time of Knox

---

[1] See local charter of 1427, transferring by excambion "the fourth part of Yester, Duncanlaw, Morham and Giffordgate," and also a confirmatory charter, dated 1441, in similar terms.

[2] Two instruments of sasine, indeed, dated 1607 and 1611, describe certain "butts" of land in Giffordgate as bounded by lands called "Knox's Walls"; so that before 1607 the name of Knox was associated with the locality. Richardson and others adduce this fact as evidence of the antiquity of the testimony to the Giffordgate site. But such connexion of the name of Knox with the district is not decisive; for the name was common in East Lothian; and the association of Knoxes with Giffordgate might be held to have given rise to the tradition of the Reformer's birth there.

[3] Pont's map of the county made in the time of Charles I. (see Chalmers's *Caledonia*, iv., 535; ed., 1889), and Monipennie's *Scots Chronicles*.

and the reign of Charles I., had become extinct.[1]
A claim may also be advanced in favour of Morham, four miles from Haddington—the site preferred by Dr. Hume Brown.[2] Morham was within
Haddington constabulary; so that a parishioner of
the former might consider himself to be "of Haddington." In the fourteenth century, the Morham
estate came through marriage into the possession
of the Giffords; and it is inferred by those who
favour this site that the lands acquired might, in
consequence, come to be known as Gifford. The
birth of Knox in Morham, moreover, would account most adequately for the Reformer's apparent acknowledgment of the Earls of Bothwell as
entitled to receive feudal service from his family [3];
for in 1490–1 half of the Morham property passed
into the hands of the Bothwells [4]; whereas Giffordgate does not appear ever to have been theirs.[5]

---

[1] The case for Gifford village has been well stated by
the late Mr. Kerr, minister of Yester, in a pamphlet entitled
Where was Knox Born? He and Dr. McCrie, however,
wrote before attention had been called to the omission of the
village from ancient maps.

[2] *Life of John Knox*, i., 10.

[3] Knox, *H. of R.*, ii., 323, where he states that his "grandfather, goodshir [mother's father] and father had served
under the Bothwells"; and he adds, "This was part of the
obligation of our Scottish Kyndness."

[4] There is a charter in Register House, Edinburgh, record-
ing a grant to this effect by James IV. to Patrick, Earl of
Bothwell, and to his heirs.

[5] The facts and arguments favourable to Morham have
been presented by Mr. David Louden, formerly schoolmaster

Against these considerations, however, must be placed not only the lack of evidence that Morham ever was called Gifford, but positive testimony to its retention of the original name long after its conveyance to the Gifford family: for, as we have seen, local charters of the fifteenth century refer to the estate as "Morham." It is highly improbable, therefore, that any native of Morham would speak of himself on that account as "born in Gifford." The "obligation of Scottish Kyndness," on the part of Knox's father and grandfather, to follow the Bothwell standard may have been based on the fact that the Earls of Bothwell had been for three generations sheriffs of the county; the phrase being fairly understood not in the technical sense of feudal allegiance, but in the more general meaning of dutiful loyalty, arising out of close relationship combined with territorial subordination. On the whole, Giffordgate is the site for which most and against which least can

---

of the parish, in *History of Morham* (1889), pp. 34–51. In addition to what is stated above, he draws attention to the indisputable fact that Morham was a habitation of Knoxes. Nine old tombstones in the parish churchyard commemorate persons of that name, the oldest dating back to 1660. Giffordgate, however, with its "Knox's Walls," may also claim to be an abode of members of the clan (see note, p. 26). Mr. Louden adduces, further, the oral testimony of an old man, Nelson, born about 1800, who remembered his grandfather pointing out a spot in the parish which in his (*i. e.*, the grandfather's) boyhood was spoken of as John Knox's birthplace: but in favour of Giffordgate a similar local tradition has existed.

be urged; and Carlyle's oak still "holds the field." [1]

III. John Knox's parentage, although not distinguished, was respectable. "Descendit but of lineage small" is the testimony of a personal friend and admirer, John Davidson of Prestonpans.[2] The Reformer's father, William, and both his grandfathers served, as we have seen, under Earls of Bothwell; and two of these died under the standard of that family. This was probably on what Knox describes as "that unhappy field" of Flodden, in 1513; for an Earl of Bothwell was slain in the battle, with most of his followers, in a gallant attempt to retrieve the fortunes of the day.[3] Of the Reformer's mother all that we certainly know is that her name was Sinclair—a name which Knox occasionally used for concealment in times of trouble [4]; but she may have been related to Marion Sinclair, wife of George Ker of Samuelston, for whom Knox acted repeatedly as

[1] The writer is indebted for information regarding ancient documents connected with Haddington, and also for several suggestions embodied in this paragraph, to Dr. J. G. Wallace-James, Provost of Haddington, whose archæological research-work regarding the charters of the burgh is well known.

[2] In his *Breif Commendation of Uprichtness*, Stanza xiv., reprinted as an appendix to McCrie's *Life of John Knox*. Archibald Hamilton describes the Reformer as *obscuris natus parentibus* (*De Conf. Calv. Sectæ*, p. 64). Had there been anything discreditable in Knox's parentage, Hamilton would have stated it.

[3] Knox, *H. of R.*, ii., 313; Laing, *W. of K.*, vi., p. xvi.

[4] Laing, iv., 245.

notary, and whose daughter married the second
Lord Home, Chancellor of Scotland. On his
mother's side, therefore, the Reformer may have
been well connected.[1] We know of only one
brother of John Knox,—William,—who became a
merchant of considerable standing at Preston
(East Lothian), and was the father of three sons
who became ministers of the Church of Scotland.[2]

IV. At the period of Knox's birth and boyhood, Haddington was a prosperous burgh. Its
position, indeed, on one of the main roads leading
from England to Edinburgh, had exposed it repeatedly to English ravage and incendiarism: but
the fertility of the soil in the surrounding district
enabled the town always to rise out of its ashes
into renewed prosperity. It was already distinguished as the birthplace of King Alexander
II., in 1198, and of the historian, Walter Bower,
in 1385. Haddington was a notable ecclesiastical
centre. About a mile east of the town stood a
Cistercian Abbey, founded in 1170 by Ada, the

---

[1] Laing., vi., p. xv.; *Proceedings of Soc. of Antiq.*, iii., 67.

[2] Rogers, *Geneal. Memoirs of John Knox*, pp. 60–70. In
the Record Office there is a letter from Regent Arran to
Edward VI., dated Feb., 1552, and seeking "letters of safe
conduct" for "our lovit William Knox in Prestoun"; and in
Sept. 1552, he received liberty to trade in any part of England. His eldest son, William, became minister of Cockpen
(Midlothian) in 1567; the second son, Paul, of Kelso in 1574;
the youngest, John, was minister successively of Lauder and
of Melrose between 1576 and 1623, and signalised himself by
opposition to episcopacy and to the Five Articles of Perth.

mother of William the Lion.[1]   Within the burgh
itself was a church, consecrated to the Virgin, old
enough to have been mentioned in 1134; three
chapels dedicated respectively to St. John, St.
Catherine, and St. Anne; a chapel of St. Martin
on the east of the Nungate, whose ruins remain;
and a church and monastery belonging to the
Blackfriars.[2] Chief of all was a church of the
Greyfriars, dating from the thirteenth century
—the "Lamp of Lothian," of which the present
parish church by the riverside, with ruined choir,
but with nave still used for worship, is in part a
survival.[3] Educationally, as well as ecclesiastically, Haddington was well equipped. It had a
grammar school, at which Walter Bower probably, and the more illustrious John Major, certainly, had received their education.[4] At this
institution, even if his birthplace was a few miles

---

[1] Wyntoun, *Orig. Cronyk.*, vii., 960.

[2] Barclay, *Trans. of Soc. of Ant.*, i., 64–66; Chalmers,
Caledonia, iv., 515.

[3] D. Miller, *Lamp of Lothian*, pp. 377–385.   The name
was given to the edifice either from its architectural beauty,
or from the tower being visible from afar by travellers, or
from the moral illumination which the church imparted.
The ground adjoining the churchyard is still called "Friars'
Croft."

[4] In the dedication of his treatise on Book IV. of Lom-
bard's *Sentences*, Major refers to Haddington as "the town
which fostered the beginnings of my own studies, and in
whose kindly embraces I was carried on in my education
to a pretty advanced age." See Æneas Mackay's translation of Major's *Greater Britain*, p. xxxii.

distant, Knox acquired, we may presume, his facility in speaking and writing Latin.

V. There is no evidence that during Knox's boyhood the Reformation had extended to Haddington, where even in 1546 the movement met with a cold reception [1]; but if the year 1513–14 be accepted as the date of the Reformer's birth, he must have heard something, before leaving school for university, of the great religious question of the time. The degeneracy of the Franciscans, who held the chief place, ecclesiastically, in the town, had been satirised by William Dunbar and David Lyndsay, both connected with East Lothian.[2] By 1525, the circulation of Lutheran books and tracts in Scotland had become so notorious that the subject was brought before Parliament [3]; and in the following year copies of Tyndale's English New Testament found their way to seaports on the east of Scotland.[4]

In 1527, while John Knox would be still at

---

[1] Knox, *H. of R.*, i., 136–138.

[2] Dunbar's *Visitation of St. Francis*, and the *Friars of Berwick*, usually attributed to him, were written early in the sixteenth century. His connection by birth with East Lothian is mentioned by himself in his *Flyting*, line 110. Lyndsay's earliest printed satire against the clergy and religious orders (the *Papyngo*) was published about 1530; but as he was born in 1490, and his father had an estate two miles from Haddington, he was doubtless locally notable before 1530 for his exposure of clerical immorality.

[3] *Acts of Parl. of Sc.*, ii., 295; Lorimer, *Scott. Ref.*, pp. 2, 3.

[4] A. F. Mitchell, *Scott. Ref.*, p. 23.

school, or, if the traditional date of his birth be
adhered to, a student preparing for the priesthood, the brief ministry was inaugurated of a
leading pioneer of the Scottish Reformation—
Patrick Hamilton, the son of a Linlithgowshire
knight, and a kinsman of the noble families of Hamilton and Albany.   He preached at St. Andrews,
in the spring of 1527, the Lutheran doctrine which
he had imbibed at Paris under Lefevre, and had
afterwards studied more fully in Luther's own
controversial tracts.   The Primate, James Beaton,
was not anxious to come into conflict with a representative of two powerful families: yet he dared
not incur the suspicion of countenancing heresy.
He sent, accordingly, to Hamilton a citation to
appear, which was probably intended, and at any
rate was accepted, as a warning to disappear.
During the greater part of the year 1527 Hamilton
lived at Marburg in Hesse, under the potent protection of Landgrave Philip.   He signalised his
Protestantism there by the publication of a series
of theses on Justification, which were afterwards
eulogised by Fryth, the English martyr, as containing the " pith of all Divinity." [1]   Late in the autumn he returned to Scotland, fortified by further
study of Reformed doctrine, as well as by intercourse with Protestant divines.   He resolved now,
at whatever risk, to vindicate the truth in which

---

[1] Foxe, iv., 563.   The theses are embodied by Knox in his
H. of R., i., 21–35.

3

he believed. To crowded congregations in Linlithgow he preached the evangelical doctrine of
justification by faith. The Primate refrained at
first from renewing the former citation. He invited the young Reformer to a friendly conference
and treated him at the outset with conciliation, in
the hope, doubtless, that he would be induced to
retrace his steps. When this expectation proved
vain, Hamilton was ensnared into such a definite
declaration of his views as sufficed to bring home
to him the charge of heresy. The old summons
was then reissued [1] and was boldly faced. A single
day witnessed his trial, condemnation, and martyrdom. At the stake he prayed that God would
open the eyes of his fellow-citizens; and when
unable any longer to speak he held up his half-
burnt hand, in response to the appeal of a sympathetic bystander,—as a token of steadfast faith.[2]

VI.   It was a common saying at the time that
the "reek of Patrick Hamilton infected as many
as it blew upon"; and we can hardly imagine that
Knox, who reports this saying, was himself en-

---

[1] The citation is given in full by Prof. Mitchell in his
Scottish Reformation, App. B. Among the charges against
Hamilton were (1) denial of any reward of salvation for good
works—a misrepresentation of his doctrine of justification;
(2) repudiation of image-(worship) and prayers for the dead;
(3) assertion that tithes were not exigible, sacraments in
themselves not reliable, and Church censures not authoritative.

[2] Alesius (Hamilton's friend), *Comm. on Psalm xxxvii.*;
Lorimer, *Patrick Hamilton*, Appendix 2.

tirely unaffected.¹   If he became a student at St.
Andrews in 1529, the memory of Hamilton would
still be fresh in the city: even if he entered the
university a year or two later, the impression
would not have become faint. The following
warm words in Knox's *History* have the appearance of a personal reminiscence:

"When those cruel wolves had, as they supposed,
clean devoured their prey, they found themselves in
worse case than they were before: for then, within
St. Andrews, yea almost within the whole realm,
there was none found who began not to enquire
wherefore was Master Patrick Hamilton burnt? And
so, within short space many began to call in doubt
that which they held for a certain verity." ²

During the seventeen years, however, which followed Hamilton's martyrdom, there is no evidence
of Knox having said or done anything which involved adherence to the cause for which Hamilton
died. He refrained, indeed, from taking his degree as "Magister Artium," not improbably on
account of the oath against "Lollardism" which
the university demanded from its "Masters." ³
It appears also, as already has been incidentally
indicated, that at this period (possibly under
the influence of Gavin Logie, Principal of St.
Leonard's College) Knox became a student of the

¹ Knox, *H. of R.*, i., 42.
² *Ibid.*, 36.
³ See page 17.

ancient Fathers, especially of St. Augustine, from whom he would learn to crave for a more scriptural theology than the Church then supplied.[1] At some date, however, prior to December, 1540, he was ordained as a priest of the Church of Rome [2]; and in 1543 he is found signing himself a "Minister of the Holy Altar." [3] During the five years or more which succeeded his ordination he exercised, like many other priests of that time, the office of notary; and also acted as a private tutor.[4] Up till the latter part of the year 1545, no public support, so far as is known, was given by him to the Reformation movement.

---

[1] Beza, *Icones*, Ee. iii.; Spottiswoode, *Hist. of Ch.*, ii., 180; D. Buchanan, *Life and Death of Knox*, p. 1.

[2] The requisite age was twenty-five, so that he might have been admitted in 1538; moreover, Spottiswoode, as we have seen, declares (*Hist. of Ch.*, ii., 180) that "he was held worthy to enter into orders before the years allowed"; but the earliest evidence of his priesthood is a legal document, dated December, 1540, in the burgh archives of Haddington. In this document Knox is called Sir John Knox, a title given to priests who were not "Masters." See Laing, *W. of K.*, vi., p. xxi.

[3] *Ibid.*, p. xxii., and Facsimile. Ninian Winzet (*Certane Tractatis*, ii.) describes Knox as "esteeming that ordination null, by which sometime ye were called Sir John."

[4] Laing, *W. of K.*, vi., p. xx.; Archibald Hamilton, *De Conf. Cal. Sect.*, p. 64. As Knox appears to have exercised notarial functions repeatedly at Samuelston, three miles from Haddington, Dr. Laing conjectures that he lived with the Kers of Samuelston (one of whom was married to a Sinclair), and may have acted as priest in the little Chapel of St. Nicolas on the estate.

VII. This long period of reserve and reticence in a man (as the issue proved) of strong convictions, ardent temper, and openness of speech, has been an enigma to all students of the Reformer's history. The difficulty is enhanced if we adhere to the traditional date of Knox's birth, and thus postpone his avowal of Protestant views until he was forty years of age. Even, however, if we accept 1513–14 as his birth-year, his inaction throughout early manhood and professional life is remarkable and calls for explanation.

(1) Some restraint may have been exerted at first over Knox by John Major, who, after an absence of six years, returned to St. Andrews University in 1531. His name and fame as a distinguished ex-alumnus of Haddington Academy, and as the "Prince of Paris Masters"[1] must have been previously familiar to Knox, who testifies, that Major's "word was then holden [*i. e.* at St. Andrews after 1531] as an oracle in matters of religion."[2] His influence over the future Reformer, who at some period was his scholar, can be traced in various spheres of thought. From Major, who was a Schoolman, Knox probably learned that dialectic resourcefulness which George Buchanan—also a pupil of Major—disparages somewhat unfairly as "sophistry." Such argumentative aptitude, blended with moral

---

[1] So he is called by Melanchthon, Op. i., 398.

[2] Knox, *H. of R.*, i., 37.

earnestness, rendered Knox afterwards a potent controversialist as well as a heroic Reformer. From Major, also, Knox apparently first imbibed those advanced views of the limitations of monarchy, which the Reformer afterwards unfolded and vindicated. "From the people"—so this "Master" declared—"kings have their institution, and on them [the people] royal power depends." "The nation is above the king, who exists for the people's good, not they for his." [1] In the sphere of religion, Major had been the leader in France of the ecclesiastical party who united loyal adherence to Roman doctrine with strenuous opposition to papal despotism and urgent demand for practical reform. [2] While Knox, therefore, might hear from his teacher a free disparagement of papal bans and denunciation of clerical abuses, he would also receive from him a scholastic defence of transubstantiation, saint-worship, compulsory celibacy for the priesthood, and other Roman Catholic tenets; without any word of sympathy for that Reformed teaching which Hamilton had recently vindicated. Major's prestige as an "oracle," along with his

---

[1] Major, *Greater Britain*, Book IV., 17; *Comm. on Lomb. Sent.*, Book IV., 76.

[2] *Comment. on Matthew*, fol. 18. In later years Major's zeal against the Papacy cooled, owing probably to his alarm at the Protestant doctrine of the right of private judgment. A disputation against papal assumption, contained in the original edition of the above-mentioned commentary, is significantly omitted in the later edition of 1529.

personal influence as a native of East Lothian,
may have contributed to prevent Knox from
publicly committing himself, during his academic
course, to the Reformation cause.

(2) The burning of Hamilton was the inau-
guration in Scotland of a stern policy of repression
and persecution such as constrained many reformers to conceal their convictions. Beaton and
the hierarchy, having crossed the Rubicon, were
impelled to go forward, both by increasing symp-
toms of revolt and by influential approval of their
policy. On the one hand, even within the archiepiscopal precincts of St. Andrews, Gavin Logie
taught doctrine so suggestive of Protestant truth
that suspected heretics were said to have "drunk
at St. Leonard's well." [1] On the other hand,
John Major, although fully alive to the Church's
abuses, congratulated Beaton on having "man-
fully removed" Hamilton; while the University of
Louvain, sent a warm letter of approbation. [2]
The young King, moreover, James V., endorsed
the episcopal policy, not from any favour for
persecution, but from his obligation to support
the hierarchy as the price of their co-operation
in resisting the encroachments of the nobility.
During the fourteen years, accordingly, which
intervened between the martyrdom of Hamilton and the death of James in 1542, frequent

---

[1] Calderwood, *Hist. of Kirk*, i., 104; Knox, *H. of R.*, i., 36.
[2] Calderwood, i., 80–82.

"inquisition" was made, under the primacy of James Beaton and that of his nephew David, for those who showed any leaning towards Reformed views.[1] Various repressive enactments were passed by Parliament[2]; numerous martyrdoms of priests, friars, and laymen took place[3]; many escaped death only by flight and exile.[4] Was it wonderful that amid such persecution not a few remained reticent who sympathised intellectually with the Reformation movement, but who had not experienced those deep spiritual aspirations which the evangelical truth, proclaimed by the Reformers, awakened?[5]

(3) Neither of these two influences, however, adequately accounts for a man of Knox's temperament refraining so long from any act or word which would commit him on the great religious

---

[1] See *Diurnal of Occurrents*, p. 15, which records "a great abjuration of the favourers of Martin Luther."

[2] See Chap. II., p. 52.

[3] Among notable martyrs were Henry Forrest, a Benedictine of Linlithgow; Thomas Forret, Norman Gourlay, and Duncan Simpson, priests; John Keillor, John Beveridge, and Jerome Russell, friars; D. Straiton and N. Kennedy, gentlemen of Kincardine and Ayrshire respectively. (Knox i., 52–62).

[4] Among distinguished exiles were Gavin Logie, James Hamilton, the brother, and Alexander Alane (Alesius), the friend, of Patrick Hamilton; Alexander Seaton, the King's confessor, George Buchanan, the historian, and John MacAlpine, a Dominican, who as Machabæus became Professor of Theology at Copenhagen, and one of the translators of the Bible into Danish. (*Ibid.* 36, 54–71).

[5] See Chap. II., pp. 51, 53.

question of the time.   His self-reliant disposition
would prevent him from being unduly restrained
by Major, especially after his entrance into
the priesthood.   On the other hand, any natural
" fearfulness " [1] would in his case be more than
counterbalanced by that impatience of secrecy and
time-serving, and that habit of "speaking his
mind" whether men approved or not, which
were apparently essential features of his character.   In a time of religious conflict, moreover,
it is difficult for any earnest man, even although
without the highest kind of spiritual experience,
to maintain for years a position of neutrality
regarding matters which intimately concern his
profession.   The solution of the problem of Knox's
long reserve is to be found mainly, we believe, in a
prominent characteristic of the future Reformer,
which appears throughout his entire public career,
—his warm patriotism.   While other Protestants of
the period who fled from Scotland—Alesius,
Seton, Logie, MacAlpine, William, and many
more—found permanent spheres elsewhere, and
"did never after" (as Knox pathetically expresses
it) "comfort their country with their bodily
presence," [2] he, on the contrary, as we shall
see, repeatedly declined permanent promotion in

[1] Knox spoke of himself (on his death-bed) as a "fearful
man," but immediately afterwards qualified the confession
by the statement that he "feared not the faces of men"
(Laing, *W. of K.*, vi., 637).

[2] Knox, *H. of R.*, i., 56.

England; kept himself through correspondence in
constant touch with his countrymen; and thrice
left his Genevan flock when Scotland claimed
his service. There is a suggestive passage in a
treatise written by Knox in 1554, when religious
work in Scotland was impracticable. "Sometime
I thought that it had been . . . impossible
that any realm or nation could have been equal
dear unto me." [1] Throughout his correspondence
anxiety for the welfare of his own country is frequently revealed; and his *History of the Reformation in Scotland* is a continuous manifestation of
a keenly patriotic as well as of an earnestly religious character.

Now, during the period with which we are engaged, there was not a little to cause a patriotic
Scot to refrain from identifying himself with the
Protestant party, even although he might be in
sympathy with the Protestant cause. For the
question of religious reformation was then complicated with politics, and in particular with the
rival policies of England and of France. Ever
since the marriage of James IV. to Margaret
Tudor in 1503, there had been a Scottish party
favourable to friendlier relations with English
neighbours than with more distant French allies.
The endeavour of James V., moreover, to humble
a too powerful aristocracy had issued in a section
of the nobility identifying their interests with the

---

[1] Laing, *W. of K.*, iii., 133.

policy of Henry VIII., and in some cases even transferring to him their allegiance.[1]   Through the rupture between King Henry and Rome, in 1534, a fresh bond of connection was constituted; many who favoured the Reformation in Scotland now looked to England for sympathy and support. Henry VIII. saw in this altered attitude an opportunity of reviving the old project of Edward I. to incorporate the northern with the southern kingdom, or at least to establish over Scotland an English suzerainty.   He proposed a marriage between his daughter Mary and his nephew, James V., just as at a later stage, after James's death, he proposed a betrothal between his son Edward and the infant Mary Stuart.   He attempted to wile James V. into England for conference, with the object (as State Papers have revealed) of getting the Scottish King into his power.   Repeatedly he sent an army across the Border, with the design, if not of subjugating Scotland, at least of forcing upon it a civil and ecclesiastical policy.[2]

The result of Scottish disloyalty, real or apparent, and of English aggression, open or disguised, was a strong patriotic sentiment among the nation against the English alliance.   The Beatons,

---

[1] Burton, *H. of Sc.*, iii., 150–152 (edit. 1876); *State Papers,* Henry VIII., vol. iv.

[2] Burton, iii., 162, 178, 181–183.   At a later stage, in 1542, Henry actually published a manifesto, claiming the Scottish throne on essentially the same grounds as those advanced by Edward (*Ibid.*, iii., 365.)

and the Scottish hierarchy as a whole, who promoted an alliance with France and had rescued the
King from English control and from Scottish allies
of England, were widely regarded as bulwarks of
Scottish independence.[1] The Reformed party, on
the other hand, being associated so far with the
unpatriotic English faction in Scotland, lost meanwhile the support of many who believed in the
necessity of reformation, but were influenced for
a time more by patriotic feeling than by Protestant conviction. Among these we may with considerable probability include John Knox; and he
would be more likely to avoid identifying himself
with any movement which encouraged, even indirectly, English aggression or interference, if he
knew of a remarkable interview which took place
in 1531 between the Sheriff of his native county—
the Earl of Bothwell—and the Earl of Northumberland, Henry's trusted agent in regard to Scottish affairs. At that meeting substantial aid, to
the extent of at least seven thousand men, was
promised to the King of England by Bothwell,
on behalf of himself and other noblemen, in the
event of an English invasion of Scotland; and the
hope was held out that ere long Henry would be
crowned in Edinburgh.[2] There were many to

---

[1] Herkless, *Cardinal Beaton*, p. 162.

[2] *State Papers*, Henry VIII., iv., 597, 598; Burton, iii., 151.;
Herkless, 115. Even if such promises were never meant to
be fulfilled, the rumour of their having been made would
strengthen the Roman and anti-English party.

whom the Reformation was no more than a highly
desirable event, for which the country might
wait; whereas the virtual, if not actual, annexation of Scotland by England was a near and
imminent peril. For all such Scotsmen, Cardinal
Beaton, notwithstanding his heinous faults, could
not but appear a more trustworthy political
leader, on the whole, meanwhile, than nobles
whose reforming sympathies were associated with
unpatriotic self-seeking, if not with the yet graver
delinquency of treason.

ADDITIONAL NOTE ON THE DATE OF KNOX'S BIRTH

The contempory and local testimony of Sir Peter
Young, in itself stronger than that of Spottiswoode,
is fortified by the following considerations:

1. When Young sent his letter to Beza in 1579,
George Buchanan, his senior colleague in the royal
household, with whom he must have been in constant communication, was still alive. Can we sup-
pose that Young wrote about Knox's age (especially
if any doubt existed), without consulting Buchanan,
who was Knox's friend,[1] and born in 1506? and is it
likely that the historian would misstate the age of a
friend and contemporary by eight years?

---

[1] Knox submitted part of his *History* to Buchanan's revisal (*H. of R.*, ii., 134), and bears witness to "the rare graces
of God given to that man, His servant" (*ibid.*, i., 71). Buchanan, on the other hand, refers repeatedly to Knox in
favourable terms, particularly testifying to his excellence as
a preacher (*Hist. of Sc.*, Book xvi.). It was with Knox's
good-will, doubtless, that Buchanan was chosen Moderator
of Assembly in 1567.

2. Beza was on terms of friendship with Knox, whom he must have known in Switzerland; and the friendship was kept up by correspondence (Laing, *W. of K.*, vi., 565, 613). We can readily believe that from imperfect memory, or through inadvertence (notwithstanding Young's letter), he represented Knox as dying in his fifty-eighth instead of in his fifty-ninth year. But that an intimate friend should have deliberately declared Knox to be nine years younger than he really was, is not very credible.

3. Young's testimony as to the date of Knox's birth, and Beza's statement that the Reformer studied in St. Andrews under Major, who returned to the university of that city in 1531, harmonise suggestively with certain records in the Reformer's *History* relating to the time during which he would most probably have resided there as a student. Knox's account of proceedings at St. Andrews between 1529 and 1535 is particularly detailed and graphic. He knows what was said then and there about the recent burning of Patrick Hamilton in 1528. He refers to the teaching of Gavin Logie, who left Scotland about 1535 and to the "novices of the Abbey," who under the influence of the sub-prior (probably Wynram, the future Reforming leader) " began to smell somewhat of the verity." He recalls a private interview in St. Andrews at that time between John Major and a friar, William Airth, who shared Major's views about clerical abuses; he mentions the names of the chief auditors on a particular occasion in the parish church; and he gives details of discourses preached in St. Andrews at this period by friars Airth and Seaton, who both fled soon afterwards to England, and ceased

to have further connection with the Scottish Reformation (Knox, *H. of R.*, i., 36–47). In reading this portion of Knox's *History*, it is difficult to avoid the impression that he is drawing material from the storehouse of personal reminiscences at St. Andrews.

4. If Knox was born in 1513, instead of 1505, and if his connection with Glasgow University be surrendered, several circumstances in his life become more easy of explanation. (*a*) His apparent lack of interest in Glasgow, whose university was supposed to be his Alma Mater. He was very seldom there in after life; whereas St. Andrews, next to Edinburgh, was his favourite abode (Laing, *W. of K.*, i., 185, 228, 347; vi., 70, 79–85, 602–606, 615–620). (*b*) If he was not born until 1513, the statement of Spottiswoode and of David Buchanan (see p. 23) that he received orders before the usual age (*i. e.*, twenty-five) becomes more credible; for the earliest reference to his priesthood relates to 1540, when, according to the traditional date of his birth, he would have been already a priest for over ten years. (*c*) The very long period during which, if the date 1505 be correct, there is absolutely nothing known about the future Reformer is substantially shortened. (*d*) The difficulty involved in a man of Knox's ardent nature not committing himself to the Reformation cause until 1545, is lessened by the acceptance of Young's date. (*e*) Knox's attitude of discipleship towards Wishart, and his practice of attending that Reformer with a "two-handed sword" (see p. 60) are more natural if Wishart, whose birth is usually assigned to the year 1513, was Knox's senior, or at least his equal as to age, and not his junior, as would be the case if the traditional date of 1505 be

maintained as the year of Knox's nativity. The Reformer's attitude of docile reverence towards Calvin
(see Chap. V.), who was born in 1509, is also more in
keeping with the supposition that he was junior and
not senior to the great Swiss divine. (See articles by
Andrew Lang and the present writer in the *Athenæum*
of 5th Nov. and 3rd Dec., 1904).[1]

---

[1] Since the above was printed, Mr. D. Macmillan, in his
John Knox (p. 311), has argued that Beza, although living at
Lausanne, near Geneva, could not have known Knox personally. Otherwise Young would not have thought it necessary
to send Beza a " pen-portrait of the Reformer " in 1579.
But Knox had left Geneva twenty years before; and Young,
doubtless, considered it desirable, in view of Beza's forthcoming memoir of Knox, to recall the details of the latter's
appearance.

CHAPTER II

1543–1546

THE death of King James V. in December,
1542, issued in a political crisis. Cardinal
Beaton, the leading counsellor of James, in
his anxiety not only to frustrate Henry VIII.'s
designs against Scottish independence, but to keep
in his own hands the government of the country,
aroused against himself a jealousy and hostility
which imperilled at once his person and his policy.
It was asserted at the time, and widely believed,
that the royal testament, which appointed Beaton
as Regent during the minority of Mary Stuart, had
been drawn up by the Cardinal after the King's
death; and that the parchment, while still blank,
had been signed by the dying or dead sovereign's
hand, guided by Beaton himself.[1] According to

---

[1] Knox, *H. of R.*, i., 91–93; Spottisw., *H. of Ch. of Sc.*, i.,
141. Bishop Lesley admits that the Cardinal's appointment
by the King could not be proved (*H. of Sc.*, ii., 264, Sc. T.
Soc.). Hay Fleming (*Mary Queen of Scots*, pp. 3, 180, and

another contemporary report, endorsed by Knox,
there was found on the King's person after his
death a long list of nobility and gentry, prepared
by the Cardinal with a view to their prosecution
and the confiscation of their property.[1] Even if
these charges were calumnious, there was a general and well-founded belief at the time that Beaton was determined to rid the Court of every man
of position who could not be won over to his
party. A temporary reaction, accordingly, against
both the hierarchy and the French alliance
ensued. In January, 1543, the nobility, forgetful
for the time of private jealousies, nominated to
Parliament as Regent the Earl of Arran, whose
sentiments were believed to be strongly against
both Rome and France. Three weeks later, the
Cardinal was arrested and imprisoned as a con-
spirator against the welfare of the realm.[2]

I. The new Government proceeded without delay to manifest its willingness to enter into an English alliance, as well as to favour the Reform cause.
When the Estates met in March, 1543, and
confirmed Arran's regency, they declared, at his
instigation, their readiness to inaugurate negotiations, as King Henry proposed, for the betrothal
of the infant Mary Stuart to the boy who became

"Cont. Rev.," Sept., 1898) and Hume Brown (*H. of Sc.*, ii.,
4) favour the charge of forgery against Beaton; Andrew
Lang takes the other side (*H. of Sc.*, i., 459–461).

[1] Knox, *H. of R.*, i., 82.

[2] Lesley, *H. of Sc.*, ii., 265; Hume Brown, *H. of Sc.*, ii., 4, 5.

Edward VI.[1] Certain important stipulations, however, were laid down as essential. The young Queen of Scots was not to be removed to England, as Henry had demanded, until she had completed her tenth year; the English proposal that certain Scottish fortresses should be surrendered meanwhile, as guarantees, was rejected; Scotland was to remain an independent kingdom always under the government of a native ruler: and if issue from the marriage failed, the next Scottish heir was to succeed to the throne.[2] Henry was irritated at conditions which prevented him from recognising the betrothal as a virtual acknowledgment by Scotland of English suzerainty; and he accepted the stipulations only because he hoped to secure their eventual withdrawal.

What caused dissatisfaction to the King of England, however, removed a ground of suspicion from many in Scotland who favoured the Reformation movement, but had disliked its apparent association with subservience to a rival people. This change of sentiment manifested itself in a remarkable alteration of attitude. Not a few who from patriotic reasons had hitherto supported, or at least refrained from opposing, the hierarchy were now ready to promote legislation in favour of the Protestant cause. In 1535 Parliament had passed a stringent law against the introduction,

---

[1] Knox, *H. of R.*, i., 102; Lesley, *H. of Sc.*, ii., 266.
[2] *Acts of Parl. of Sc.*, ii., 411–413; Tytler, *H. of Sc.*, v., 325.

possession, or use of any heretical books, among which Tyndale's New Testament was known to be included.[1]   So recently as 1541, in James V.'s last Parliament, repressive statutes had been enacted prohibiting even private conventions for the discussion of Holy Scripture; declaring it criminal to help or harbour persons cited to answer a charge of heresy; and imposing the penalty of death on all who questioned the Pope's supreme authority or spiritual infallibility.[2]   Now, in 1543, the Estates ordained the lawfulness of possessing and of reading Holy Scripture in the vernacular; an enactment which Knox describes as "no small victory of Christ Jesus, nor small comfort to such as before were holden in bondage."   "The Bible," he continues, "might now be seen on almost every gentleman's table, instead of being hid away in some out-of-the-way corner."   The Regent Arran was esteemed to be "the most fervent Protestant in Europe."[3]

---

[1] *Acts of Parl. of Sc.*, ii., 342.

[2] *Ibid.*, ii., 370; Tytler, *H. of Sc.*, v., 285.

[3] Knox, *H. of R.*, i., 100, 101.   The version circulated was that of Tyndale.   According to Knox, the Spiritual Estate made a very ineffective resistance to the enactment regarding vernacular Scripture.   The prelates first contended that the Church had forbidden the Bible to be read except in Hebrew, Greek, or Latin.   When confronted with Christ's command that His Word be "preached to all nations," they pleaded that vernacular versions must be certified as "true."   When it was demanded "what could be reprehended" in Tyndale's translation, "nothing could be found but that *Love* was put in the place of *Charity*" (in 1 Cor. xiii.).

It was at this juncture that we find the earliest trace of John Knox's sympathy with Protestant truth; and it is not unlikely, as already suggested, that the emphatic dissociation, under Regent Arran, of the Scottish Reform movement from an unpatriotic policy, was in his case, as in that of others, one cause of an altered ecclesiastical attitude. A more personal and spiritual motive contributed to Knox's new departure. The Regent had appointed as his chaplains two evangelical friars, Thomas William of Athelstaneford, in East Lothian, whom Knox describes as a man "of wholesome doctrine" and "prompt utterance"; and John Rough, "not so learned," but "more vehement against all impiety." These chaplains were not mere Court officials: they preached frequently in Edinburgh, and sometimes apparently elsewhere.[1] William probably included Haddington, four miles from his home, within the sphere of his evangelistic activity. At all events, the Haddington notary-priest (possibly a former school-fellow) was somewhere among the hearers of this Dominican friar; and we have it on testimony which, although not contemporary, is sufficiently ancient to command acceptance, in the absence of any evidence to the contrary, that while listening to William, Knox first received a "taste" and a "lively impression of the truth,"

[1] Knox, *H. of R.*, i., 95–96 (with Laing's Note); Spottisw., i., 143–144; Foxe, *Acts*, etc., viii., 433.

and was much moved thenceforth to the "earnest study of the Holy Scripture." [1]　The passage of the Word of God on which he "cast" his "first anchor" (according to his own testimony) was the seventeenth chapter of St. John. [2]

II. The Reforming policy inaugurated by Arran in the Parliament of 1543 was short-lived. The Regent was a man of no stability of character. He was unable to withstand the combined influence of the Queen Dowager, Mary of Guise, to whom the Reformation and the proposed English marriage were alike distasteful; of the hierarchy, who interdicted the mass during the Cardinal's imprisonment; [3] of all thorough Romanists, in whose eyes the treatment of the Primate was sacrilege; and of the party who, without any strong ecclesiastical convictions, preferred the time-honoured alliance with France to the new-born alliance with England.　The Regent's illegitimate brother, John Hamilton, Abbot of Paisley, who arrived in Scotland from France soon after the meeting of Parliament, added his personal influence on the side of Romanism.　He alarmed Arran by reminding him that the legality of his mother's marriage, and therefore his own legitimacy, depended on the validity of the divorce granted by the Pope to his father from a former

---

[1] Calderw., *H. of the Kirk.*, i., 156; Dav. Buch., in *Life and Death of Knox*, p. 18.

[2] Laing, *W. of K.*, vi., 643.

[3] *Hamilton Papers*, i., 426.

wife. If the papal authority—so the Abbot argued—were repudiated by Scotland, then the Regent was a bastard with no legal claim either to the earldom, to the regency, or (in the event of Mary Stuart's death without issue) to the throne.[1] Before the end of April, the English ambassador, Sadler, observed tokens of Arran's tergiversation. The Cardinal had been virtually released, and was conspiring against the English party[2]; the Protestant chaplains had been dismissed from the Court[3]; men with reforming aspirations, like Sir David Lyndsay and Henry Balnaves, who had been admitted to the Regent's confidence, were now replaced by Romanist counsellors[4]; ten thousand adherents of the French faction assembled in Leith to intimidate the vacillating Earl.[5] Up to the 25th of August, however, when the terms of the betrothal were approved by the Regent, the semblance of a policy favourable to the Reformation and to England was retained: but eight days later, in the Franciscan Church of Stirling, Arran recanted his Protestantism, renounced his policy of alliance with England, and received absolution

[1] Knox, H. of R., i., 105; Spottisw., i., 146; Ham. P., i., 49.

[2] Ham. Papers, i., 483; Sadler Papers, i., 83–90.

[3] Knox, H. of R., i., 105; Spottisw., i., 44. According to the latter, Rough was not dismissed from the Regent's service, but " on some colour dimitted to preach " in Ayrshire.

[4] Knox, H. of R., i., 106.

[5] Diurnal of Occur., p. 28.

from the Primate himself.[1]   The political outcome
of the Regent's apostasy was the repudiation of
the matrimonial proposal by the Scottish Parliament in December, 1543 (nominally on account of
the seizure of certain Scottish ships by the English), and the devastation in the following May
of part of Scotland by an English army, as
a chastisement for alleged broken faith.[2]   The
ecclesiastical issue was the renewal of persecution, particularly in Perth and Dundee, under the
auspices of the triumphant Cardinal, and with the
reluctant acquiescence of the humiliated Regent.[3]

III.   The seed of evangelical truth, which had
been sown in Knox's heart by Chaplain William,
fructified under other husbandry.   In May, 1544,
or possibly in July, 1543, George Wishart, the
son or nephew of a laird of Pitarrow, in Kin-
cardineshire,[4] returned, after long absence, to his

---

[1] Knox, *H. of R.*, i., 109; *Sadler Papers*, i., 277–278; *Ham. Papers*, i., 522.

[2] *Diurn. of Occur.*, 30; Tytler, v., 353.   It was on this occasion that Melrose, Dryburgh, Kelso, and Coldingham Abbeys were destroyed by English soldiers, and not, as is often supposed, at the time of the Reformation by fanatical Scottish Protestants (Burton, *H. of Sc.*, chap. xxxv.).

[3] Knox, *H. of R.*, i., 117; Foxe, *Acts*, v., 623; Spottisw., i., 147; Herkless, *Cardinal Beaton*, 283–285.   Four men were hanged and one woman drowned at Perth, early in 1544, for alleged heresy.

[4] The date of Wishart's return is disputed, and the question has some bearing on the controversy (see pp. 64 sqq.) as
to his alleged complicity in the assassination of Cardinal
Beaton.   See Laing's *W. of K.*, i., 125 and App. ix.; A. Petrie,

native land. Six years before, while a teacher of Greek in Montrose, Wishart had come under the suspicion of heresy, through his practice of reading the Greek New Testament with his pupils. He was cited to appear before the Bishop of Brechin; fled to England; visited subsequently Germany and Switzerland; and eventually became a tutor in the University of Cambridge. An admiring pupil there, Emery Tylney, describes him in 1543 as a man of tall stature, comely in person, courteous, lovely, glad to teach, desirous to learn, fearing God, hating covetousness. "If I should declare his love to me, and all men, his charity to the poor in giving, relieving, caring, helping, providing, yea infinitely studying how to do good to all and hurt to none, I should sooner want words than just cause to commend him." [1]

The immediate occasion, probably, of Wishart's resolve to return to Scotland was the Regent's original Protestant policy, which appeared to promise opportunities of freely propagating Reformed doctrine. Prior to his actual return, Arran's apostasy and the Cardinal's restoration to power had completely changed the situation. Wishart, however, was not deterred from delivering his testimony, first at Montrose in a private house; afterwards more publicly at Dundee, in spite of

Compendious History, ii., 182; *N. B. Rev.*, xlix.; Rogers, *Life of Wishart*, p. 19; Hay Fleming, in *Contemp. Rev.*, lxxiv., 380; Andrew Lang, *H. of Sc.*, i., 469.

[1] Foxe, *Acts*, v., 625–626 ; Rogers, *Life of Wishart*, 6, 7, 17.

pestilence and attempted assassination, of ecclesiastical malice and magisterial opposition; in numerous parishes, also, of Ayrshire, under the protection of the Earl of Glencairn, Hugh Campbell of Kinyeancleuch, and other influential friends of the Reform movement. Sometimes he preached in churches, occasionally in the fields, and once, at least, in the street at the East Port of Dundee, so that he might be heard both by the plague-stricken crowd outside the gate, and by the healthy multitude inside.[1] Early in December, 1545, he ventured, against the remonstrance of friends, to preach in Leith, under the shadow, as it were, of the Regent's palace; and afterwards at Inveresk, a few miles from Edinburgh.[2]

It was at this stage that Knox came under Wishart's potent influence. The former had become tutor some time before in the family of Hugh Douglas of Longniddry in Haddingtonshire, an ardent adherent of the Reform cause; and he had "waited upon Wishart from the time he came to Lothian."[3] The house of Douglas was Wishart's abode during a portion of his five-weeks' stay in the district.[4] Knox was probably present at the service in Inveresk, about eight

---

[1] Knox, *H. of R.*, i., 125–133; Cook, *H. of R.*, i., 272–278.
[2] Knox, *H. of R.*, i., 134, 135.
[3] *Ibid.*, i., 137, 139.
[4] *Ibid.*, p. 134.

Haddington Parish Church ("Lamp of Lothian"), in which Knox attended George Wishart on the occasion of the latter's last sermon, in January, 1546, a few hours before his arrest.

miles off; and he could hardly fail to be one of the congregation in the neighbouring church of Tranent on the two succeeding Sundays, when, as he testifies, Wishart "preached with the like grace, and like confluence of people." We are expressly told that he was with the Reformer on the occasion of the latter's evangelistic visit to Haddington in January, 1546.[1] The acquaintance between the two men speedily ripened; on Wishart's side into a fulness of brotherly confidence which throws significant light on the sympathetic phase of Knox's character; on Knox's part into a warmth and chivalry of personal devotion, which prove that Tylney's eulogy of Wishart rested on a solid foundation. He was "a man" according to Knox, "of such graces as before were never heard [of] within this realm, yea, and are rare to be found yet in any man." On the Sunday before his arrest, while he was preparing his thoughts for his last service in Haddington church, Wishart was in a state of deep depression, caused partly by the apparent lukewarmness of the people of the town as compared with those of other places, and partly by a letter which he had just received, and which he interpreted as a sign that "men began to weary of God." Knox was the friend whom Wishart summoned to his presence, to whom he imparted his disappointment, and from whom he sought strengthening sympathy. When "the time of sermon approached," Knox "left the preacher for the present to his meditation"; but he remained near enough to know that "Master George spaced up and down before the high altar more than half an hour, and that his very visage declared the grief of his mind." Many years afterwards Knox recalled vividly Wishart's solemn judgments on the town which would not "know the time of God's merciful visitation," along with his "exhortation to patience, to the fear of God, and to works of mercy" on the part of God's people.[1]

It had been arranged that the preacher should pass the night at the house of Cockburn of Ormiston (about six miles off), and Knox relates his departure on foot with that laird on a night "of vehement frost," when riding was impracticable. Knowing Wishart's depression and foreseeing danger (for Cardinal Beaton was then in the vicinity, with five hundred armed men), Knox "pressed to have gone with Master George" and appeared with a "two-handed sword," which he or others carried about for the Reformer's defence. But Wish-

---

[1] *H. of R.*, i., 137–138. The letter which had depressed Wishart was from certain "gentlemen of the West," including the Earl of Cassilis, who had undertaken to meet the Reformer in January at Edinburgh, and to procure for him the opportunity of "disputation" with the bishops at the Provincial Synod (Knox, i., 131). The letter informed Wishart of the inability of these friends to keep the engagement.

art, also foreboding trouble, unselfishly declined
the valued company of his chivalrous friend.
"Nay, return to your bairns [*i. e.*, his pupils at
Longniddry]; one is sufficient for one sacrifice." [1]
There is no evidence that the two friends ever
met again; but the disciple heard of the midnight
arrest of his master by Lord Bothwell in the Cardinal's name; of the prisoner's transference from
Bothwell's castle, Elphinstone Tower, first to
Edinburgh, and eventually, with the Regent's
sanction, to St. Andrews; of Wishart's trial on the
last day of February (the anniversary of Patrick
Hamilton's condemnation and martyrdom) in the
cathedral of that city, before the two archbishops
and other dignitaries of the Church.[2] Wishart's
condemnation was a foregone conclusion; and the
execution, illegally carried out without the sanction of the Regent,[3] took place on the day after
the trial. If Knox was not present on the occasion, eye-witnesses doubtless reported to him the
particulars recorded in his *History*, including the
martyr's Christ-like declaration at the stake, "I
forgive them [his accusers] with all my heart";

---

[1] Knox, i., 137–139.

[2] *Ibid.*, i., 139–167. The reconciliation of the Primate and
the Archbishop of Glasgow (Dunbar) at this time, after
a recent quarrel, is compared by Knox to the restoration of
friendship between Pilate and Herod over the trial of Christ.

[3] See Pitscottie, *H. of Sc.*, ii., 56 (Sc. Text Soc. ed.), where
it is stated that the Regent "would not consent that any
'skaith' shall be done to that man at that time."

his prayer to Christ to "forgive them that have condemned me to death this day ignorantly"; and his solemn warning to the prelates and those associated with them, that "if they will not convert themselves from their wicked error, there shall hastily come upon them the wrath of God." [1]

If Wishart's teaching corresponded with the testimony which he gave at his trial, we know what doctrines Knox would specially receive from him. He would learn the supremacy of Holy Scripture above all fallible ecclesiastical councils;

---

[1] Knox, *H. of R.*, i., 169, 170. The words last quoted contain, probably, the germ out of which the myth of Wishart's alleged prophecy of the death of the Cardinal was afterwards developed: "He who from that high place feedeth his eyes with my torments, within few days shall be hanged out at the same window, to be seen with as much ignominy as he now leaneth there in pride." This "prediction" is not contained in the original and anonymous account of the martyrdom published in London in the following year, and attributed by Rogers (*Life of Wishart*, p. 49) and by Andrew Lang (*H. of Sc.*, i., 488) to Knox himself. It is not referred to in Knox's narrative of the proceedings—an omission the more significant because Knox elsewhere credits Wishart with foreknowledge. It is also not found in the first edition of Foxe's *Acts*, (1563). The earliest reference to the alleged prophecy occurs in a reprint of Foxe's work (1570), where the words occur in the margin: "Mr George Wishart prophesieth of the death of the Cardinal." George Buchanan, in his *History of Scotland* (Book xv., fol. 178), expands this into the sentence: "He who looks down upon us so proudly, will within a few days lie no less ignominiously than he now arrogantly reclines." Not till 1644, in the edition of Knox's *History* by David Buchanan (who takes many liberties with the text), does the saying appear in full form (p. 171).

the universal priesthood of believers, as distinguished from any exclusive sacerdotalism; the doctrine of justification by faith, as unfolded in the Epistle to the Romans; the recognition of "those Sacraments only which were instituted by Christ"; the rejection of transubstantiation, purgatory, "saint-worship," compulsory celibacy, enforced auricular confession to a priest; and the disavowal of superstitious belief in exorcism, holy water, the duty of abstaining from flesh on Friday, and other mere ecclesiastical observances.[1]

Through Wishart, moreover, Knox would become acquainted with an important doctrinal manifesto of Swiss Protestantism—the earliest Confession of Faith of the Helvetian churches, prepared by Bullinger and other Reformers for the Congress of Basel in 1536. Wishart had translated this Confession into English,[2] and he could hardly have failed to show it to his loyal follower. To this early embodiment of Protestant doctrine, with its emphatic testimony against images, altars, elaborate vestments, and "unprofitable ceremonies," as well as to Wishart himself, who was doubtless in substantial accord with what he had been at pains to translate, may be traced primarily the radical and Puritanic character of Knox's Reformation, as distinguished from the more

---

[1] Knox, *H. of R.*, i., 153–167.

[2] See *Wodrow Miscellany*, pp. 7–23. The MS. was printed after Wishart's death.

conservative and moderate policy which guided
the founders of the Lutheran and Anglican
churches.

ADDITIONAL NOTE TO CHAPTER II

*Alleged complicity of George Wishart in the con-
spiracy against Cardinal Beaton.*

The charge of complicity beforehand was made by
the Roman Catholic Dempster (*Hist. Eccl. Gentis
Scot.*, ii., 599), in the seventeenth century; and it has
been endorsed in recent times, to the extent, at least,
of the expression of grave suspicion, by Tytler
(*H. of Sc.*, v., chap. v.), Burton (*H. of Sc.*, iii., chap.
xxxvi.), Cunningham (*H. of Ch. of Sc.*, i., chap. viii.),
Stephen (*Scot. Ch.*, i., 527, 528), and others. Andrew
Lang regards the question as unsolved (*H. of Sc.*, i.,
487).

The unauthenticity of Wishart's alleged prophecy
of Beaton's death "within few days" removes one
foundation of the charge. The other two grounds
of suspicion are: (1) Documentary evidence (*a*)
that in April, 1544 "a Scottish man called Wishart" carried from Scotland to England a letter from
Crighton of Brunston, the contents of which referred
to a conspiracy against the Cardinal, and (*b*) that
the said Wishart had an interview with Henry VIII.
(*State Papers*, Henry VIII., v., 377). If George
Wishart did not return to Scotland until May, 1544
(see p. 56), he could not, of course, have been the
bearer of this letter. But, even if he returned in
July 1543, there is no evidence that he was the man
referred to. Dr. Burton argues that "if there had

been another Wishart so important as to get private
audience of Henry VIII., he could be identified."
But secret agents, even between nobles and kings,
when the business on hand is discreditable, need
not be persons of social distinction. The vague
designation, moreover,—"a Scottish man called
Wishart,"—hardly suggests a Master of Arts in Orders
who had been a tutor in Cambridge University. It
has been ascertained, however, that there were
several Wisharts of standing at that time, including
a second George Wishart, who became a baillie of
Dundee some time before 1560; a third George
Wishart (connected with the Pitarrow family), who
was a procurator in 1565; and John Wishart, a
kinsman of the martyr, who was a member of the
Reforming Parliament of 1560. Any one of these
may have been the Wishart referred to in the *State
Papers;* particularly the last, who became an as-
sociate of Kirkcaldy of Grange, one of the assassins
of the Cardinal (Rogers, *Life of Wishart*, pp. 58, 82–
87; Laing, *W. of K.*, i., 536).

(2) Wishart was undoubtedly, at the close of his
life, on terms of some intimacy with Crighton, of
Brunston; but with the actual assassination of the
Cardinal, Crighton had nothing to do; and even
if he still cherished a murderous purpose against
Beaton, there is no indication of his having confided
his designs to Wishart. The Reformer was also on
intimate terms with the Earls of Glencairn and
Cassilis, and with other members of the English
party in Scotland. These were in frequent correspondence with representatives of Henry VIII., and
there is evidence of the Earl of Cassilis having, in

5

May 1545, corresponded with Sadler, the English ambassador, regarding a "killing of the Cardinal" (Tytler, *Hist.*, v., 460). But Wishart's relations with this nobleman and others of the English faction appear to have been in connexion only with his preaching, at which they acted as his protectors.

While the arguments for Wishart's connivance are thus without substantial weight, the following considerations point strongly in the opposite direction: (1) The Cardinal was well aware of plots against his life. Had he suspected Wishart of complicity he would have made the most of these, especially with a view to securing the Regent's sanction (which was withheld) to Wishart's trial and execution. (2) No contemporary writer, Catholic or Protestant, alludes to Wishart's supposed connexion with the conspiracy. (3) What is otherwise recorded of Wishart militates against his complicity. Apart from the general testimony of Tylney and Knox to his gentleness of character, we have (*a*) his demeanour at Mauchline, when he was excluded from the church there, and when his friends were about to force an entrance. "It is the word of peace that God sends by me," he declared: "the blood of no man shall be shed this day for the preaching of it" (Knox, *H. of R.*, i., 128). (*b*) At Dundee, when a priest attempted to assassinate him, and when the infuriated multitude would have lynched the assassin, Wishart "took him in his arms, and said, 'Whosoever troubles him shall trouble me'" (*Ibid.*, i., 131). (*c*) We have seen (p. 62), how, prior to his martyrdom, he besought Christ to forgive those who had condemned him. Unless Wishart was the most shameless of hypocrites (which

is not asserted by his accusers), he could not have
uttered that prayer, if all the while he was acces-
sory to a plot against Beaton's life.   It was not the
living Reformer, but the dead martyr, through the
natural resentment excited by his execution, who
conspired to kill the Cardinal.[1]

---

[1] In addition to works quoted, see a tract by William
Cramond of Cullen (1898), *The Truth about George Wishart;*
Andrew Lang's article in *Blackwood*, March, 1898, on *The
Truth about the Cardinal's Murder;* and Hay Fleming's reply
in *Contem. Rev.*, lxxiv., 375–389.

CHAPTER III

1546–1549

THE assassination of Cardinal Beaton followed within three months after the martyrdom of Wishart. Plots had long been devised against him, but Wishart's death was the immediate occasion of the final and successful conspiracy. Early in the morning of the 29th May, 1546, the Primate's castle was surprised by an armed band headed by Norman and John Leslie of Rothes, Kirkcaldy of Grange, and James Melville of Raith. The Primate was found in his bedchamber and solemnly summoned to repent of his wicked life, especially of the shedding of Wishart's blood.

"That blood," said Melville, "cries for vengeance, and we are sent from God to revenge it: for here before God I protest that neither hatred of thy person nor love of thy riches, nor fear of any trouble thou couldest have done to me, moveth me to strike thee, but only because thou hast been and remainest an obstinate enemy against Jesus Christ and His holy evangel."

"And so," adds Knox, "he struck him twice or thrice; and so he fell; never a word heard out of his mouth but 'I am a priest, I am a priest: fy, fy, all is gone.'" [1]   That Melville and perhaps others of the conspirators sincerely believed themselves to be divinely appointed instruments of just retribution, need not be disputed; but the familiar lines attributed, although on inadequate authority, to Sir David Lyndsay, express probably the sentiment of most contemporary Reformers, and the general verdict of Protestant posterity:

> "As for the Cardinal, I grant,
>   He was the man we weel could want,
>   And we'll forget him soon:
>   And yet I think that sooth to say,
>   Although the loon be weel away,
>   The deed was foully done." [2]

What bearing has the *Tragedy of the Cardinal* on the character of Knox ? He had no share in the conspiracy and assassination[3]; but unquestionably he condoned the murder after it had taken place. Ten months later, as we shall presently see, he identified

---

[1] Knox, *H. of R.*, i., 174–177.

[2] The stanza is not contained in any edition of Lyndsay's *Tragedy*, and the metre is not the same. Wodrow is the earliest author who ascribes the verse to Lyndsay. See Hay Fleming's editorial note in A. F. Mitchell's *Scott. Ref.*, p. 81.

[3] Knox's Roman Catholic detractor, James Laing, expressly accuses him of instigating the "removal" of the Cardinal (*De Vita et Moribus Hereticorum*, p. 113); but his charges against the Reformers generally are so virulent as to be untrustworthy in the absence of distinct evidence.

himself with the conspirators by repairing to the Castle of St. Andrews, of which they had taken possession after committing the crime; and in his *History* he refers to the deed as a "godly fact" of which he was able to write even "merrily" as one of God's "just judgments, whereby he would admonish the tyrants of this earth that in the end he would be revenged of their cruelty." [1] Knox apparently justified the killing of Beaton on the ground that when cruel oppressors, instead of being punished, are protected and supported by the civil authority, that authority ceases so far to have any claim to be the "minister of God" and the sole executive of public justice. In such circumstances the individual has the right to intervene, in order to discharge a neglected corporate duty; so long as he avoids acts of revenge for private wrongs and confines himself to retribution for public evil-doing. The principle is obviously a dangerous one and liable to gross abuse in its application. It may partly explain, but cannot justify, Knox's condonation of the murder; and in any case his "merriness" in the narration of the tragedy must be condemned. One may charitably believe that his ardent affection for the martyred Wishart helped to obscure his vision and to distort his judgment. [2]

---

[1] Knox, *H. of R.*, i., 177, 180.

[2] On another occasion, Knox was careful to declare that even prisoners unjustly confined must not "shed any man's blood for their freedom" (Knox, *H. of R.*, i., 229).

Knox had continued, after Wishart's arrest and
martyrdom, to discharge the duties of tutor to
Francis and George Douglas, sons of the Laird of
Longniddry, as well as to Alexander Cockburn,
son of John Cockburn of Ormiston.[1]   The ruins
of a chapel near the site of the former mansion-
house of Longniddry still bear the name of " John
Knox's Kirk." [2]   In that chapel, doubtless, were
held those readings from the Gospel of St. John
with which Knox supplemented his instruction in
"grammar" and "human authors," and to which
others besides his three pupils were admitted.[3]
As a disciple of Wishart, however, Knox must
have felt, even before the Cardinal's death, that his
liberty, if not his life, was in danger: and after the
assassination the peril increased.   His continuous
residence at Longniddry became impracticable:
he had to "remove from place to place by reason
of the persecution that came upon him," at the
instance, he believed, of Beaton's successor,
Archbishop Hamilton.   His original purpose, accordingly, was to leave Scotland for a time.
"Of England," he declares, "he had then no

---

[1] Knox, *H. of R.*, i., 185.   Of Knox's three pupils, the last-
named alone attained to distinction.   An inscription on his
tomb at Ormiston commemorates his "insignem linguarum
professionem" and includes a testimony to his learning by
George Buchanan.   Dempster (*Hist. Eccl.*, p. 182) speaks of
having seen three literary works by Alexander Cockburn,
who died in 1564, at the age of twenty-eight.

[2] Laing's note 2 in *W. of K.*, i., 185.

[3] Knox, *H. of R.*, i., 186.

pleasure"; "the Pope's name being suppressed,
his laws and corruptions remained in full vigour";
but he intended "to have visited the schools of
Germany." The anxiety, however, of the lairds
of Longniddry and of Ormiston to retain him as
the tutor of their sons induced Knox to acquiesce
in their proposal that he should avail himself
of the protection of the Castle of St. Andrews,
and should take his three pupils thither.[1] To
this deviation, at the instance of others, from his
original purpose was due, humanly speaking, the
transformation of Knox out of a mere sympathetic adherent into the protagonist of the Scottish Reformation.

Knox and his pupils arrived in April, 1547.
During the autumn of 1546 the Castle had been
ineffectually besieged by the Regent, whose own
son, captured at the time of the Cardinal's death,
had been detained as a hostage. In December,
however, a truce had been arranged, according to
which the Castle was to remain in the hands of
the conspirators and their friends until a "sufficient absolution" should be received from the
Pope "for the slaughter of the Cardinal."[2] Such
absolution was deemed necessary before the
surrender of the fortress and the delivery of the
hostages could be accepted as the price of civil
indemnity for those implicated in the crime.

---

[1] Knox, *H. of R.*, i., 185.
[2] *Ibid.*, i., 183, 184.

II. The company within the Castle numbered
at this time 150,[1] including the conspirators
themselves and those who had joined them out of
sympathy or from fear of persecution. Among
the most notable of the latter were John Rough,[2]
ex-chaplain of the Regent, who acted as minister of the Castle congregation, and Henry Balnaves, the Regent's ex-Secretary of State, a
leading promoter of the Act of Parliament in
1543, authorising the use of vernacular Scripture.
Among frequent guests at the Castle, although
not constant inmates, was Sir David Lyndsay,
the unsparing castigator, as we have seen, of
clerical vice and ecclesiastical abuse, whose *Tragedy of the Cardinal* had been issued shortly before
Knox's arrival.[3] The "Castilians" appear to
have been rather a "mixed multitude" as regards character. On the one hand, there were
godly men in whom Knox recognised a genuine
"Congregation of the Faithful"; on the other
hand, regarding a large proportion of the garrison,

---

[1] Keith, *Church and State in Sc.*, i., 124.

[2] Rough, who retired to Kyle in Ayrshire after the Regent's recantation, had repaired to St. Andrews on hearing
of Beaton's death. He left St. Andrews prior to the capture
of the Castle, and resided for six years in England, holding
a benefice near Hull. At Edward VI.'s death, he fled to
Friesland; but during a visit to London in 1557 he was arrested, and burnt at Smithfield. (Calderwood, *H. of the
Kirk*, i., 251; Laing's note in Knox's *H. of R.*, i., 187.)

[3] Compare line 267 with date of printing as given by Laing,
Works of Sir David Lyndsay, i., 371.

he testifies sorrowfully to "their corrupt life"; [1]
and George Buchanan accuses them of "depreda-
tions with fire and sword" as well as of gross
impiety and immorality, "from which they could
not be restrained by Knox's frequent admoni-
tions." [2]   The Reformer continued in the Castle
chapel at St. Andrews those semi-public exposi-
tions of the Gospel of St. John which he had
begun in the chapel at Longniddry. His pupils
were also instructed in a Catechism,[3] "an account
of which he caused them to give publicly in the
parish Kirk"; an incidental evidence that the relations between the "Castilians" and the ecclesiastical authorities were at this juncture moderately
friendly.[4]   It was not long before the tutor of
boys was called to become the leader of men.
The Bible readings and catechetical exercises
were attended by a numerous audience: and the
more intelligent hearers soon discovered that

---

[1] Knox, *H. of R.*, i., 204.

[2] *H. of Sc.*, Book xv., folio 179.

[3] Possibly the Catechism of Calvin (published in Latin,
1538), which Wishart might have brought home from Switzerland along with the Helvetian Confession. The First
Book of Discipline directed it to be introduced into the
Scottish Church (1560) as "the most perfect that ever yet
was used" (Knox, *H. of R.*, ii., 239).

[4] Knox, *H. of R.*, i., 186.   Prior to the settlement in 1549
of the recently appointed Primate Hamilton, the ecclesiastical government was in the hands of the Vicar-general Wynram (afterwards a Protestant Superintendent of Fife), who
already sympathised with the Reformation.

Pulpit from which Knox preached in the town church of St. Andrew's.
(Now in the University Building.)

they had among themselves a man of gifts and
power. Rough, in particular, a preacher "without corruption" and "well liked of the people,"
but "not the most learned," soon realised that
for pulpit ministry to the Castle garrison, for
the conversion of the citizens to evangelical
doctrine, and above all for controversy with
the divines of the Church and University, a
preacher more eloquent, more erudite, and more
powerful in argument than himself was required.
With fine self-abnegation, accordingly, he joined
with Balnaves in pressing on Knox privately the
office of preacher. At first Knox "utterly refused." His ordination as a priest by Roman
hands was for him no adequate warrant: and he
declared to his friends that he "would not run
where God had not called him;" meaning—so he
himself interprets the utterance—that he would
do nothing "without a lawful vocation." [1]

The "lawful vocation" was not long of coming.
Rough and Balnaves took counsel with Lyndsay
and others; and the outcome was a formal call
to the ministry of the Castle congregation. Knox
himself gives a graphic description of the scene.
It was at the ordinary service, and apparently
Knox had received no warning of what was
intended; but the subject of Rough's sermon—
the right of a congregation to choose as their
minister one in whom they discerned the gift of

---

[1] Knox, *H. of R.*, i., 184–186.

God, and the heavy responsibility of refusing such
a call—prepared him for the personal application.

"Brother, ye shall not be offended," said Rough,
"albeit I speak unto you that which I have in charge,
even from all those that are here present, which is
this: In the name of God and of His Son Jesus Christ,
and in the name of these that presently call you by
my mouth, I charge you that ye refuse not this holy
vocation: but that as ye tender the glory of God, the
increase of Christ's kingdom, the edification of your
brethren and the comfort of me, whom ye understand
well enough to be oppressed by the multitude of
labours, that ye take upon you the public office and
charge of preaching, even as ye look to avoid God's
heavy displeasure, and desire that He shall multiply
His graces with you."

The preacher concluded by publicly asking those
present whether he had not fulfilled their charge.
When an answer in the affirmative had been given,
"the said John, abashed, burst forth in most
abundant tears and withdrew himself to his chamber"; and "no man saw any sign of mirth of him,
neither yet had he pleasure to accompany any
man, many days together." [1]   The call, however,
was not declined: and an occasion for the inaugur-
ation of Knox's ministry soon presented itself.

III.   Among the notable divines of St. Andrews at this time was Dean John Annand, Principal of St. Leonard's College, who "had long

[1] Knox, *H. of R.*, i., 186–188.

troubled Rough in his preaching." Knox had already supported his colleague in some controversy with a tract, which has perished; and the Dean had been constrained to fall back on the authority of the Church, whose condemnation, he argued, of the new doctrine rendered further disputation superfluous. At the close of a sermon to this effect by Annand, Knox publicly offered to prove that "the Roman Kirk, as now corrupted, was the synagogue of Satan"; that "the Pope was the Man of Sin, of whom the Apostle speaks," and that neither accordingly possessed the authority which the preacher had claimed. Scotsmen are notoriously fond of a theological tournament; and those present "cried with one consent: 'let us hear the probation of that which ye have now affirmed'." The following Sunday was appointed for the purpose. Knox has preserved a summary of this first sermon after his call, preached before his now aged preceptor, John Major, before his future colleague in the Reformation, Vicar-general Wynram; and before numerous canons and friars, as well as lay enquirers. Taking Daniel vii., 24, 25 as a text, he showed how the lives of clergy, from popes downwards; how the doctrines of the Church, particularly that of justification through "works of man's invention"; how ecclesiastical enactments such as clerical celibacy, compulsory fasting, and observance of days; and how such "blasphemous" pretensions as those which claimed papal infallibility and power over purgatory—all combined to prove that the Roman Church was not Christ's body, but the "whore of Babylon," and the Pope not the "Vicar of Christ" but "Antichrist." Knox's sermon became the talk of the town. "Others," it was said, "sned [lopped] the branches of the Papistry; but he strikes at the root, to destroy the whole." "Wishart," some declared, "spake never so plainly, and yet he was burnt: even so will he be"; while others warned the dignitaries of the Church not to rely on "fire and sword" as "defences"; since "men now have other eyes than they had then." [1]

Archbishop Hamilton heard with astonishment of the heresy allowed to be preached in his metropolitan city, and he sent to his Vicar-general a letter of remonstrance against such scandalous toleration. Wynram found himself constrained to take some action. He summoned Rough and Knox to a theological convention in St. Leonard's College; but he stated at the outset that the object of the gathering was not a judicial trial, but a friendly colloquy. Passing by the main points at issue, regarding which he was anxious, probably, to avoid committing himself, the Vicar-general opened discussion on the comparatively minor question of the lawfulness of certain ecclesiastical ceremonies. On this subject Wynram main-

[1] Knox, *H. of R.*, i., 189–192.

tained the moderate position that ceremonies
which have a "godly signification" are lawful,
although not prescribed by the Word of God;
while Knox took his stand on what afterwards
became known as the Puritan doctrine, that
nothing in worship is pleasing to God or lawful
for man except what "God in express words has
commanded." At this stage the Vicar handed
over the argument to a Franciscan friar, Arbuckle
by name, who had probably shown himself eager
to enter the lists. Arbuckle, less cautious than
Wynram, undertook to demonstrate not merely
the lawfulness but the divine institution of various
ceremonies (such as the use of oil, salt, candles,
spittle, etc., in baptism); and ere long was en-
tangled by his opponent into the position that
when the Apostles wrote their Epistles, in which
there is no reference to such observances, "they
had not yet received the Holy Spirit." "Father,
what say ye?" interposed the Vicar-general. "God
forbid that ye affirm that; for then farewell the
ground of our faith." The discomfited friar
failed to recover himself: the discussion was not
prolonged: other things were "scooft over"; and
after this (so Knox declares) the Roman party
"had no great heart for further disputation."
The Vicar-general did not encourage discussion;
and the Roman clergy adopted the prudent arrangement that henceforth the Sunday sermon
in the parish church should always be preached

by one of themselves. Knox's teaching was thus relegated to week-days, when the congregation was smaller, and the Roman preachers avoided controversial topics, delivering "sermons penned to offend no man." [1]

The labours of Knox were abundantly fruitful. "A great number of the town openly professed" Reformed doctrine; and he was emboldened to take a step which inaugurated a significant development in Protestant organisation. Hitherto adherents of the Reformation movement either abstained from a participation in the Holy Communion, at least in public, or took part in the mass with an express or a tacit repudiation of the superstitious observances connected with the celebration. Knox was the first, apparently, in Scotland to introduce the public celebration of the Sacrament (probably in the Castle chapel) according to a Reformed ritual and without any acknowledgment of transubstantiation. The Protestant movement began thus to be transformed into the establishment of a Reformed Church. [2]

[1] Knox, *H. of R.*, i., 192–201. Knox himself is our sole authority for the incidents above described; but we may presume he would be particularly careful to relate accurately proceedings in which Wynram, his own colleague in the ministry of the Reformed Church, was concerned.

[2] *Ibid.*, pp. 201–202. Wishart is said to have privately celebrated the Holy Communion in the Castle on the morning of his execution (Geo. Buchanan, *H. of Sc.*, B. xv., folio 178; but Knox is silent as to this incident. It is probable that Wishart celebrated the Lord's Supper privately at Dun (see A. F. Mitchell, *Scott. Ref.*, p. 78).

Ruins of the Castle of St. Andrew's,

IV.   Meanwhile, about midsummer, the papal
absolution of the conspirators arrived; but owing
to the ambiguous terms—"*remittimus irremis-
sibile*"—the garrison refrained from making a
surrender, which they were now inclined to postpone through fresh hope of succour from England.   Before the end of June, however, foreign
intervention took place from a different quarter.
In response to the Regent's repeated appeals, a
fleet of twenty-one French galleys arrived before
St. Andrews; while the Scottish army co-operated
on land.   Eventually (after a month) the simul-
taneous assault by land and sea, combined with
an outbreak of pestilence and the cutting off of
supplies, led to the garrison (120 in all) surrender-
ing on fair conditions.   According to Knox, their
lives were to be spared: they were to be trans-
ported to France: thereafter they were to be
removed at the French king's expense to any
country except Scotland which each prisoner
might select.[1]

Knox had forewarned the garrison of impending trouble, as the manifestation of divine displeasure at their evil doings.   Before any French
galley had appeared, "from the time he was called
to preach," he testified that "their corrupt life
could not escape punishment of God."   While the
garrison were rejoicing over early successes, "he
lamented, and ever said they saw not what he

---

[1] Knox, *H. of R.*, i., 203–206.   See note, p. 82.
6

saw." When they boasted of the Castle's strong
and thick walls, he replied that these would prove
to be "egg-shells." When they reckoned confidently on rescue by an English army, he had
predicted, "Ye shall be delivered into your
enemies' hands." [1]

The conditions on which the garrison are stated
to have surrendered were not faithfully fulfilled.
The lives of the "Castilians" were spared: but
instead of liberty on arrival in France, and the
choice of an abode thereafter, all were either committed to prison or consigned to the galleys.[2]
Among those who endured the latter form of
bondage was Knox. About a year and a half of

---

[1] Knox, *H. of R.*, i., 204–205.

[2] Tytler (*H. of Sc.*, vi., 17) and Andrew Lang (*H. of Sc.*, ii.,
18) decline to accept Knox's statement of the conditions,
and therefore question his charge of bad faith. Buchanan
(B. XV., fol. 179) speaks of the garrison as "*incolumitatem
modo pacti,*" a phrase which may mean either that they
were guaranteed merely against personal injury, or that their
lives only were to be spared. Lesley (*Vern. Hist. of Sc.*,
p. 194) limits the promise to the sparing of their lives
"if the King of France thought this to be done." It is
of course *possible* that Knox confused the terms asked for
with the terms granted (as Lang suggests); but the Reformer's
statement on a matter in which he was personally concerned
is very precise; and it is more probable, that the descriptions of Buchanan and Lesley were founded on what actually
was done with the captured men. Knox, moreover, accounts
definitely for the alleged breach of faith, as owing partly to a
letter from the Pope to the King of France counselling
"severity," and partly to an embassy from Scotland demanding that "those of the Castle should be sharply handled"
(Knox, *H. of R.*, i., 207).

his life, from September, 1547, were spent in the galley service. What his normal experience probably was may be realised from the description of a Huguenot galley-bondman during the persecution which followed the revocation of the Edict of Nantes in 1685. Food and clothing were scant and coarse: shelter from the elements was allowed only in winter. The galleymen were "chained by the neck in couples," and were so bound to the benches that they could "neither sit nor stand upright," nor yet "lie down at full length." At night they slept under the benches, closely packed together, "on a little straw gnawed by rats and mice." They were sometimes obliged to row ten or twelve hours without interruption; and their labours were stimulated by frequent strokes of the cowhide whip and by fear of the more terrible bastinado. Any galleyman who professed to be wounded or infirm was lashed "to discover whether he was not feigning." All the time their faith was tried by constant assurances poured into their ears by the chaplain, that by renouncing Protestantism they would obtain immediate liberation.[1] Long afterwards Knox referred to the "torment" which he sustained in the galleys; to the "sobs of his heart"; to his feet "chained in the prison of his dolour"; and

---

[1] See *Autobiography of a French Protestant* (Jean Marteilhe), trans. from the French (*R. T. S.*), pp. 69, 81, 134, 203, 209, 213.

to his "lying in irons, sore troubled by corporal infirmity, in a galley named *Notre Dame*." [1]

Knox, however, was not the man to sink under tribulation. "From the very day they entered into the galleys"—so he testifies [2]—he declared that God would deliver them "from that bondage to His glory, even in this life." Through three recorded incidents during this period we catch glimpses of his uniform hopefulness amid occasional depression, of his power of mental effort amid bodily affliction, and of that vein of humour which helped him, to bear patiently misfortune and malice. (1.) Persistent efforts were at first made to entice or threaten the Scottish captives into conformity to Roman usages. One Saturday, at Nantes, the *Salve Regina* was sung, and a painted wooden image of the Virgin was brought to be devoutly kissed. When the image was "presented to one of the Scottish men" (not improbably to Knox himself, who relates the incident)

---

[1] *H. of R.*, i., 349; Epis. Dedic. prefixed to Knox's summary of Balnaves's *Justification by Faith* (Laing, *W. of K.*, iii., 8). We can hardly doubt, also, that the Reformer had this period of his life in mind when in his *Treatise on Prayer* (Laing, *W. of K.*, iii., 89, 101) he speaks of having called to God "with sore oppressed heart from the deep pit of tribulation," and when in the same writing he recalls the "grudging and murmuring complaints of the flesh," and the "anger, wrath, and indignation which it conceiveth against God, calling all His promises in doubt." Partial relief, indeed, must, occasionally, have been given, for Knox was able to do some literary work (see p. 85 and Stalker, *John Knox*, 27).

[2] *H. of R.*, i., 228.

he refused to touch what he called "ane idol accursed." The "painted brod" was then violently thrust in his face and put between his hands; whereupon the indignant Protestant threw the image into the Loire, exclaiming, "Let our Lady now save herself; she is lycht aneuch." "After that," adds Knox, "was no Scottish man urged with that idolatry." [1]   (2) A second notable incident took place in the winter of 1548, when Knox's galley lay at Rouen, and his fellow-captive, Henry Balnaves, was imprisoned in the palace of that city. Balnaves had been occupying his leisure with the composition of his treatise on *Justification by Faith*, and had somehow got it put into the Reformer's hands for revisal. In spite of what, with grim humour, Knox calls "incommodity of place, as well as imbecility of mind" (the result of excessive manual labour and bodily infirmity), he contrived to edit his friend's treatise, dividing it for convenience into chapters, drawing up a "summary," adding annotations, and preparing a "commendatory Epistle." The work thus revised and supplemented was despatched to Scotland: it constitutes a remarkable memorial of literary labour in circumstances the most unfavourable.[2]   (3) The third incident occurred while the *Notre Dame*

---

[1] *H. of R.*, i., 227.

[2] Laing, *W. of K.*, iii., 4, 8, 9. For some unexplained reason the work was not published until after Knox's death.

happened to be lying between Dundee and St.
Andrews.[1] Knox was so ill at the time that
"few hoped his life." Sir James Balfour, then a
trusted friend and fellow-captive, although afterwards he proved himself unworthy of the Reformer's confidence,[2] bade him "look at the land,
and asked him if he knew it."

"Yes," was the reply, "I know it well; for I see
the steeple of the place where God first opened my
mouth in public to His glory: and I am fully persuaded, how weak that ever I now appear, that I
shall not depart this life until my tongue shall glorify
His godly name in the same place." [3]

Knox had no scruple about advising some of his
friends who asked his counsel—Kirkcaldy, Kirk-
michael, Robert and William Leslie,—to make
their escape from prison, provided they could do
so without bloodshed; and in this, eventually, they
succeeded. For a chained galley-man to escape
was much more difficult; and Knox does not

---

[1] It was probably one of the galleys which in June, 1548,
brought over from France an army of 6000 to help the Scots
in their conflict with England (And. Lang, *H. of Sc.*, ii., 12).

[2] Spottiswoode (*Hist.*, i., 177) states that he obtained his
freedom by "abjuring his profession." He returned to
Scotland, was appointed Official of Lothian by the Primate,
and eventually in 1567 became Lord President of the Court
of Session (Laing, notes on Knox's *H. of R.*, i., 202, 235).

[3] Knox, *H. of R.*, i., 228. He states that Balfour reported
this incident "in presence of famous witnesses many years
before" his (Knox's) final return to Scotland.

appear ever to have attempted it. He was
"assured that God would deliver them," and was
content to "abide for a season upon His good
pleasure." [1]   There is some uncertainty about the
circumstances of his release, which took place in
February or March, 1549 [2]: but there can be no
doubt of its being due to negotiations for the
exchange of prisoners. These negotiations were
initiated by the English [3] with the Scottish and
French Governments so early as the spring of
1548; and they issued ultimately in the deliverance of all who had surrendered at St. Andrew's,
except James Melville of Carnbee who had died a
natural death in the Castle of Brest.[4]

---

[1] Knox, *H. of R.*, i., 228–230.

[2] Laing, *W. of K.*, iii., 31.

[3] Knox and his gifts would become known to the English
Government through Balnaves, who had twice visited the
English Court on business during his abode at the Castle of
St. Andrews (Laing, *W. of K.*, iii., 410).

[4] See Bain, *Calendar of State Papers*, i., 102, containing
letter of Huntly to Somerset, 29th March, 1548; Tytler,
Reigns of Edw. VI. and Mary, i., 295; Knox, *H. of R.*, i., 233.

CHAPTER IV

JOHN KNOX IN ENGLAND—THE PIONEER OF PURITANISM

1549–1554

DURING the year and a half of Knox's servitude as a galley-man the Reformation cause in Scotland made little progress, owing partly to the lack of any notable Reforming preacher, and partly to renewed suspicion, among many otherwise inclined towards Protestantism, of the English alliance with which the religious question had been complicated. The vindictive devastation of Scotland by the English in 1544, after the matrimonial negotiations had been broken off, had not been forgotten; and Romanism was still widely identified with patriotism. Henry VIII. had died early in 1547; but his favourite policy of annexing Scotland to England by marriage contract did not die with him. About a month after the capture of St. Andrews by the French, a large army under Protector Somerset crossed the Border. It came to force upon Scotland a renewal of that betrothal between Edward VI. and Mary Stuart,

to which the Scottish Parliament had assented in
1543, during the brief period of Protestant ascendency. Somerset had counted on the support of
the Reformers in Scotland: but even those who
approved of the marriage did not welcome the
invasion: it was "not the right way to woo
and win a woman."[1] At such a juncture the
Roman clergy showed themselves at their best.
The Primate united with the Regent in raising an
army to resist the English. The sinews of war
came largely from the higher clergy: and at the
battle of Pinkie, on 10th September, 1547, as
Knox records, with involuntary admiration which
tempers his detestation, "No men were stouter
than the priests and canons."[2] The battle resulted in the defeat of the Scots with the loss of
10,000 men: but the issue, nevertheless, was a moral
discomfiture for England and the English policy,
while it added moral strength to the Roman cause
in Scotland. Somerset was not strong enough to
follow up his victory: he effected nothing but the
humiliation and irritation of the people whom it
was his interest to conciliate. The Primate and
his fellow-prelates, on the other hand, were glori-
fied in the eyes of the nation, as the patriotic,
even if unfortunate, champions of Scottish inde-

---

[1] Mary of Guise, in an interview with Edward VI., in November, 1551, expressly attributed to Somerset's invasion
the final withdrawal of Scotland from the proposed matrimonial alliance. See Keith, *Ch. and State in Sc.*, i., 138.

[2] Knox, *H. of R.*, i.. 209. 210.

pendence; while the cause of Reform was injured by its association, even indirectly, with English aggression. The Roman party, moreover, made the most of a document, found among the papers of Balnaves in the Castle of St. Andrews, containing the signatures of two hundred noblemen and gentlemen who had secretly bound themselves to the service of England.[1] Renewed English invasions in the winter and spring of 1547–48, and the arrival in June of a French army of 6000 to assist the Scots in their straits, strengthened the Romanist party in Scotland which favoured a French against an English alliance. The way was thus prepared for the betrothal in July of Mary Stuart to the Dauphin with the approval of the Estates; and before the end of that month the young queen was despatched to the country which for thirteen years was to be her home.[2]

Even before the capture of St. Andrews, in the summer of 1547, the resumption of persecution had been foreshadowed by a resolution of the Privy Council, in response to a petition from the clergy, to enforce the laws against heresy.[3] After

[1] Tytler, *H. of Sc.*, vi., 19, 20. Among the two hundred were the Earls Marischal, Cassilis, and Bothwell. Comp. Hay Fleming, *Mary Queen of Scots*, p. 192, who gives evidence of Argyll having "received a thousand crowns to incline him to the marriage." For evidence of Glencairn's treachery see Bain, *Cal. St. Pap.*, i., 10.

[2] Knox, *H. of R.*, i., 214–216; *Diur. of Occur.*, pp. 46, 47.

[3] Robertson, *Statuta*, i., p. cxlvi.

Hamilton's settlement in his See, accordingly, it
was only to be expected that Church and State
would combine in a policy of repression. At a
Provincial Church Council held at Edinburgh in
November, 1549, along with the laudable enactment of some reforming canons, it was resolved to
make a "diligent inquisition as to heresies." [1]
The return of Knox to Scotland at this time, even
if the terms of his liberation allowed it, must thus
have appeared perilous for himself and useless
for the cause. Gratitude to the English Government which had secured his release: sympathy so
far with Cranmer and other Reformers who were
endeavouring to make the English Church not
merely anti-papal but genuinely Protestant; and
the conviction that his vocation to the ministry
could not meanwhile be effectively fulfilled in his
native land—combined to induce Knox to accept
an invitation to settle in England. [2]

At the time of Henry VIII.'s death the Church
of England differed from the Church of Rome in

---

[1] Robertson, *Statuta*, ii., 81, 127. For reasons afterwards
to be stated, however, there was only one very notable outcome of this fresh inquisition. See Chap. VII., p. 183.

[2] Knox, *H. of R.*, i., 231; Lorimer, *John K. and the Church
of England*, p. 5. Knox's anxiety to resume the vocation of
the ministry somewhere is shown by his prayer, written
towards the close of his servitude in the galleys, and incor-
porated in the Epistle Dedicatory prefixed to Balnaves's
Justification by Faith : "Continue, O Lord, and grant unto us
that as now with pen and ink, so shortly we may confess
with voice and tongue, the same [Confession of our Faith]
before Thy Congregation" (Laing, *W. of K.*, iii., 9).

little more than the repudiation of the papacy, the suppression of the monasteries, and the authorised use of a vernacular Bible and liturgy. By the spring of 1549, when Knox arrived, considerable progress had been made, under the direction of Cranmer and the Protector, notwithstanding the indifference or opposition of the majority of the English clergy. Images which had been idolatrously venerated were removed; Reformed Homilies and a Protestant Catechism had been introduced; the Cup had been restored to the laity in Holy Communion; the earlier English Prayer-book of Edward VI. had come into use; marriage of the clergy had been legalised. Knox was conscious of his gifts; and England presented a favourable field of labour with a fairly congenial environment.

The Reformer was by no means the first Scottish Protestant who entered the service of the English Church. In 1535, under Henry VIII., through Cranmer's influence, Alexander Alane, the friend of Patrick Hamilton, held a lectureship in divinity at Cambridge: he is believed to have been the first in that university who expounded the Old Testament in the original.[1] During the same reign and in the same university, as we have seen, Wishart had propagated evangelical truth. Four distinguished Scottish Dominicans, also, had rendered similar service

[1] A. F. Mitchell, *Scott. Ref.*, 266.

in England. Alexander Seton, had become
chaplain to the Duke of Suffolk and a popular
London preacher.[1] John MacAlpine had been
presented to a canonry of Salisbury Cathedral.[2]
Thomas William, Knox's earliest instructor in
the Reformed faith, had become a Protestant
evangelist in Bristol.[3] John McDowel, whom
Knox eulogises for his "singular prudence" as
well as "learning and godliness," had been appointed chaplain to the Bishop of Salisbury, and
was the first in the diocese to assail publicly the
doctrine of papal supremacy.[4] In the earlier portion of Edward VI.'s reign three other Scots were
enrolled in a list of eighty accredited preachers—
John Willock, a Dominican from Ayrshire, afterwards one of Knox's leading colleagues in Scotland [5]; John McBriar of Galloway, eventually
Vicar of Newcastle ; and John Rough, the ex-
chaplain, and future martyr under "Bloody
Mary."[6] It is evident that at a time when the
mass of the English clergy were either lukewarm
or hostile, the Protestant cause benefited substantially by Scottish refugees.

The chief service, however, which England

---

[1] Knox, *H. of R.*, i., 54, 55, 531; Lorimer, *Precursors of
Knox*, 184. See p. 40.

[2] Knox, i., 55; Spottisw., *Hist.*, i., 131; Lorimer, 186.

[3] Knox, i., 105; Lorimer, 189.

[4] Knox, *H. of R.*, i., 55; Lorimer, 187.

[5] Knox, *H. of R.*, i., 245 and note 2; Lorimer, 190.

[6] Laing, *W. of K.*, i., 529, 530, 538–9.

received at this period from Scotland was rendered
by Knox.   His first sphere of labour was Berwick,[1]
which had been finally ceded by Scotland about
seventy years before.   This town, with its mixed
population partly of English, partly of Scottish,
extraction, was doubtless regarded as an appropriate pastoral charge for a patriotic Scot in
England, who desired to keep in touch with his
own fellow-countrymen.   Knox ministered there[2]
from the spring of 1549 to the spring of 1551,
Berwick lay within the diocese of Durham, of
which Tunstall[3] was the Bishop.   He was one of
the reactionary prelates who acquiesced in the
Reformation of Henry VIII., but had no sympathy with Cranmer's moderately progressive policy, and adhered to Roman doctrine and ritual.
The licensed preachers, however, held their commissions directly from the Privy Council, and were
virtually independent of diocesan jurisdiction.

Knox's parishioners at Berwick, like his congregation at St. Andrews, consisted of two distinct sections—garrison [4] and citizens.   The field

---

[1] Laing, *W. of K.*, i., 231; vi., p. xxvi.

[2] The Church has been transformed through repeated
restoration; and the old pulpit, popularly believed to be that
from which Knox preached, belongs probably to the early
part of the seventeenth century.

[3] Tunstall was imprisoned and deprived in 1552 through
Northumberland's influence for alleged treason; was restored under Mary, and again deprived for non-compliance
under Elizabeth (Froude, chaps. xxviii., xxx., xxxvii.).

[4] The normal strength of the garrison in time of peace was

Ruins of the Castle of Berwick-on-Tweed.

was not favourable for spiritual husbandry. The
northern counties of England were less affected by
the Reformation than most other districts of the
country; the influence of the Bishop was hostile;
and the moral tone of both soldiers and civilians
was bad. Sanguinary quarrels were common
among the garrison; disorder and robbery prevailed among the townsmen. In a letter addressed to Protector Somerset, in November, 1548,
it is declared that "there is better order among
the Tartars than in this town; and that a stern
disciplinarian as well as a stirring preacher will be
required to work out a moral and social reform." [1]
Knox was well fitted by character to fulfil these
requirements; and his brief ministry in the Castle
of St. Andrews had prepared him for his work in
the Border town. The earnest spirit in which he
laboured may be discerned from a letter addressed by him to the congregation in 1552,
after his departure. He declares that he had
"preached Christ among" them "in much weak-
ness and fear," yet "with rude boldness and zeal
towards God's glory and" their "salvation." [2]
Long afterwards, when Queen Mary Stuart re-

600; but during the first year of Knox's ministry, prior to
the Treaty of Boulogne (March, 1550), the number of soldiers
required for defence against Scottish invasion by land and
French assault by sea must have been abnormally large.

[1] Lorimer, *John Knox and the Ch. of E.*, 18; Knox, *H. of
R.*, ii., 280.

[2] Lorimer, 263.

peated to him some calumny about his having been "the cause of great sedition and slaughter in England," he was moved to testify regarding the visible fruits of his ministry: "I shame not, Madam, to affirm that God so blessed my weak labours that in Berwick, where commonly before there used to be slaughter, by reason of quarrels among soldiers, there was as great quietness, all the time I remained, as there is this day in Edinburgh." [1] The repeated promotion and offers of further promotion which Knox—no place-hunter or time-server—received in Engand, indicate that the efficiency of his pastorate at this period was fully recognised.

The preachers appointed by the Privy Council, when stationed in some town, were expected to propagate Reformed doctrine also in the surrounding district; and in such work Knox appears not to have spared himself. Evidence will be given afterwards [2] of his aggressive Protestantism in the diocese of Durham: and a casual letter appears to indicate his evangelistic diligence even in its less frequented parishes. In May, 1551, John ab Ulmis, then in England as a refugee, refers incidentally in correspondence to the Island of Lindisfarne as a place "not far from the town of Berwick," where, notwithstanding its isolated situation, he found the "inhabitants rightly

---

[1] Knox, *H. of R.*, ii., 280.
[2] See page 103.

instructed in religion." [1] To John Knox, directly
or indirectly, we may ascribe, with the highest
probability, such instruction; and it is interesting
to think of the island which, in the seventh century, under the Scottish monk Aidan, became a
second Iona, receiving now, after nine hundred
years, from a Scottish Reformer, a fresh diffusion of
the light which in the interval had become obscured.

Knox was instrumental at Berwick, not only in
propagating Protestantism, but in sowing some of
the earliest seeds of English Puritanism.   When
he arrived in the town the First Prayer-book of
Edward VI. had already been sanctioned and
issued.   Apart from its being composed in English, it diverged considerably from the old Roman
service-book: but it retained kneeling at Communion, prayers for the dead, the ceremony of
exorcism, and the use of the ancient vestments.
The public employment of this liturgy was ordered
to commence on Whitsunday, 1549: but in many
dioceses and districts the strong opposition to the
book by Romanists on the one hand, and a section
of Protestants on the other, prevented its widespread introduction. [2] Among the leading dissen-
tients from the Act of Uniformity which imposed
the new service-book was the Bishop of Durham. [3]

---

[1] Lorimer, 46. By "rightly instructed in religion" John
ab Ulmis evidently meant instructed in religion according to
Reformed doctrine.

[2] Perry, *Ref. in Engl.*, pp. 72–76.

[3] Froude, *H. of E.*, iv., 386.

For once, although on very different grounds,
Knox agreed with Tunstall. The Privy Council
do not appear to have constrained the Scottish
preacher to use a book to which he had strong
objections. An extant fragment of the "Practice
of the Lord's Supper used in Berwick-upon-Tweed
by John Knox" shows that he introduced into
the worship there forms of service distinctly Puritan in character. The Communion office is partly
borrowed from Swiss and German sources: probably it was based on materials privately used and
supplied to Knox by Wishart.[1] Prominent among
the features of Knox's service was the discontinuance of kneeling at the Holy Communion. He
regarded this attitude as a symbolical endorsement of transubstantiation and of the idolatry of
the host.[2] Objection to this posture became one
of the distinctive "notes" of Puritanism in Britain: and it is interesting to find the earliest practice, so far as is known, of sitting at Communion
in the Berwick service[3] conducted by a Scottish

---

[1] Lorimer, 290–297; A. F. Mitchell, *Scott. Ref.*, 77, 78.

[2] "Kneeling in that action, appearing to be joined with
certain dangers in maintaining superstition, I thought good
amongst you to avoid; and to use sitting at the Lord's
Table, which ye did not refuse" (Letter of Knox to the
Congregation of Berwick, Lorimer, 201).

[3] In 1550, Bishop Hooper advocated the same posture;
but a letter sent from England in 1552 from the Reformer
Utenhove to Bullinger indicates a sermon of a Scot (presumably Knox) as the chief occasion of the movement against
kneeling (Drysdale, *Presbyterians in England*, 66).

Reformer. This was the first of a series of acts
and testimonies which justify Carlyle's designation of Knox as the "chief priest and founder"
of English Puritanism.[1]

III. The Reformer's ministry at Berwick was
a memorable period, not only in his public career,
but in his domestic life. Among his congregation was Mrs. Elizabeth Bowes, the daughter
of Sir Roger Aske of Yorkshire. Her husband, Richard Bowes, was Captain of Norham
Castle, a few miles from Berwick, and belonged
to a Northumbrian family of whom one
had been knighted for his prowess at Flodden.
Husband and wife, as often happened at that
time, were differently affected on the great religious question of the day. Richard Bowes, like
most of the northern gentry, was a keen Romanist: Elizabeth Bowes, even before the arrival of
Knox, sympathised with the Reformation. Under
his ministry this sympathy developed; it issued
eventually, as we shall find, in separation from a
husband with whom she could dwell in peace only
at the cost of fidelity to truth.[2] Mrs. Bowes had
ten daughters, and at some date prior to 23rd
June, 1553, Knox and the fifth daughter, Marjorie,
had "pledged themselves to one another before
witnesses"; although, in consequence of her
father's opposition, the marriage did not take

---

[1] Carlyle, *Heroes and Hero-Worship*, p. 133.
[2] Knox, *H. of R.*, i., 253.

place till 1555 or 1556.[1]   No record remains of the
early period of Knox's acquaintance with his future
wife. The marriage, so far as appears, was a happy
one : but from incidental references one receives
the impression that the engagement was due to
the arrangement of the prospective mother-in-law
rather than to any ardent mutual affection, at first,
on the part of the young lady and the ex-priest,
who was probably her senior by many years. Certainly this was the view taken by friends, as Knox
himself candidly declares.[2]   It cannot be said that
even according to the prosaic standard of modern
courtship Knox was a model lover. The defect-
iveness of his ardour may be inferred from a
curious and suggestive expression in his earliest
extant epistle to his betrothed : " I *think* [!] this
be the first letter ever I wrait to you "; and the
writing, is entirely occupied with warnings against
" false teachers " and references to her mother's
conflicts with " the accusatour of God's elect "![3]
It must be remembered, however, in extenuation,
that when Knox wrote this letter he was forty or

---

[1] Knox's first extant letter to Mrs. Bowes as his future
mother-in-law is dated 23rd June, 1553; but the betrothal
may have been considerably earlier (Laing, *W. of K.*, iii.,
343). His first letter to Marjorie Bowes is undated (*ibid.*,
395). As to the time of the marriage, see p. 134.

[2] Laing, *W. of K.*, iii., 37. "It is supposed that all the
matter [of the betrothal] comes by you and me." So Knox
writes to Mrs. Bowes; and he is at no pains to deny the
truth of the "supposition."

[3] *Ibid.*, *W. of K.*, iii., 395.

more; and that he had been accustomed to fulfil
the office of pastor to Marjorie Bowes for some time
before he entered into the relationship of lover. In
his correspondence with her, amid much spiritual
counsel there gleams from time to time a sober af-
fectionateness. Thus, in one letter he writes to his
"most dear sister," "Be sure I will not forget you
and your company,"—adding, however, as if he
had gone too far, "so long as mortal man may
remember any earthly creature." [1]　In another
letter, addressed to his mother-in-law, he declares
that "there is none with whom I would more
gladly speak," *i. e.*, than with Mrs. Bowes; but
he at once corrects himself with the addition,
"only she excepted whom God hath offered to me,
and *commanded* me to love as my own flesh." [2]
Lovers do not usually base their affection on offers
and commands!

Knox's correspondence discloses his mother-in-
law as a kind-hearted and devout woman, whose
converse was a source of comfort and edification
to her future son-in-law; yet at the same time as
a spiritual valetudinarian, morbidly introspective,
constantly complaining about her religious condition, and living in habitual dread of reprobation.
On the one hand, he bears grateful witness to the
"motherly kindness ye have shewn unto me at
all times since our first acquaintance" [3]; and

---

[1] Laing, *W. of K.*, iii., 358.

[2] *Ibid.*, iii., 370.

[3] *Ibid.*, iii., 378.

when he was in straits, after Mary Tudor's accession, she offered him pecuniary aid, which he had
the self-respect to decline.[1]   He testifies, also, to
her helpfulness in higher ways.   He declares that
from "the first day that it pleased the Providence
of God to bring you and me in familiarity, I have
always delighted in your company, . . . for I
find a congruence betwixt us in spirit."[2]   In one
pathetic passage he relates that the unfolding by
her of her own spiritual troubles and infirmities
was "a very mirror" wherein he beheld himself
"so rightly painted that nothing could be more
evident": and he recalls how "often when with
dolourous hearts we have begun our talking,
God has sent great comfort to us both."[3]   On the
other hand, he naïvely admits that "her company," although "comfortable, yea honourable,
and profitable," was "not without some cross";
for his "mind was seldom quiet for doing somewhat for the comfort of her troubled conscience."[4]
The Reformer's careful and patient treatment of
her doubts and "desperation," as revealed in his
long letters, indicates an amiable feature of his
character; but one can readily understand the
depressing influence of even a "dearly beloved
mother" who was in constant dread of "apostasy"; in continual "battle with Satan"; com-

[1] Laing, *W. of K.*, iii., 372.

[2] *Ibid.*, iii., 337–339.

[3] *Ibid.*, iii., 338.

[4] *Ibid.*, vi., 514.

paring herself with the people of Sodom, and groaning with more force than taste over her spiritual "adultery."[1]

IV.   During the ministry of Knox at Berwick he paid at least one memorable visit to Newcastle. This visit exerted considerable influence on his career, occasioned his earliest conspicuous effort in literary controversy, and placed him in the front rank of the more thorough English Reformers.   It was natural that a reactionary prelate like Tunstall should regard with disfavour Knox's aggressive Protestantism.   As the latter, however, held a commission direct from the Privy Council, the Bishop, in his episcopal capacity, had

---

[1] Laing, *W. of K.*, iii., 361, 364, 372, 382, 385.   The relations subsisting between Knox and Mrs. Bowes occasioned, prior to his marriage at least, some unfounded scandal which in its turn formed the basis of vile insinuations by the renegade Archibald Hamilton (*De Conf. Calv. Sect.*, p. 65).   The scandal was magnified through the dislike of some of the Bowes family towards Knox, on account of his Protestant views and influence over his future mother-in-law.   "The slander and fear of men," so he writes, "hath impeded me to exercise my pen so often as I would; yea very shame hath holden me from your company when I was most surely persuaded that God had appointed me to feed your hungry and afflicted soul" (Laing, *W. of K.*, iii., 390–391).   A few months before his own death, after Mrs. Bowes had passed away, he felt impelled to "declare to the world what was the cause of our great familiarity"; which was "neither flesh nor blood, but a troubled conscience on her part which never suffered her to rest but when she was in the company of the faithful, of whom (from the first hearing of the Word at my mouth) she judged me to be one" (Laing, vi., 513).

no power to interfere; and probably he would have been content to remain quiescent but for the complaints of a section of his clergy that Knox was denouncing the mass as idolatry. These complaints led Tunstall to summon Knox, in April, 1550, before the Council of the North, of which the Bishop was a leading member. This Council was composed of twenty-three representative clergy, nobility, and gentry; and one of its functions was to secure conformity to the parliamentary enactments about religion.[1]

Knox, however, was not cited as an ecclesiastical offender, but to "give his confession why he affirmed the mass to be idolatry," and a large congregation assembled in the Church of St. Nicholas at Newcastle to hear his address. The Bishop had furnished the preacher with an opportunity of effectively propagating his views on a burning question of the time.[2] In the First Prayer-book of Edward VI., the elevation and adoration of the host were significantly discontinued. Accordingly, when Knox declared that the mass, as celebrated by Romanists, was idola-

---

[1] Burnet, H. of R., ii., 36, 310; Strype, Memorials, ii., Part II., 161. The headquarters of the Council were at York, but annual sessions were held at Hull, Durham, and Newcastle; and it was presumably to the regular session at Newcastle that Knox was cited. The Earl of Shaftesbury was President of the Council, and Sir Robert Bowes was a member of it

[2] Laing, W. of K., iii., 33–70 (where the discourse is given in full); Lorimer, Knox and the Ch. of E., pp. 51–65.

Church of St. Nicholas (now the Cathedral), Newcastle.
(From an eighteenth-century print.)

trous, he was in harmony with a parliamentary
statute, and his declaration could not be made
the ground of a charge against him. It is significant, however, that in his discussion of the question he goes far beyond the standpoint of the
Prayer-book. He uses the term "idolatry" in a
wide sense, embracing not a little which Cranmer and his colleagues would have declined to
condemn. The latter were content to omit from
the Communion office whatever involved or suggested transubstantiation. With this part of the
subject Knox deals effectively in the latter portion of his discourse, and shews the unscriptural
character of the doctrine of the mass, as an
alleged "sacrifice for the sins of the quick and the
dead." [1] But in the earlier part of the address
he adopts by anticipation the Puritan position
that "all worshipping, honouring, or service in-
vented by the brain of man in the religion of
God, without His own express commandment, is
idolatry." [2] On the basis of this contention he
includes under "idolatry of the mass" all the
non-scriptural ceremonial with which the Communion had been associated, and thus con-
demns not only what the Prayer-book proscribed

---

[1] Laing, *W. of K.*, iii., 65.

[2] *Ibid.*, iii., 34. This is the position taken up by the *Westminster Confession* (XXI., l.) and by the *Shorter Catechism*
(Qu. 51). The unlawfulness of unprescribe modes of worship had already been affirmed by Knox at St. Andrews
(see p 79).

but also not a little which it approved. He denounces the introduction and consecration of altars, the use of candles and certain vestments, the unauthorised addition of certain words to the scriptural formula of institution, and various "ungodly invocations and diabolical conjurations." [1] At the close of the discourse, he calls

"God to record that neither profit to myself, hatred of any person or persons, nor affection or favour that I bear towards any private man, causeth me to speak as ye have heard, but only the obedience that I owe unto God in ministration, and the common love which I bear to the salvation of all men." [2]

The discourse of Knox, so far from occasioning any interference with his liberty, brought him prominently before Court, Church, and people as a powerful champion of Reformed doctrine. Early in 1551, he was removed, by order, doubtless, of the Privy Council, from Berwick to Newcastle. In this more influential sphere he continued, along with the preaching of Protestant truth, to celebrate worship in conformity, not with the authorised Prayer-book, but with his own Puritan ideas. In addition to the propagation of evangelical doctrine among the citizens of Newcastle and the population of the North gen-

---

[1] Laing, iii., 49. The reference is to the pleading of the merits of saints and to exorcism.

[2] *Ibid.*, iii., 69.

erally, he attracted to the town numerous Scots "chiefly for his fellowship." [1]

V. The ecclesiastical standing and distinction of John Knox in England at this period are illustrated by two offers of promotion, one of which was accepted, the other declined, and also by two instances of his influential intervention in Church affairs. At some date between December, 1551, and October, 1552, he was appointed one of six royal chaplains.[2] Two of these chaplains at a time resided at Court; the other four itinerated in various districts of the country. Through this office Knox's influence was largely increased. He had as frequent listeners to his preaching not only the King himself, but ministers of the Crown and officials of the Court, while he had also the opportunity of delivering his testimony at important centres in different parts of the country.[3]

Before the close of 1552, a yet more important charge was within the Reformer's reach. The Duke of Northumberland, who, after Somerset's fall, became the most powerful statesman in the kingdom, occupied the post of Warden of the Borders. In that capacity he was often in

---

[1] See Lorimer (p. 78), who quotes a letter from the Duke of Northumberland to Cecil, Sept., 1552.

[2] Lorimer, 79–80. Knox was not one of the original six, appointed in Dec., 1551; but on 27th Oct., 1552, there is an entry in the Register of the Privy Council authorising the payment to him of £40 "in way of the King's Majesty's reward."

[3] Laing, vi., p. xxix.; Lorimer, 48.

contact with Knox, whose headquarters, after he became chaplain, continued to be in the North, and the Duke repeatedly heard the Reformer preach. Partly to strengthen the Protestant cause in the south, and partly to rid the Borders of a preacher whose independent spirit and Puritan attitude he did not like, Northumberland recommended him for the vacant See of Rochester.[1] Knox appears to have had no objection to episcopacy as such, but he disapproved of "your proud prelates' great dominions and charge, impossible by one man to be discharged."[2] He gives a further reason—"foresight of trouble to come."[3] He had also, one may assume, no desire to come under obligations to a statesman whose unprincipled character, afterwards disclosed, he seems already to have discerned; and,

---

[1] In a letter from Northumberland to Cecil (*State Pap. Edw. VI.*, xv. 35; Tytler, *Reigns of Edward VI. and Mary*, ii., 142), of date 28th Oct., 1552, the former writes: "he [Knox] would not only be a whetstone to quicken and sharp the Archbishop of Canterbury, whereof he hath need, but also he would be a great confounder of the Anabaptists lately sprung up in Kent." He adds, as a further reason for the Reformer's promotion, that Knox "should not continue the ministration in the North contrary to this set forth here" [*i. e.*, the prescribed liturgy]; "and that the Scots now inhabiting Newcastle chiefly for his friendship would not continue there."

[2] Laing, *W. of K.*, v., 518; comp. iii., 26, where Knox declares that no bishop should mix himself with temporal or secular business, but should continually preach, read, and exhort his flock.

[3] *Ibid.*, iii., 122; comp. iv., 221.

moreover, as a patriotic Scot, he would be unwilling to undertake responsibilities which might
have permanently severed his connection with
his native land. Accordingly, after a personal
interview with the Reformer Northumberland
later reports that he had found Knox "neither
grateful nor pleasable," adding, "I mind to have
no more to do with him, but to wish him well." [1]
The offer of the See of Rochester was thus declined. Nearly twenty years afterwards, when
Knox was requested to take part in the installation of John Douglas as Bishop of St. Andrews,
and when his refusal to do so was ascribed to
personal disappointment, he was moved to recall
this long-past incident in his career, and to declare that he had refused a greater bishopric than
ever it [St. Andrews] was." [2]

The Second Prayer-book of Edward VI., sanctioned in April, 1552, and the Forty-two Articles
promulgated in the following year, bear each
some mark of Knox's influence. The practice of
sitting instead of kneeling at Communion had
become frequent by 1552, among those who
favoured it being Hooper, Bishop of Gloucester.
The Puritan party were not strong enough to pro-

---

[1] Letter of 7th Dec., 1552, from Northumberland to Cecil,
(*State Pap. Edw. VI.*, xv., 66) quoted by Tytler, *Reigns of
Edward VI. and Mary*, ii., 148. The Duke, however, did not
cease to regard Knox as a man worthy of consideration (see
Tytler, ii., 158, 159).

[2] Richard Bannatyne's *Memorials*, p. 256 (Bann. Club ed.).

cure the introduction of any change of posture
into the new service-book, but an important concession was secured which so far met their views.
There was inserted what High Churchmen have
called the "Black Rubric," deleted after the accession of Elizabeth to propitiate Catholics, replaced at the Restoration to conciliate Puritans,
and still retained. This rubric significantly declares that by kneeling "no adoration is intended
either of the sacramental bread and wine," or
"of Christ's natural flesh and blood." The insertion of the caveat was assigned in 1554 by
Dr. Weston (afterwards Dean of Westminster) to
the authority of a "run-a-gate Scot."[1] That this
Scot was Knox appears from the fact that about
this time he preached before the King a sermon
against kneeling, and that a memorial to the Privy
Council, dated 1552, in favour of sitting at Communion was substantially Knox's work.[2] His influence appears in another kindred matter.   In
October, 1552, the Forty-five Articles (afterwards
reduced to Forty-two, ultimately to Thirty-nine)
were submitted for consideration to the royal

---

[1] Foxe, *Acts, etc.*, vi., 510; Laing, iii., 80.

[2] Lorimer, pp. 99–107, 267–284; Gairdner, *Eng. Ch. in Sixteenth Cent.*, p. 307; Drysdale, *Presbyterians in England*, p. 68.
Having secured the insertion of the rubric, Knox soon after
advised his former congregation at Berwick to adopt the
kneeling posture for the sake of peace (Lorimer, 259–263):
but he appears never himself to have conformed. (See
below.)

chaplains. Knox could not but object to Article
Thirty-eight, which, in the original draft, endorsed
the *ceremonies* of the Prayer-book, as "in no way
repugnant to the wholesome liberty of the Gospel." In the final form this clause is significantly
altered; all reference to ceremonies has disappeared.[1] These are probably only specimens, ac-
cidentally disclosed, of the ecclesiastical influence
exerted by the Scottish chaplain. They corroborate the testimony of a friendly Flemish resident
in England [2] that Knox "wrought upon the minds
of many," and they account for the complaint of
the hostile Weston that "this one man's authority
so much prevailed." [3]

The standing and influence of Knox are further
illustrated by the vain efforts made to get rid
of him, and by the toleration which he received,
notwithstanding his nonconformity, from the
Privy Council. The earliest attempt to dis-
place him was made by the Mayor of Newcastle,
Sir Robert Brandling, after a sermon by Knox on
Christmas Day, 1552. The Reformer had dis-
coursed on the "obstinacy of the Papists" who
were "thirsting for the King's death"; and had
affirmed that whoever opposed the Reformed doctrine was not only an "enemy to God," but a
"secret traitor to the Crown and Common-

---

[1] Lorimer, pp. 108–110, 126–129; Gairdner, p. 308.

[2] John Utenhove in letter to Bullinger, dated Oct., 1552
(quoted by Lorimer, p. 98).

[3] Foxe, vi., 510; Lorimer, p. 134.

wealth." [1]   The proceedings against Knox failed,
largely through the intervention of Northumberland, who, in spite of the Reformer's refusal
of a bishopric, held over him the ægis of his influence and condemned the Mayor's "malicious
stomach." [2]   Two or three months later, "heinous
delations," laid against the Reformer before the
Privy Council, equally failed to undermine his
credit, and issued, as he himself expresses it, in
"Satan's confusion" and the "glory of God." [3]
Once more, in April 1553, he was summoned before
the Council to explain his refusal of a presentation to the vicarage of Allhallows in London.
He replied that while he was ready to fill an
office like that of royal chaplain, which gave
him the opportunity of preaching Christ's Gospel, he considered that no beneficed minister
could discharge his office before God in England
without fuller power of discipline—authority
to "divide the lepers from the whole." There
was another reason, however, for his citation.   He
was asked to explain "why he kneeled not at
the Lord's Supper"; and when he pleaded the
example of Christ at the original institution,
he was dismissed with "gentle speeches" and a
recommendation to reconsider the question, but

---

[1] Laing, *W. of K.*, iii., 297.

[2] Tytler, *Reigns of Edward VI. and Mary*, ii., 158.

[3] Laing, *W. of K*, iii., 364 (letter to Mrs. Bowes, 23rd March,
1553).

without any threat of deprival.[1]   Obviously, notwithstanding his Puritanical nonconformity in some details, Knox was regarded as a valuable champion of the English Reformation.

VI.   Before Easter, 1553, Edward's approaching death had been anticipated, and Northumberland's plot to disinherit Mary Tudor had already been devised.   The Reformer and his fellow-chaplains appear to have discerned at an early stage the Duke's unprincipled policy, and were not afraid to allude from the pulpit to iniquity in high places.[2]   It was the turn of Knox to officiate in April, 1553; and in the last sermon which he preached before Edward and his Council, he boldly referred to the "young and innocent king being deceived by crafty, covetous, wicked, and ungodly counsellors, whom he compared to Ahithophel, Shebna, and Judas.[3]

Edward's death in July was to Knox, as to other Protestants in England, a grievous calamity, which he interpreted as a divine judgment.   "We had a king," he writes, "of so godly disposition towards virtue and the truth of God that none from the beginning passed him"; and he accuses "no less his own offences than the offences of others," as the "cause of the away-taking of that most godly prince."[4]   No fear, however, of what

---

[1] Calderwood, *Kirk of Scot.*, i., 280, 281.

[2] Laing, *W. of K.*, iii., 176, 177.

[3] *Ibid.*, *W. of K.*, iii., 282; Lorimer, 169–172.

[4] Laing. *W. of K.*, iii., 175.

might happen under Mary Tudor tempted Knox
to give any countenance to the usurpation which
was forced on the unfortunate Lady Jane Grey;
and he was careful not to omit public prayer that
God would "illuminate the heart of our Sovereign
Lady, Queen Mary." "Inflame the hearts of her
Council," he added, "with Thy true fear and
love," and "repress the pride of those that would
rebel." [1] Yet he was not blind to impending
peril. Amid the "joy and riotous banqueting at
the proclamation of Mary" he foresaw "troubles"
and "destructions" all the more certain to follow
on account of the conspiracy which had proved
futile.[2] He was in no hurry, however, to leave
his post. On the 26th of July, a week after Mary's
accession, we find him preaching at Carlisle; in
August he speaks of himself as labouring in Kent;
in September he asks the prayers of Mrs. Bowes
for his ministry in London.[3] In November a reactionary Parliament enacted that from the 20th
December there "should be no other form of service but what had been used in the last year of

---

[1] Laing, *W. of K.*, iii., 107.

[2] *Ibid.*, 168.

[3] *Ibid.*, 365, 374, 376. On 16th Aug., a proclamation of
the Queen forbade Protestants and Catholics to interrupt
each other's services, but prohibited all preaching on either
side without a royal license (Froude, *H. of E.*, v., 236). Knox,
however, probably regarded his chaplaincy as a virtual
license, until it became clear that his appointment was not
to be renewed under Mary.

Henry VIII." [1] Before that date the mass had
been restored; and the majority of Reforming
leaders were in prison or in exile. Yet Knox remained and continued to preach after the interval
of toleration had expired. On the 22nd of December he writes that "every day of this week I must
preach, if this wicked carcase will permit " [2]
With the death of Edward, however, his royal
chaplaincy, as well as his commission as a preacher,
came to an end; and neither appointment was
renewed. His special responsibility as regards
England accordingly ceased; and when the in-
tercepting of his letters convinced him that his
apprehension impended, he yielded, although re-
luctantly, to the counsel of friends and escaped
to Dieppe early in 1554.[3]

That Knox left England with some misgiving
appears from his anxiety to vindicate himself by
anticipation from the charge of faint-heartedness.
"Some," he writes, "will ask, Why did I flee?
Assuredly I cannot tell; but of one thing I am
sure; the fear of death was not the chief cause.
. . . By God's grace I may come to battle

---

[1] Lorimer, p. 186; Perry, *Ref. in Eng.*, p. 116.

[2] Laing, *W. of K.*, iii., 113.

[3] There is some doubt as to the date of Knox's departure
from England. On the authority of a P. S. to his "Exposition of Ps. VI., "Upon the very point of my journey, the last
of February" (Laing, iii., 156), Professor Hume Brown dates
the Reformer's flight on that day. But Knox probably refers
here to his departure from *Dieppe*.

before all the conflict be ended."[1] We catch
from his correspondence some incidental glimpses
of the circumstances and motives under which he
acted. He mentions on the 6th January his
"very weak health," and he may not have been
in a physical condition to face a conflict.[2] He
seems, also, to have felt the responsibility of
remaining when this could not be done "without
danger to others," referring probably to some of
his future wife's kindred and to some intimate
friends in London.[3] But what weighed doubtless
above all with Knox was his consciousness that
he was a man with a mission, endowed with
gifts which would enable him to take, in the
future, an effective part in the Reformation
of the Church. With this expectation deeply
rooted in his soul, and with a Scotsman's practical instinct moving him to reserve his life
until he could surrender it for the manifest good
of the Church of Christ, Knox was not inclined
to throw himself and his power away on a hopeless contest in a country not his own. Cyprian
and Athanasius, in early Christian times, had fled
for a while from the dioceses to whose ministry
they had been solemnly consecrated, in order to
preserve themselves for later conflicts. Knox,
with no official responsibility to discharge, escaped

---

[1] Laing, *W. of K.*, iii., 120.

[2] *Ibid.*, 120.

[3] *Ibid.*, iii., 236; iv., 219-222.

from what was, after all, a foreign land, in order
not to forfeit the opportunity of afterwards aiding
his fellow-countrymen.

"My prayer is," he writes, "that I may be restored
to the battle"; and "my hope is that I shall be so
encouraged to fight that England *and Scotland* shall
both know that I am ready to suffer more than either
poverty or exile for that doctrine whereof it has
pleased His merciful Providence to make me a
witness-bearer." [1]

---

[1] Laing, iii., 154.

CHAPTER V

KNOX ON THE CONTINENT OF EUROPE—A LEADER
AND PASTOR OF BRITISH PROTESTANT
EXILES—LITERARY ACTIVITY

1554-1559

THE four years and some months which Knox
spent on the Continent were far from being
merely an interval of exile and of comparative
inactivity. They constitute in three respects a
memorable part of the Reformer's active life.
During this period he contributed at least one
notable service to Continental Protestantism; his
personal ministry among refugees, and his letters
as well as other writings, exerted a considerable
influence over the English, a powerful influence
over the Scottish, Reformation; and he received
impressions which were afterwards communicated
by him to the Reformed Church of Scotland, and
helped to mould its character and polity.

I. "Out of sight" with Knox was not "out of
mind." On his arrival at Dieppe his chief anxiety
appears to have been to minister in absence to
those who had been deprived of his presence. An

Exposition of Psalm VI., begun before his departure from England, was now completed and despatched to Mrs. Bowes, for whose melancholic
temperament and trying circumstances Psalm and
commentary were deemed to be specially appropriate.[1]   This work was his fulfilment of domestic
duty.   "A Godly Letter to the faithful Christians in London, Newcastle, Berwick, and to all
others within the realm of England that love the
coming of our Lord Jesus Christ" was simultaneously prepared for publication.[2]   "From a sore
troubled heart" he recalls past religious privileges
and national unworthiness, providential warnings and national disregard of them; and he
exhorts the faithful to avoid the contamination of
prevalent "idolatry."   That was the Reformer's
fulfilment of pastoral responsibility towards his
former congregations in England.   Scotland was
not forgotten, although no record of any Scottish
correspondence at this period remains.   Part of
Knox's time at Dieppe was occupied with the
preparation of four questions "concerning the
Kingdoms of Scotland and England" for submission to the Swiss divines; and three of those questions related to his native land.[3]

II.   We may assume that on his arrival at
Dieppe, Knox would not fail to communicate with
the Scottish colony who resided in the long street,

[1] Laing, *W. of K.*, iii., 113–156.

[2] *Ibid.*, 159–215.

[3] *Ibid.*, 219–226; see below, p. 121.

still called Rue d'Ecosse, close to the harbour of
that town; and he may have lodged there with
some former Scottish acquaintance, or friend of an
acquaintance. The relations, commercial as well
as political, between Scotland and France were
close, and he doubtless received—probably from
a fellow-countryman—news about his native land,
of later date than any which he was likely to have
heard in London. Knox's stay at Dieppe, however, on this occasion was limited to a few weeks
at most. The Reformation had not yet secured
for itself any visible footing in the town; and
by the 1st of March he had set out for the more
congenial atmosphere, spiritually at least, of
Switzerland.[1]

His Swiss tour lasted fully two months. There
was little appreciation in that age of romantic
scenery; and the Reformer would have been surprised if any one had asked him about his impressions of Mont Blanc, the Bernese Oberland, or the
lakes of Lucerne and Geneva. "I have travelled,"
he writes, "through all the congregations of Hel-
vetia, and reasoned with all the pastors and many
other excellently learned men." [2]   At Geneva he

---

[1] Laing, iii., 159. In 1547 Knox thought of visiting Germany (p. 72). In the interval he had come to know more
about Lutheranism and Calvinism, and now showed his
preference for the latter. His attitude towards Lutheranism
incidentally discloses itself, when he complains that "persecutors have *imposed* on us the name of Lutherans, schis-
mastic and heretics." (Laing, *W. of K.*, iv., 310).

[2] Laing, *W. of K.*, iii., 235.

met with John Calvin, then in the plenitude of his
power as religious dictator of the city, and spiritual director of a large part of Reformed Christendom. At Lausanne he probably saw Theodore
Beza, who wrote to him in after years as "my
Knox, my very dear brother," and included
the Reformer among his *Portraits of Illustrious
Men.*" [1]   At Zurich he became acquainted with
the leader of German Swiss Protestantism (after
Zwingli's death in 1531)—Henry Bullinger, to
whom Calvin had commended Knox: and to Bullinger the four questions previously referred to
were immediately addressed. The questions indicated in what direction Knox's thoughts were
running. The first related to the obedience due to
sovereigns in their minority, and had a present
reference to Mary Stuart, as well as a retrospective
application to Edward VI., and to the validity of
ecclesiastical arrangements made in his reign.
The second question referred to the propriety, or
otherwise, of female sovereignty, and to the right
of a queen to "transfer" the government to her
husband; with an obvious bearing on the position of Mary Tudor, who was about to marry a
Romish fanatic, and of Mary Stuart, who was
affianced to the Dauphin of France. The third
and fourth questions asked counsel as to the duty,

---

[1] Beza, *Epist.*, i., 79; *Icones*, Ee. iii.   The portrait of Knox
was sent to Beza by Sir Peter Young in 1579, and is recognised as authentic (Hume Brown, *John Knox*, ii., 322).

or otherwise, of submitting to a sovereign who enforced "idolatry," and as to the kindred obligation, or non-obligation, to aid and abet a religious nobility in resisting an idolatrous ruler. The latter enquiry was obviously suggested by the condition of Scotland at the time: the former referred to the position of Protestants both in Scotland and in England. Bullinger answered cautiously. A lawfully appointed ruler, he holds, even if a minor, is to receive "obedience": and although the law of God ordains woman to be in subjection, "it is a hazardous thing for godly persons to oppose political regulations." "We must not obey commands opposed to God and His lawful worship"; but any "rash attempt" at resistance is discouraged; the "only and the true deliverer" is God.[1] Knox did not accept Bullinger's moderate dicta without qualification. Soon after receiving the answers he wrote to his "afflicted brethren in England" that all is not lawful or just which is statute by civil law, neither yet is everything sin which ungodly persons allege to be treason.[2] At a later period, Bullinger's caution about opposition to female sovereignty was signally disregarded.

By the 10th of May Knox had returned to Dieppe. He was anxious to "learn the estate of England and Scotland" through letters from his

---

[1] Laing, iii., 219–226.
[2] *Ibid.*, iii., 236.

friends.[1] From England he would receive tidings
of the imprisonment of all the leading Reformers in that country, and also of the approaching marriage of Mary and Philip of Spain—the
prelude to the bloody persecution which was the
outcome largely of Spanish influence.   From
Scotland he would learn that, the regency had
passed out of Arran's hands into the stronger grasp
of Mary of Guise.   From the new Regent the Reformer had little hope of toleration for Protestants;[2] her policy of temporary conciliation until
her daughter's marriage with the Dauphin had
been consummated, was not yet generally known.
To neither country, therefore, the path appeared
open for Knox.   No record remains of any communications from him to fellow-countrymen at this
time; but in two "Comfortable Epistles to his
Afflicted Brethren in England" he exhorts them to
bear patiently the cross of Christ, and uses strong
language against the "false" Tunstall and the
"cruel" Gardiner.[3]   In the course of the summer
he was in "great anguish of heart," owing to tidings that many English Protestants "began to fall
before that idol" (*i. e.*, the mass).[4]   He followed
up his "Comfortable Epistles" accordingly, with
a "Faithful Admonition to the professors of God's
truth in England.[5]   In his address he speaks very
plainly of the Queen as one who "under an English

[1] Laing, iii., 253.   [3] *Ibid.*, iii., 231–249.
[2] *Ibid.*, iv., 217.   [4] *Ibid.*, iii., 345.
                    [5] *Ibid.*, iii., 263–330.

name beareth a Spaniard's heart," and of episcopal "traitors" who, after solemnly swearing that
they would never consent to a foreigner reigning
over England, had "adjudged the imperial crown
of the same to appertain to a Spaniard." [1]

III. In the lingering hope, probably, that some
brightening of the ecclesiastical horizon might
take place either in England or in Scotland, Knox
remained for more than two months in Dieppe.
Before the end of July, however, when the government of Mary Tudor had been firmly established,
notwithstanding her unpopular marriage, and
when no prospect of useful service in Scotland
had as yet been assured, the Reformer repaired to
what had become the metropolis of Reformed
Christendom and a chosen resort of persecuted
refugees—Geneva. He was instinctively drawn
towards the man who was destined to exert a
potent influence over him, and through him over
Scotland. Within a few weeks, however, this
second visit to Geneva was brought to a close by
an invitation which came to him in September
from Frankfort. [2]

The English Protestant refugees on the Continent at this period are believed to have been
nearly one thousand in number. [3] Of these a

---

[1] Laing, iii., 296, 297.   [2] Knox, *H. of R.*, i., 231, 232.
[3] See Burnet, *H. of R.*, ii., 502. Article by Froude in
Ed. Rev., lxxxv., 398. The chief resorts, besides Geneva
and Frankfort, were Emden in Friesland, Wesel in Rhine-
land, Strassburg, Zurich, and Basel.

considerable proportion settled in Frankfort, on account of its tolerant government, its central position, and its commercial connexions which facilitated communication with home. Twenty-one of these exiles, including John Bale, Bishop of Ossory, Thomas Cole, Dean of Sarum, and William Whittingham, afterwards Dean of Durham, despatched to Geneva a call to Knox to accept office as one of two pastors of the refugee congregation.[1] Permission had been obtained from the magistrates to hold service in the Church of the "White Ladies" (Cistercian nuns), the use of which had already been granted to a Walloon congregation under the ministry of Valérand Pullain. The original membership of the English community belonged chiefly to the Puritan section of Reformers; and the privilege of worshipping in the church was accorded to them on condition of their adherence to the Walloon doctrine and ritual, which were modelled on those of Geneva. It was natural, therefore, for the refugees from England to choose as their pastor a gifted preacher like Knox, who had already manifested Puritan tendencies.

Knox was at first unwilling to accept the invitation. He had already recognised in Calvin one from whom he could learn much; and, in the hope that an opportunity might ere long come to him of service at home, he was probably

---

[1] Laing, *W. of K.*, iv., 13.

reluctant to hamper himself with pastoral responsibilities. But the masterful will of the Genevan dictator operated effectually on the Scottish refugee. "At the commandment of that notable servant of God, John Calvin,"—so Knox himself relates,—he obeyed the call and arrived at Frankfort in November, 1554.[1]

It was in keeping with Knox's chequered fortunes throughout life that he found in his new sphere not a haven of rest, but a sea of troubles. Frankfort became the scene of a contention which presented a forecast in miniature of the conflict between Puritanism and Anglicanism. The English congregation, with mingled generosity and self-importance, had written to other refugee communities, informing them of the privileges which they enjoyed, and inviting exiles to join them. Negotiations commenced with the English at Zurich; but a service-book which Knox and his friends had drawn up for congregational use,[2] on the basis of the Liturgies of Calvin and of Pullain, stood in the way. These exiles were unwilling to set aside the Prayer-book of Edward, to which they had been accustomed at home, and which their Protestant brethren in England continued to use at the peril of their lives. The refugees at Strassburg were somewhat more accommodating; but they made it a condition of

---

[1] Knox, *H. of R.*, i., 231, 232.
[2] A. F. Mitchell, *Scott. Ref.*, p. 124.

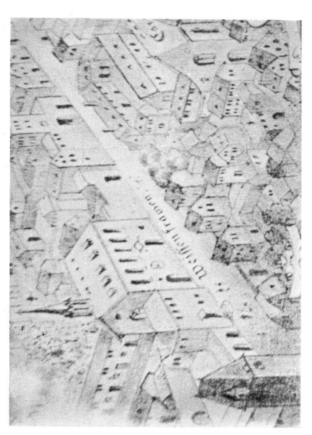

Church of the Weissen Frawen ("White Ladies," Cistercian order) in Frankfort, where Knox officiated in 1554. (From a print of the sixteenth-century.)

their adherence that the substance of the English
Prayer-book should be accepted. Negotiations,
in consequence, were broken off and Knox offered
to retire with a view to peace. Meanwhile, however, Thomas Lever, one of the Zurich community,
accepted a call to be Knox's colleague, and became the leader of a section of the Frankfort congregation who favoured the introduction of the
English Liturgy. Both parties agreed to submit
the question to Calvin, who deprecated contention
about forms of prayer as "too much out of season," but gave it as his opinion that the Prayer-
book contained many "foolish things which might
yet be tolerated" (*tolerabiles ineptias*) and "had
not that purity which was desired." [1] A compromise was adopted in February, 1555, according
to which the Liturgy as a whole was to be used,
but the litany, congregational responses, and
commemoration of saints were to be omitted; the
surplice was not to be worn, and sitting was
to be substituted for kneeling at the Lord's
Supper. "Thanks were given to God; the Holy
Communion was, upon this happy agreement,
ministered." [2]

Hardly, however, had this settlement been attained when the conflict was reopened through the
arrival in March of a fresh company of exiles
under the guidance of Richard Cox, Chancellor of

---

[1] Laing, *W. of K.*, iv., 28, 29.

[2] *Ibid.*, iv., 31.

Oxford University. The new-comers insisted on
uttering the responses, as they had been accustomed to do at home; and one of them suddenly
entered the pulpit and read the litany. Knox restrained himself at the time; but in his sermon at
afternoon service on the same day, he reproved
those by whom the "godly agreement was ungodly
broken." Owing to the recent accession, the
majority were now in favour of the English
Prayer-book. They found their action, however,
hampered by the intervention of Johann von Glau-
burg, an influential Calvinistic magistrate. So
long as peace prevailed he had abstained from interference; but he now warned the congregation
that unless the condition on which the use of the
church had been given was fulfilled, the doors of
the building would be closed against them.[1]

The discomfiture of the party led by Cox
tempted them into an unworthy retaliation.
In his "Faithful Admonition" published in the
preceding July, the Reformer, with intemperate
exaggeration, had referred incidentally to the Emperor Charles V. as "no less an enemy to Christ
than ever was Nero."[2] Two members of the
congregation[3] brought this epistle under the notice

---

[1] Laing, *W. of K.*, iv., 32–37.

[2] *Ibid.*, iii., 308.

[3] Edward Isaak, afterwards Sheriff of Kent, and Henry
Parry, Chancellor of Salisbury (Laing, iv., 47). Among
those by whose counsel they acted, Knox includes "Jewell of
Oxford," afterwards Bishop of Salisbury.

of the Frankfort magistracy. The magistrates were in a difficulty. Knox was the leader of the party who were loyal to municipal directions; his accusers belonged to the section whose advent had introduced dispeace and disregard of civic injunctions. On the other hand, Charles was then in Augsburg, within one hundred and sixty miles of Frankfort. He might receive an account of Knox's description of him; and the magistrates shrank from incurring the charge of having put the calumniator of the Emperor into a position of authority. Knox, accordingly, was first interdicted from preaching; and when his opponents urged the magistracy to take further action, the latter, unwilling to prosecute, yet afraid to let Knox alone, requested him to relieve them from their difficulty by voluntary departure. Whittingham, Cole, Foxe, and others followed him in his withdrawal from the city, some going to Basel, others to Geneva.[1]

---

[1] Laing, iv., 38–51. The removal of Knox and his friends was not followed by "peace and prosperity." "Cox and his partisans were not long of suffering from internal divisions. Robert Horne, one of the party, in a letter dated February, 1556, speaks of the Church of our exiles at Frankfort as almost ruined." See Etienne Huraut, *John Knox et ses relations avec les églises reformées du continent*, p. 49. It is an interesting circumstance (kindly communicated to me by the present English Chaplain at Frankfort, the Rev. G. W. Mackenzie,) that for nine months, in 1881–82, the still existing White Ladies' Church was occupied by the English congregation of the city.

9

In reviewing Knox's procedure at Frankfort, one cannot but regret that he allowed himself to be persuaded by Calvin to accept a position the difficulty of which he must have foreseen. That a representative body of English Protestants should discard (except through local constraint) the reformed ritual, established in England prior to Mary Tudor's accession, in favour of any other form of worship, was a "divisive course" which could not but weaken the Reform cause. On the other hand, that Knox, after being called to the pastorate of a congregation with whose form of worship he was in accord, should be constrained to efface his own and others' convictions, in order to satisfy the scruples of new-comers, was unjustifiable and intolerable. His position at Frankfort was an impossible one. The comparison of Charles V. to Nero was equally unjust and imprudent; but in that age even godly men, in the heat of controversy, often wrote of opponents with offensive rancour [1]; and Knox's fault sinks into insignificance compared with the spiteful meanness of those who dragged into public notice one rash word of a man whom their fellow Reformers had invited to be their pastor, and with whom, in things essential, they themselves were agreed. Both parties were anxious to have Calvin on their side; their letters to him are extant.

---

[1] In 1540, Luther wrote about the Emperor as a "servant of the servants of Satan." *Luthersbriefe*, v., 275.

Calvin's sympathies, on the question of ritual, were with the Puritans, but he refrained from "moving a new contention of a matter which is well ended." "One thing," however, he adds significantly, "I cannot keep secret, that Master Knox was, in my judgment, neither godly nor brotherly dealt withal." [1]

IV. Knox returned to Geneva about the end of March, 1555. He arrived at a notable juncture in the history of the town. A few weeks before, the closing scene had been enacted in a prolonged conflict of Calvin and his Puritan supporters with the "Libertines" who inclined towards Antinomianism, and the "Patriots," who disliked the influx of foreigners. The two main points of controversy had been the authority of the Church, apart from the State, to inflict excommunication—an authority essential, as Calvin insisted, to spiritual independence; and the admission of strangers to the full rights of citizens—a measure advocated by him as desirable both for the material prosperity of the city, and for its prestige as a chosen refuge of persecuted Protestants. Calvin and the Reform party had triumphed on both issues; the right of excommunication had been conceded to the Church; and early in 1555 fifty foreigners had been admitted to citizenship. A few weeks after Knox's arrival the leaders of the Patriots and the Libertines

---

[1] Laing, *W. of K.*, iv., 59.

attempted to secure by lawless violence what they had failed to accomplish by constitutional procedure. On the night of the 13th of May, a riot was organised. By means of the watchword, "Geneva for the Genevese!" it was attempted to stir up the baser patriotism of citizens to revolution and bloodshed. The conspiracy failed; the revolutionary forces were mastered; the intended assassination of foreigners was prevented; four of the rebels were beheaded; other leaders of the insurrection escaped execution only through flight; and Calvin's ascendency in Geneva was effectually established.[1] Three years afterwards, when Knox was composing his treatise on *Predestination*, the events of that memorable night were still fresh in his memory. He declares that beneath hatred of strangers there lay, as the real cause of the conspiracy, hatred of the "reformation of manners" by men "filthy in life," and he describes the remarkable intervention, as he believed, of Providence, through which a rebel multitude were overcome and dispersed by a little band of loyal citizens.[2]

The spectacle of Calvin's triumph could not fail to impress itself upon Knox, and fortified him afterwards, doubtless, in his own ecclesiastical conflicts. Calvin's influence over him in the spheres of doctrine and Church government will afterwards

---

[1] Henry, *Life of Calvin*, ii., 315–317.
[2] Laing, *W. of K.*, v., 212–214.

come before us; what impressed him in the first
instance was the Swiss Reformer's moral power.
The Church of Geneva—so Knox wrote in 1556—
" is the most perfect school of Christ that ever was
in the earth since the days of the Apostles. In
other places I confess Christ to be truly preached;
but manners and religion so sincerely reformed I
have not yet seen in any other place." [1] As one
result of the triumph of Calvin's party, the council not only admitted the English refugees to
citizenship, but ordered accommodation to be provided for their common worship. Knox's position as ex-pastor of the exiles at Frankfort led
to his selection as minister of the Geneva congregation, a portion of which had been under his pastorate in the former town.[2] Before many weeks had
elapsed, however, he resolved somewhat suddenly
to return, at least for a time, to Scotland. We
have Knox's own testimony that this journey
was " most contrarious to my own judgment," and
that his future mother-in-law was the instrument
to " draw me from the den of my own ease " at
Geneva.[3] Scotland was not yet ripe, he believed

[1] Letter to Mrs. Locke, in Laing, iv., 240.

[2] In June, 1555, Calvin applied to the Council of Geneva,
on behalf of the English congregation, for the use of a church.
The church was not officially granted till five months later;
but Knox probably began about the time of Calvin's application to minister to a congregation already in course of
formation, although he was not formally appointed as pastor
until November, during his visit to Scotland (*Ibid.*, 51).

[3] Letter to Mrs. Bowes, in *Ibid.*, 217.

for an aggressive Reformation movement. Mrs. Bowes, apart from any personal reason for desiring Knox's return, had fuller means of knowing the more hopeful ecclesiastical condition of the country.

V. Knox's visit to Scotland in 1555–56 will be described in the following chapter. He left Geneva in the end of August, and paid a visit to Berwick on his way to Edinburgh.[1] His marriage to Marjorie Bowes appears to have taken place on this occasion, or during his residence in Scotland. In the summer of 1556 he received a summons, which he obeyed, from his congregation at Geneva; and on the eve of his departure in July, he sent on before him, to Dieppe, not only his wife but his mother-in-law.[2] Mrs. Bowes's position in Berwick, as a zealous Protestant amid Catholic environment, had apparently become more difficult than ever to maintain. The party, accompanied by a pupil called Patrick and a man-servant, James, arrived in Geneva early in September.[3] The congregation of English exiles there had never ceased to regard Knox as their minister. In the preceding November, indeed, Christopher Goodman and Anthony Gilby [4]

---

[1] Letter to Mrs. Bowes, in Laing, iv., 217.

[2] Knox, *H. of R.*, i., 253.

[3] *Livre des Anglois*, p. 3 (A. F. Mitchell's ed.).

[4] Goodman and Gilby had both been adherents of Knox at Frankfort. Goodman, a native of Chester, followed Knox to Scotland in 1559, became minister of St. Andrews at the

L'Auditoire, Geneva, in which Knox and his congregation worshipped, 1556–59.

had been elected to "preach the Word of God and minister the Sacraments"; but Gilby was expressly appointed only "to supply the room till Knox returned"; and in December, 1556, the latter was reappointed, with Goodman as colleague, to the pastorate.[1]

During Knox's absence the English exiles had been accommodated in the little Church of Notre Dame la Neuve, situated close to the Cathedral of S. Pierre, and used by Calvin as a lecture hall.[2] The *Livre des Anglois* enumerates 212 persons who composed the regular membership of this Anglo-Genevan congregation. Among the "Seniors" or Elders (for the Genevan church polity had been adopted) were Miles Coverdale, the translator of the Bible, whose version of the Psalms is still used in the Church of England; Thomas Sampson, formerly Dean of Chichester who afterwards declined the Bishopric of Norwich on account of his Puritan convictions; William Whittingham, the husband of Calvin's sister-in-law, and Knox's successor in the Geneva pastorate; John Bodley of Exeter, and his son Thomas, the founder of the Bodleian Library; Thomas Bentham, a distinguished Hebraist, afterwards Bishop of

---

Reformation, and returned to England in 1565. Gilby belonged to Lincolnshire. After the accession of Elizabeth, he became Vicar of Ashby de la Zouch.

[1] *Livre des Anglois*, 49; Laing, *W. of K.*, iv., 51.

[2] Hence its more usual designation—*L'Auditoire*. The building, with some structural alterations, still exists.

Lichfield; and James Pilkington, one of the Frankfort refugees, who became Bishop of Durham. The
roll of members included ten persons in Orders besides the pastors; ten students preparing for the
holy ministry; and numerous representatives of
the gentry and mercantile class.[1] Among the women
of the congregation one merits special notice—
Mrs. Anne Locke, who arrived in Geneva with her
son and daughter in May, 1557. Her husband
was a London merchant, with whom Knox had
become acquainted in England. In a letter written
from Geneva in 1556 to Mrs. Locke and another
lady, the Reformer gratefully recalls the "special
care" of the two women over him, comparing it to
that of mother over child.[2] His strong views regarding the unfitness of women to "bear rule"
were united with a full appreciation of womanly
ministry; and Mrs. Locke appears to have been
particularly helpful through her intelligent sympathy with his religious work and aspirations.
In return he aided her with counsel in religious
matters; and four days after her settlement in
Geneva she needed his comfort on the sudden
death of her daughter.[3] The form of service used

---

[1] A. F. Mitchell's ed. of the *Livre des Anglois*, 6–11.

[2] Laing, *W. of K.*, iv., 220.

[3] *Livre des Anglois*, p. 15. Knox's extant letters to Mrs.
Locke extend from 1556 to 1562. He kept her informed of
his proceedings, sent to her more than one of his writings,
confided to her his hopes and fears, and asked repeatedly to
be remembered in her prayers. "The correspondence [so an

Church of S. Pierre, Geneva.

by the congregation—the *Book of Geneva*—was substantially that which had been originally in use at Frankfort prior to the "troubles"; and it was the Service-book which, with some modification, became in 1560 the Book of Common Order in the Scottish Church.

Knox's life at Geneva was no idle one, although he called it, by comparison with life in his native land, a "den of ease." Three months after his return from Scotland, he excuses himself for "bare and brief letters" on the ground of family cares and congregational work. The presence in his household of a mother-in-law who habitually required his spiritual counsel would not

---

eminent author declares] testifies to a good, sound, downright friendship between the two"; and in one of Knox's letters occurs what the same writer calls the "truest touch of personal humility in all Knox's extant writings." Referring to his own constancy in friendship, although "of nature churlish," he modestly accounts thus for such constancy: "I have rather need of all than any have need of me" (R. L. Stevenson, *Men and Books*, 272, 273; Laing, *W. of K.*, vi., 11). It must be admitted, however, in connection with Mrs. Locke's coming to Geneva, that Knox was somewhat selfishly inconsiderate of her husband's wishes and comfort. After hearing of Mrs. Locke's earnest desire to see himself, and expressing the "thirst and languor" which he had for her presence and sympathy, he writes to her: "Were it not that partly ye are impeded by empire of your head [*i. e.*, her husband] . . . in my heart I would have wished, yea and cannot cease to wish, that it would please God to guide and conduct yourself to this place" (Laing, *W. of K.*, iv., 238, 240). This was a virtual encouragement to Mrs. Locke to extort from her husband permission to go to Geneva.

lighten his burden; and there is a mixture of
pathos and comedy in his reference to "daily
troubles occurring in my domestic charge, where-
with before I have not been accustomed and
therefore are they the more fearful." [1] The standard of clerical public duty in Geneva was somewhat exacting. Calvin himself, besides his
academic work preached thrice a week, and on a
fourth day expounded Scripture. [2] The appetite
for services (and these not remarkable for brev-
ity), among a congregation of foreigners, many
of whom were without any stated occupation,
was not likely to be less keen than that of an assembly of busy Genevese. Knox accordingly, we
may presume, followed Calvin's example; and to
minister acceptably to a flock which included a
score of divines and divinity students, involved
exposure to abundant criticism, and demanded no
mere superficial preparation. During the two and
a half years, moreover, of Knox's Genevan ministry he was constantly engaged in literary work.
Not to speak of numerous private letters which,
although described by himself as "bare and
brief," occasionally reached the dimensions of a
modern sermon, [3] the Reformer's literary publica-

---

[1] Laing, *W. of K.*, iv., 239.

[2] Schaff, *Swiss Reformation*, 445; Beza, *Opera*, xxi., 132.

[3] One letter is a long reply to "Sisters in Edinburgh" who
enquired about "women's apparel." Knox pleads that the
subject is "difficill and dangerous"; declares that there is
"no uncleanness" in "silks, velvet, gold"; and that the

tions at Geneva included his *First Blast against
the Monstrous Regiment* [*i. e.*, Rule] *of Women*,[1] the
amplification of a letter addressed by him to the
Regent Mary of Scotland in 1556; an *Appellation*
from a sentence pronounced against him in his
absence by the Scottish hierarchy in the same

---

evil lies in the "abuse of the same to ostentation" and
"affectation of beauty other than nature has given." He
commits himself, however, to the condemnation of hair-dye,
farthingales, and wearing the "claithing of men." (Laing,
W. of K., iv., 225–236).

[1] "To promote a woman to bear rule . . . above any
realm, is repugnant to nature, contumely to God, a thing
most contrarious to His revealed will and approved ordinance; and finally it is the subversion of good order, of all
equity and justice" (Laing, *W. of K.*, iv., 373). He founds
his main argument on the saying of St. Paul: "I suffer not a
woman . . . to usurp authority over the man," and on
the sentence pronounced upon woman after the fall, "Thy
will shall be subject unto thy husband"; since "she that is
subject to one may not rule many"; but he ignores the
modification of the law of subjection in such particular cases
as those of Deborah and Huldah; and he supports his argument by unfair references to the "inordinate lust," "foolish
fondness and cowardice," murderous "cruelty and phrenzy"
of individual women. Knox was supported in his contention
by Goodman and Whittingham; but Foxe wrote to him
what Knox calls a " loving and friendly letter " of expostula-
tion. Beza declares that "as soon as we learned the
contents" of the *Blast*, the "sale was forbidden"; Morel
denounced it to Calvin as " *pessimum et pestilentissimum* ";
and Calvin himself censured Knox's "thoughtless arro-
gance." (Laing, iv., 356–8; v., 5; Calv. *Opera*, xvii., 541).
In 1559, after Elizabeth's accession, John Aylmer, an English exile during the time of persecution, replied to the *Blast*
in a work entitled *An Harborowe for Faithful and Trewe
Subjects.* He recognises Knox's "honesty and godliness,"

year; a *Letter to the Commonalty of Scotland*, in 1558[1]; and two treatises of a hortatory character in fulfilment of the obligations under which he lay to the people of England, and especially to "the inhabitants of Newcastle and Berwick."[2] The long and elaborate treatise on *Predestination* was published in 1560, when Knox had finally returned to his native land; but the composition of the work belongs to the period of his Geneva pastorate, when he was holding constant intercourse with Calvin.[3] Notwithstanding engrossing labours, and occasional worries, this period was probably the happiest of the Reformer's mature life. That he looked back upon it with great pleasure was shown incidentally long afterwards by a private letter written in 1568, when his work in Scotland appeared to have been completed. He writes with kindliest memory of that "little flock" at Geneva, "among whom I lived with quietness of conscience and contentment of heart;

---

but blames him for lack of "moderation" and publication of the work "out of season." Knox himself in his letter to Foxe admits his "rude vehemency"; although he never disavowed his arguments (Laing, iv., 351; v., 5). A year afterwards we find him admitting that his *Blast* hath "blown from me all my friends in England" (*ibid.*, vi., 14); and although in the interval he published the summary of a proposed Second Blast (*ibid.*, iv., 539), the intention, fortunately, was never carried out.

[1] The significance of these works is indicated in Chap. VII.
[2] Laing, *W. of K.*, v., 469–522.
[3] *Ibid.*, v., 9–468. See Note at the end of this Chapter.

among whom I would be content to end my days,
if so it might stand with God's good pleasure."[1]

In Geneva Knox's two sons, Nathanael and
Eleazer, were born: the former was baptised in
May, 1557, with Whittingham as "god-father";
the latter in November, 1558, with Coverdale
as "witness."[2] Of Mrs. Knox's life in Geneva,
no record remains, but the impression she left
upon those with whom she came in contact must
have been agreeable; for Calvin describes her
as *suavissima* and a wife whose like is not
found everywhere.[3] For Knox himself the social
and religious fellowship of Geneva and its vicinity
could not fail to be quickening. In addition to
Calvin, there were Theodore Beza, Professor of
Greek in the adjacent town of Lausanne and
afterwards Calvin's successor in the ministry;
Peter Viret, pastor and teacher for twenty-two
years in that town, which he left for Geneva in
the spring of 1559; Farel, the founder of the
Genevan Reformed Church, and at that time
chief pastor of Neuchâtel; Vico of Naples, who
had organised an Italian congregation at Geneva
a few years before Knox's arrival, and the two
brothers Colladon—Nicholas, who succeeded Calvin as Professor of Theology, and Germain, who
co-operated with Calvin in drawing up a code of

---

[1] Letter to John Wood (Laing, *W. of K.*, vi., 559).
[2] *Livre des Anglois*, p. 73.
[3] Letters of Calvin in Laing, vi., 124, 125.

laws for Geneva.[1]   Along with these were the English clergy already enumerated, most of whom afterwards exerted a notable influence in the Church of their own land.   From these divines came forth the famous Geneva translation of the Bible and an English metrical Psalter.   The former work was mainly composed by Whittingham; but others, including, doubtless, Knox, assisted in the revision.[2]   It became at once the popular version in Britain, and retained its hold for many years after the "authorised" version was issued in 1611.   The metrical Psalter formed part of the *Book of Geneva*, and consisted of fifty-one Psalms in metre.   It was the nucleus of the original Psalter of the Reformed Scottish Church.[3] To be pastor of such a congregation in such a city was for Knox both a high privilege and a source of power.   Through intercourse with men like Calvin, Beza, and Vico, Coverdale, Sampson, and Whittingham, he was prepared for the great

---

[1] Stebbing, *Life of Calvin*, i., 109; ii., 84, 129, 140; Schaff, *Swiss Reformation*, pp. 248, 446, 464, 465, 518, 851–854.

[2] G. Milligan, *English Bible*, pp. 79–82; A. F. Mitchell, *Scott. Ref.*, p. 91.   Two hundred editions of the Geneva Bible were published.

[3] Of the fifty-one Psalms, forty-four were adopted, after revision, from an earlier work of Sternhold and Hopkins; the remaining seven were supplied by Whittingham.   The completion of the Scottish Psalter, in 1564, was due, chiefly, to the labours of Robert Pont and John Craig, who contributed versions of their own composition (J. C. Hadden, in *Scottish Review* for January, 1891, pp. 5–10).

work that lay before him in Scotland. On the
other hand, his own strong convictions, religious
and political, along with his habit of fearless expression, could not be without influence even on
Swiss divines, and helped to fortify his fellow-
refugees in attachment to the principles of Puritanism and of constitutional government.

VI. The ministry of Knox at Geneva was interrupted a second time by an invitation which
reached him in May, 1557, from four Protestant
Scottish nobles—Lords Lorne, Glencairn, Erskine,
and James Stewart. The letter containing this
invitation refers to an improvement in the religious condition of the country from the Protestant standpoint. On the one hand, there was
now an absence of persecution, and those "enemies
to Christ's evangel," the friars, were "in less esti-
mation." On the other hand, there was a readiness not only to hear Reformed doctrine, but to
"jeopard life and goods in the forward setting of
the glory of God." A strong desire, accordingly,
prevailed—so the letter indicated—that the Reformer would return "to Scotland, to advance the
cause by his presence." [1]

It cannot be said that Knox hastened to obey
this summons. His religious patriotism was not
cooled; but conflicting responsibilities, domestic
and pastoral, had to be weighed. He took counsel, therefore, with other ministers of the city,

---

[1] Knox, *H. of R.*, i., 267, 268.

especially with Calvin.   When these, however, advised, with one consent, that he could not refuse the vocation "unless he would declare himself rebellious unto his God and unmerciful to his country," he prepared for his departure in September of the same year.[1]   There is no reason to doubt his anxiety to fulfil this vocation when accepted, or the reality of his disappointment when, on his arrival at Dieppe in October, he found two discouraging letters from Scotland awaiting him.   These letters indicated that the invitation received in May had been sent without the concurrence of some of the Protestant leaders; that fresh consultations were about to take place; and that it would be better for Knox to remain meanwhile where he was.[2]   His reply to these communications will come before us in a subsequent chapter.   Unwilling to return to Geneva so long as it was possible that he might be required in Scotland, Knox remained at Dieppe as headquarters until the spring of 1558.   In the course of the winter he paid a visit to Lyons, and another to Rochelle[3]; in both cases, doubtless, with a view to the propagation of Protestant truth; and it is interesting to find him, in a sermon delivered in the latter town, expressing the confident hope that within two or three

---

[1] Knox, *H. of R.*, i., 268–270.
[2] *Ibid.*, i., 269.
[3] Laing, *W. of K.*, iv., 260.

Letter from Knox to Queen Elizabeth, 6th Aug., 1561.

Grace from God the father throught our Lord Jesus, with perpetuall encrease of his holie Spiritt.

May it please your Majestie, that it is heir certainlie spoken that the Quen of Scotland travaleht earnestlie to have a treatiss intitilled the " First Blast of the Trompett," confuted by the censure of the learned in diverse realmes, and farther that she labouoreht to inflambe the hartes of princes against the writer. And becaus that it may appear that your Majestie hath interest, that she myndeht to travall with your Grace, your Grace's counsall and learned men for judgement against such a commen ennemey to Women and to thare Regiment. It war but foolishnes to me to pre-scribe unto your Majestie what is to be doune in any thing; but especiallie in such thingis as men supposs do tuech myself. But of one thing I think myself assured, and thairfor I dar not conceall it. To witt, that neyther doht our Soverane so greatlie fear her owen estate by reasson of that book, neyther yit doht she so unfeanedlie favour the tranquillitie of your Ma-jestie's reing and realme, that she wold tack so great and earnest panes; onles that her crafty counsall in so doing shot att a farther marck. Tuo years ago, I wrote unto your Majestie my full declaration tueching that work: experience since hath schawen that I am not desirus of innovations, so that Christ Jesus be not in his membres openlie troden under the feitt of the ungodlie. With farther purgation I will not truble your Majestie for the present, beseching the Eternall so to assist your Highnes in all effares that in his sight ye may be found acceptable, your regiment profit-able to the commenwealht, and your factes to be such that justlie thei may be prased of all godlie unto the cuming of our Lord Jesus, to whose myghtty protection I unfeanedlie committ your Majestie.

From Edinburgh, the 6 of August 1561.

Your Majestie's servand to command in godlines,

JOHN KNOX.

To the myghty and excellent Princess Elizabeht, the Quenes Majestie of England, be these delivered.

Facsimile (on reduced scale) of Knox's letter to Queen Elizabeth, 6th Aug., 1561. (From the original in the State Papers Office.)

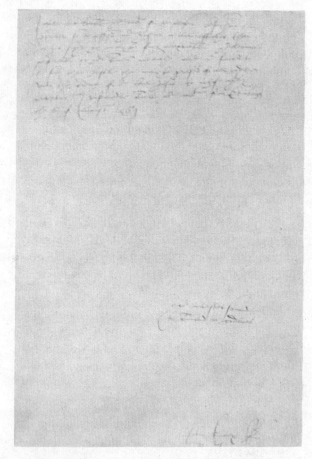

Reverse side of Knox's letter to Queen Elizabeth.

years he would be preaching the Gospel publicly in the Church of St. Giles, Edinburgh.[1]

In the interval between the first and the second visit of Knox to Dieppe, a Reformed congregation had been secretly formed in the town through the influence of a Genevan travelling merchant, Jean Venable: and while Knox was still there André de Séquéran, a gentleman of Provence recommended by Calvin, acted as pastor, preaching at night, sometimes in houses, sometimes in cellars.[2] We may be sure that Knox, who spoke French fluently, assisted in this propagation of the Reformed faith; but his time appears to have been pretty fully occupied with literary work. Three epistles of considerable length, addressed respectively to "the Nobility in Scotland" to his "Brethren in Scotland," and to "the Lords and others professing the Truth," are dated from Dieppe, and belong to this portion of the Reformer's career[3]; and his prolific pen was occupied with another subject. A few weeks before his arrival in Dieppe, a hundred and twenty Protestants had been consigned to dungeons in Paris; and several of these had been executed for meeting privately to celebrate the Lord's Supper according to a Reformed ritual. The pagan charges of immorality against the early Christians, in

---

[1] Row, *Historie of the Kirk*, p. 8.

[2] S. Hardy, *Eglise Protestante de Dieppe*, pp. 36, 37. (Paris 1897).

[3] Laing, *W. of K.*, iv., 261, 275, 286; Knox, *H. of R.*, i., 269.

10

connexion with their secret assemblies, had been reproduced, and applied to these Protestants by malignant Catholics. In the name of the victims an authoritative "Apology" was issued which Knox translated into English. In a preface of his own he attributes the vile calumnies to the Cardinal of Lorraine, the uncle of Mary Stuart.[1]

VII. The English congregation at Geneva had meanwhile become aware of Knox's position regarding Scotland; at their annual election on 16th December, he had again been chosen as one of the pastors; and at some date prior to the 16th March he was once more in Geneva. There he remained till about the end of January, 1559. Two months before, he had received a fresh invitation to return to Scotland from the leaders of the Reform movement, who simultaneously wrote to Calvin "craving that he would command" Knox to revisit his native land.[2] If previous experience might have prevented the Reformer from responding to the summons without further enquiry, his hesitation was removed by the news of Mary Tudor's death on the 17th November, 1558. The majority of the Anglo-Genevan congregation might be expected to return to England; and Knox's pastoral work would be diminished. Providence seemed to point the way back to Scotland. On the occasion of his final

[1] Laing, W. of K., iv., 289–347.
[2] Knox, H. of R., i., 274.

departure from Geneva, he was honoured with the freedom of the city.

While Knox, at this juncture, was interested chiefly in his own country, he was not unmindful of England. Soon after the accession of Elizabeth, he had addressed a *Brief Exhortation* to the nation among whom he had lived and laboured for five years, urging them to the speedy embracing of Christ's Gospel, heretofore "suppressed and banished."[1]

It was the Reformer's strong desire to visit his English friends before proceeding to Scotland. He made several attempts to procure permission to pass through England on the way home; and he remained at Dieppe (where he arrived on the 19th of February) for over two months, partly, indeed, to receive the latest information as to the ecclesiastical situation in Scotland, but chiefly in the hope of obtaining a safe-conduct from the English Government.[2] The "Monstrous Regiment of Women" barred the way. In vain Knox assured the Queen of England, through her minister, Cecil, that he was no "enemy to the person nor yet to the 'regiment' of her whom God hath now promoted"; and the work in question, although the main arguments applied to all female government, had been obviously suggested by the persecuting policy of Mary Tudor. Elizabeth

---

[1] Laing, *W. of K.*, v., 501.
[2] *Ibid.*, vi., 20.

refused to admit within her realm, even as a so-
journer, a man whose avowed political sentiments
impugned her own right to be on the throne at
all.   If Cecil showed to her Majesty Knox's letter of explanation, it is not likely that she would
be conciliated either by the Reformer's reference
to her accession as a "miraculous work of God's
comforting His afflicted by an *infirm vessel*," or
through his counsel that "only humility and de-
jection of herself before God shall be the firmity
and stability of her throne." [1]

VIII.   The ten weeks which Knox spent on
this occasion at Dieppe were very far from being
lost time.   This last visit of the Reformer to
the town constitutes a noteworthy chapter in the
history of French Protestantism.   During the
interval between his departure from Dieppe in
March, 1558, and his return in February, 1559,
the little Reformed congregation had been ministered to by various preachers; but the services
had been held, as formerly, only at night.   Knox
put an end to what he regarded as censurable
circumspection.[2]   "Under his brief ministry"—
so it is testified in a history written within a
century of Knox's time—"the number of the
faithful so increased that they dared to have
preaching in broad daylight"; and a list of
prominent converts is given, including the Lieu-

---

[1] Laing, *W. of K.*, vi., 19.
[2] Demarquets, *Mémoires Chronologiques*, p. 112.

tenant-Governor of Picardy and a descendant of
Charles Martel, who "through Knox's instruction
and influence abjured the errors of the Church of
Rome and made profession of the verity of the
Gospel." [1] Disinterested testimony, also, is borne
to the Scottish Reformer's power by a priest
of Dieppe who, in the early part of the eighteenth
century, on the authority of old manuscripts,
describes Knox as a "learned man," "vehemently zealous," and. "so eloquent that he con-
trolled the minds of men according to his will." [2]
Shortly before his departure a letter was addressed
to Calvin by one of the "faithful," in the name of
the Protestant congregation at Dieppe, requesting
a minister to be sent to them: and this request
is expressly based on the signal success of "Master
John Knox, a singular instrument of the Holy
Spirit, who, according to the graces bountifully
poured out upon him by the Lord, has faithfully
promoted, by his preaching, the glory of Christ,
during the short time that it has been in his power
to have fellowship with us." [3] The success of

---

[1] *Histoire de la Réformation à Dieppe par Guillaume et Jean
Daval* (edited by Emile Lesens), i., 10, 11.

[2] Guibert, *Mémoires pour servir à l'histoire de la Ville de
Dieppe*, p. 105.

[3] Calvin, *Opera*, xvii., 497; Duval, i., 227. According to
an old tradition, Knox preached in the Chapelle de la Mala-
drerie (of which some very scanty ruins remain) in the immediate vicinity of the town.   See L'abbé Cochet, *Repert.
archéol. du Dep. de la Seine inf.*, col. 19 (1871). It is not
probable, however, that at so early a stage any ecclesiastical

Knox's ministry at Dieppe was exhibited in changed lives as well as in Reformed belief.

"At this time God manifested wonderfully the great power of the Word; for those who formerly were incorrigibly fierce, and addicted to the indulgence of their appetites, particularly the sailors, became tractable and orderly, abstaining from blasphemy, abhorring houses of ill-fame and the customs of the tavern —a result which could not have been previously secured, whatever prohibition might have been issued by the King, with severe pains and penalties." [1]

The prosperity of the Protestant community at Dieppe continued after Knox's departure. At a celebration of the Holy Communion, a month after the Reformer had left the town, between six and eight hundred persons took part, including the Governor of the Castle and some of the leading inhabitants. Ere long two congregations were established; one of these being in the Rue d'Ecosse. Knox kept up, through correspondence, his connection with the church which, at a critical time, had been so deeply indebted to

building would be at the disposal of Protestants, and it is more likely (as suggested to the writer by M. Hardy, the Pastor of the Reformed Church at Dieppe, that Knox conducted service in the house of a wealthy Protestant lady, called Hélène Bouchard, in whose dwelling Jean Venable held his meetings in 1557 (Vitet, *Hist. des anc. villes de Fr.* i., 97, 98) (1833). The earliest historical record of any church building occupied by the Reformed community relates to the year 1608.

[1] Duval, i., 13.

Rue d'Ecosse, Dieppe.
(Several of the houses on the right existed in Knox's time.)

his active zeal: and he wrote several "comfortable" letters to the Protestant membership encouraging them to remain steadfast in the faith. Between 1625 and 1630 the number of adherents exceeded five thousand.[1]

During his entire public life Knox was resolutely opposed to a Scoto-French Alliance, which at that epoch involved the peril, if not the ruin, of the Scottish Reformation. But his brief yet effective ministry at Dieppe proves that the hardships which he had suffered from France detracted in no degree from his desire to devote freely to the genuine service of Frenchmen his time, gifts, and strength.

ADDITIONAL NOTE TO CHAPTER V

Knox on Predestination

Predestination was a burning question in Geneva during Knox's ministry there. Shortly before his settlement in the city, Castellio, Professor of Greek in Basel University, had published a trenchant criticism of Calvin's utterances on the subject; and Calvin, as well as Beza, had replied at some length. Knox, as we have seen, had benefited in earlier life by the study of Augustine, whose predestinarian views he may have imbibed, even before he came under Calvin's influence. In 1557 he had already begun the preparation of a treatise on a topic which must have been much discussed at Geneva.[2] Meanwhile,

---

[1] Huraut, *John Knox*, 69; Guibert, *Mémoires, l. c.*

[2] Laing, *W. of K.*, iv., 271.

an able anonymous work by an Anabaptist [1] against Calvinistic doctrine had been widely circulated in England; and the congregation of English exiles at Geneva received from their brethren at home a request for a reply to the work. Knox was selected for this task; and accordingly his treatise took the form of "An Answer to a great number of blasphemous cavillations written by an Anabaptist and adversary to God's eternal predestination." [2]

"How profound Knox was in Divinity," writes Calderwood, "that work of his on predestination may give evidence." [3] If the Reformer cannot be said to have added much to what "that singular instrument of Christ Jesus, John Calvin," [4] had already written, he shows much acuteness and expertness both in reasoning and in the application of Scripture. He rejects the doctrine of opponents, that "the grace of God's election is common to all, but that one receiveth it and another receiveth it not." He is not afraid to state what Calvin himself called the *decretum horribile* of reprobation in terms only a little less stern than Calvin himself. "God in His eternal and immutable counsels hath once decreed whom He would take to salvation and whom He would leave in perdition. Those whom He

---

[1] Probably Robert Cooke, who held some post about the English Court under Elizabeth (Laing, *W. of K.*, v., 16).

[2] The work must have been completed before his departure, and left in the hands of Whittingham who superintended the "imprinting." It extends to 450 pages in *ibid.*, v.

[3] *H. of the K.*, viii., 29.

[4] So Knox calls him in the treatise (Laing, v., 160).

elected to salvation, He receiveth of free mercy without all respect had to their own merits and dignity;
and them in time He calleth of purpose, who, as His
sheep, hear His voice. But to those whom He hath
decreed to leave in perdition, is so shut up the entry
of life, that either they are left continually corrupted
in their blindness, or else, if grace be offered, by them
it is oppugned and obstinately resisted." [1]

Like Calvin, Knox argues for this twofold predestination not only from Scripture (particularly from
Romans ix.), but from the analogies of nature, which
constantly elects and reprobates, and from the spiritual "necessity" of predestinarian doctrine, "to beat
down all pride," that "man may be brought to true
humility," and be "moved to praise God for His free
grace received." [2] With Calvin, also, Knox repudiates,
on the one hand, the notion that "God without just
causes doth make any man to destruction," (these
just causes, however, being admitted to be "incom-
prehensible to man" [3];) while, on the other hand, he
magnifies the divine sovereignty. The Calvinistic
obscuration of God's fatherly relation to all mankind, is reproduced in such words as these: "You
make the love of God common to all men; and that
do we constantly deny, and say that before all
beginning God hath loved His elect." [4] He emphasises the divine prescience: "all things have
ever been before His eyes; so that to His eternal
knowledge nothing is by past, nothing to come; all

[1] Laing, v., 42.
[2] *Ibid.*, v., 27, 76.
[3] *Ibid.*, v., 160.
[4] *Ibid.*, v., 61.

things are present" [1]; but he fails, like his Genevan master, to realise that the truth, "God willeth all men to be saved," is no less clearly revealed; and that we have no more right to build upon the divine fore-knowledge an eternal purpose of reprobation, than to build upon God's desire for universal human salvation the assurance that under an omnipotent government all will actually be saved.

Three things are noteworthy about Knox's treatise: 1. His scrupulous care to state his adversary's arguments at full length and in his (the adversary's) own words. 2. Amid censurable denunciations of his opponent's "profane subtlety," "impudent blasphemy," and "malicious lies," he displays a touching anxiety for his illumination. "God open your eyes that ye may see the light!" he exclaims; and solemnly assures him, "I take to record the Lord Jesus that I would bestow my own life, to join you fully to Jesus Christ." [2] 3. When Knox leaves the arena of theological controversy for the yet more responsible work of drawing up a Confession of Faith for the Church, predestination doctrine recedes into the background; for in the Confession drawn up in 1560, at the very time when his treatise was being published at Geneva, the word "predestination" never occurs; and the statement about election is so brief and general that Arminians, afterwards, could have cordially accepted it. "The same eternal God and Father, who of mere mercy elected us in Christ Jesus before the foundation of the world was laid, appointed him to be our Head, our

---

[1] Laing, v., 35.
[2] *Ibid.*, v., 247.

Brother, our Pastor and great Bishop of our souls
. . . giving power to so many as believe in Him
to be the sons of God." [1]   Calvin himself, in one of
his commentaries, when the influence of Holy Writ is
greater than that of reason upon his mind, confesses
that "predestination is a labyrinth from which the
mind of man can by no means extricate itself." [2]   In
their less argumentative moods both he and Knox
might have adopted Dante's memorable words:

> "O how far removed
> Predestination! is thy root from such
> As see not the First Cause entire; and ye,
> O mortal men, be wary how ye judge." [3]

---

[1] Chap. viii., in Laing, *W. of K.*, ii., 100.   It is possible, of
course, that the article on Election may have been modified
in revision by Knox's five colleagues to whom the first draft
(composed by him) was submitted (*Ibid.*, vi., 120, 121); but
in any case Knox endorsed the moderate statement above
quoted.

[2] Calvin on Rom. ix., 14.

[3] *Parad.*, xx., 130 *ff.*   (Cary's Translation).

CHAPTER VI

KNOX'S FIRST RETURN TO SCOTLAND

1555–1556

IN the first year of Knox's residence on the Continent, the Scottish Reformation received a stimulus from two events which might have appeared likely to operate in a contrary direction.

I. One of these events was the appointment in 1554 of the Queen Dowager, Mary of Guise, to the regency. Her brothers, the Cardinal of Lorraine and the Duke of Guise, were leading opponents of Protestantism in France, and Mary herself was a thorough Romanist. Fortunately for Scotland and for the Reformation, she was also a keen politician and an ambitious mother. For years she had aimed at supplanting the Earl of Arran, who had held the regency since her husband's death. To accomplish this purpose she privately befriended prominent Protestants, and thus established a personal influence among the Scottish aristocracy. When at length, in April, 1554, she had attained her end, after Arran's abdication, she continued by a tolerant ecclesiastical attitude to ingratiate herself with influential Reformers, in order to disarm opposition to another cardinal aim of her life—the marriage of her daughter, Mary Stuart, to the Dauphin of France.[1] The policy of conciliation, thus adopted by the head of the State, was not opposed meanwhile to any policy of severe persecution by the head of the Church. Archbishop Hamilton was neither a bigoted nor a sanguinary ecclesiastic. He realised the necessity of some kind of reformation. He endeavoured to lessen priestly ignorance and incompetence by the publication of a Catechism remarkable for moderate doctrine as well as non-controversial tone[2]; and he procured the enactment of statutes against clerical immorality—statutes, however, which, in spite of his early reputation as "chaster than any maiden," he could not enforce without condemning himself.[3] While his policy as regards

---

[1] Buchanan, *H. of Sc.*, xvi.; Lesley, (vernac.) *H. of Sc.*, 234, 244-247; Hume Brown, *H. of Sc.*, ii., 36-38; Mathieson, *Politics and Religion in Scotland, 1550-1595*, i., 40-44. Hamilton was partly constrained to resign the regency by the nobility whom Mary of Guise won over to her side, and partly bribed by the dukedom of Châtelherault, and the payment of his large debts.

[2] While distinctly Roman in doctrine, the Catechism is silent as to papal supremacy, ignores the indulgence system, refrains from forbidding or even discouraging the reading of vernacular Scripture by the laity, and. describes love and good works, in accordance with evangelical theology, as the fruit of faith rather than an independent addition to faith.

[3] Knox, *H. of R.*, i., 124.

Protestantism was of necessity so far repressive,[1] it is significant that between his appointment to the primacy in 1546 and Knox's return to Scotland in 1555, only one person in Scotland suffered martyrdom—Adam Wallace, a layman of Ayrshire, and Knox's successor in 1550 as tutor at Ormiston.[2] This comparative toleration in which Regent and Primate, from somewhat different motives,[3] concurred, issued naturally in numerous accessions to the Reform party from those whom fear had hitherto restrained from publicly professing their faith.

A further stimulus of a different kind was supplied to the Reformation in Scotland by the entrance of the English Queen, a year after her accession, on that policy of truculent persecution which has branded her character indelibly as "Bloody Mary." Under the Protestant rule of Edward VI., numerous Scots, zealous for Reform, had been attracted to the southern kingdom. Some of these naturally returned home when the conflict became fiercer in England than in Scotland. Knox mentions particularly William

---

[1] See Chap. IV., note 6.

[2] Knox, *H. of R.*, i., 237; Foxe, v., 636–641. Knox describes Wallace as "a simple man without great learning, but zealous of godliness, and of an upright life." His martyrdom took place in July, 1550.

[3] The Primate had no desire to expedite the marriage of Mary Stuart, since, failing issue from it, his own brother was heir to the throne.

Harlaw and John Willock as among the "godly" men who at this period came back to their native land for the instruction of the people and the strengthening of the Protestant cause.[1]

II. About the end of September, 1555, Knox himself arrived in Edinburgh. He preached there, privately at first, in the house of his host, James Sym, a "notable man of God."[2] But his return soon became known to the Reforming leaders, and under their auspices almost the entire winter and spring of 1555–56 were spent by him in evangelistic expeditions. Before he commenced his labours, however, there was one point on which he was anxious to have a decision. Among the memorable acts of his short ministry at St. Andrews in 1547 had been the open celebration of the Lord's Supper in accordance with Reformed doctrine and ritual. During the intervening eight years this example had not been widely imitated; and he found, on his return to Scotland, that many Protestant leaders and a large proportion of their followers still attended mass. Knox protested against such conformity as a sinful countenance of deadly error.

---

[1] *H. of R.*, i., 245. Harlaw was originally a tailor in Edinburgh; at the Reformation, he became minister to St. Cuthbert's Church in that city. As to Willock, see p. 93. Among others were Paul Methven, of Dundee, and a Carmelite friar, named Douglas, who became chaplain to the Earl of Argyle. See Bellesheim, *Cath. Ch. of Scot.*, ii., 220.

[2] *H. of R.*, i., 246. See Chap. V., p. 133.

A private conference was held in Edinburgh
at the house of John Erskine of Dun to dis-
cuss the question. There were present, besides the Reformer and Erskine himself, John
Willock, the preacher; David Forres, of Haddington, Master of the Mint, a friend of Wishart; Robert Lockhart, a lay "exhorter"; and
William Maitland of Lethington, a man, as Knox
testifies, "of good learning, and of sharp wit
and reasoning." Knox opened discussion with
the contention that it was "no wise lawful
to a Christian to present himself to that idol";
while the usage was defended by Maitland, whom
the Reformer, long afterwards on his own death-
bed, denounced for "carnal prudence otherwise
manifested." "Nothing," writes Knox, "was
omitted that might make for the temporiser."
The example of St. Paul at Jerusalem was
quoted, when he identified himself with certain
Jews in a Levitical observance. But the Reformer had no difficulty in shewing that the two
cases were not parallel. St. Paul at most counte-
nanced a practice which was abrogated for
Christians, but had been prescribed for Jews.
Moreover, it was very doubtful whether in this
instance St. Paul and St. James had acted
rightly. Eventually it was admitted, according
to Knox, by all present, that their "shifts served
nothing"; and it was resolved henceforth to meet
as Reformed congregations for separate com-

munion.[1] The decision was signal. It was an
act of ecclesiastical schism, justifiable, at this
early stage, only on the ground that the mass,
as a breach of the Second Commandment, was
not a mere imperfect mode of worship, but a
positive sin. Strategically the new departure was
a distinct gain to the Reform party in their conflict. By this significant step the Protestants in
Scotland acquired courage and consolidation.
Those who were in earnest about the Reformation became better known to each other, and
had fuller opportunity of mutual support: the
organisation of the Reformed Scottish Church
had begun.

III. The question of attendance at mass having thus been settled to his satisfaction, Knox
devoted himself with all his strength to the work
of propagating evangelical truth. He proceeded
first to Forfarshire, where the memory of Wishart
was still fresh. He resided for a month with
Erskine at Dun,[2] preaching daily to congregations

---

[1] Knox, *H. of R.*, i., 247–249.

[2] *Ibid.*, i., 249. Erskine had been "marvellously illumined"
more than twenty years before; had been the friend of
Straiton of Lauriston, who suffered martyrdom in 1534; and
had afterwards been a sympathetic supporter of George
Wishart (*ibid.*, i., 132). He was one of those Reformers who were equally zealous against English aggression
and against Roman error; for he distinguished himself in
the war of defence in 1548–49, and he was highly esteemed
and trusted by the Regent Mary (*ibid.*, i., 318; *Spalding Miscellany*, iv., 48, 49, 51). Knox describes him as "most gentle
II

which included the "principal men of the county."
We find him afterwards in Linlithgowshire,
under the protection of Sir James Sandilands
of Calder, reviving the memories of Patrick
Hamilton, and reiterating the truths for which the
"Proto-martyr" suffered. During his residence in
that county, he had as listeners to his preaching
three young noblemen who became prominent in
the history of the Reformation—Archibald Lord
Lorne, afterwards fifth Earl of Argyle; Lord James
Stuart, a natural son of James V., eventually the
"Good Regent" Moray; and Lord Erskine, subsequently sixth Earl of Mar, Governor of Edinburgh Castle, and ultimately Moray's successor
(after a brief interval) in the regency. In December Knox "taught commonly in Edinburgh"; but
after Christmas he again travelled from place to
place. He preached and administered the Holy
Communion in various parishes of Ayrshire;
among other places in the ancient town of Ayr;
in Mauchline, where he had the staunch support of Robert Campbell of Kinyeancleuch, whose
father in like manner had stood by Wishart; and

---

of nature." Buchanan speaks of him as "equally pious and
cultured." After the Reformation, he was ordained to the
ministry, and became Superintendent of Angus and Mearns.
Specimens of his discourses (S. M., iv., 101, 112) show him
to have been a preacher who united effectiveness with charity.
Queen Mary is recorded (Knox, H. of R., ii., 482) to have said
that she "would gladly hear [preaching] the Superintendent
of Angus; for he was a mild and sweet-natured man with
true honesty and uprightness."

in the House of Ochiltree, where he must have
seen the maiden who eight years later became his
second wife.   In the spring of 1556 the Reformer
was at Kilmacolm on the Clyde, by the invitation
of Lord Glencairn, whose residence, Finlayston,
was in that parish; the silver cups used on that
occasion at the Communion are still preserved.[1]
A second visit to Calder in West Lothian and
another to Dun, completed his journeyings up
till the early part of May.[2]   The welcome which
the preaching of Reformed doctrine had received
from the people during Knox's evangelistic tour
far surpassed his expectations.   "If I had not
seen it with my own eyes," so he writes to Mrs.
Bowes, "I could not have believed it."   "The
fervency here doth far exceed all others that I
have seen," he continues; and he frankly confesses that it constrained him to condemn his own
"slothful coldness." [3]

IV.   The success of "that knave Knox," as
one of the bishops called him,[4] alarmed the hierarchy; and the new practice of Protestant ab-
stention from mass revealed the magnitude
of the ecclesiastical secession which was being
consolidated into a rival church.   It was necessary to take steps to get rid of the man whom all

---

[1] Knox, *H. of R.*, i., 250 (Laing's Note).

[2] *Ibid.*, i., 249, 250.

[3] Laing, *W. of K.*, iv., 217, 218.

[4] *Ibid.*, iv., 439.   From the context the bishop appears to
have been James Beaton of Glasgow.

regarded as the *origo mali*. The laws against
heresy were still unrepealed; although, since
the change in the regency, they had no longer
been enforced. While Knox was still the guest
of Erskine at Dun he received a citation to trial
before an ecclesiastical court at Blackfriars'
Church, Edinburgh, on the 15th of May.[1] The
object of the bishops was probably the same as
that of Primate James Beaton, thirty years before, when he sent a similar citation to Patrick
Hamilton—to drive an inconvenient intruder out
of the way. As their procedure was unsupported
by the Regent, the flight of Knox from Scotland
was the issue which probably they most desired.
They mistook their man: Knox arrived, openly,
in Edinburgh, accompanied by Erskine and other
gentlemen, a few days before the date fixed for
his "compearance." The discomfited bishops departed from the trial, either, as Knox suggests, on
the ground of some "informality in their own
proceedings," or because "they feared danger to
ensue." The fiasco was an admirable advertisement. On the very day on which he was
to have been tried the Reformer preached to
a larger audience than ever had listened to him
in the city before; and, emboldened by non-
interference, he continued to preach for ten days
in succession.[2] Such a triumph was enough to

---

[1] Knox, *H. of R.*, i., 251.
[2] *Ibid.*, i., 251.

exhilarate a much less ardent nature than that of Knox.

"Rejoice mother"—so he writes to Mrs. Bowes after three days' ministrations—"the time of our deliverance approacheth. The trumpet blew the old sound three days together, till private houses of indifferent largeness could not contain the voice of it. Sweet were the death that should follow forty such days in Edinburgh as I have had three." [1]

V. Success fosters ambition. Knox had evangelised a large portion of the people; he had fortified the Reforming nobility and gentry; the Protestant party had been transformed into a Church; the hierarchy had been constrained to cower in the conflict and to beat a humiliating retreat. Not content with these triumphs, the Reformer was bold enough to essay the conversion of the Regent herself. One recalls the journey of St. Francis of Assisi to Egypt for the conversion of the Mohammedan Sultan. The suggestion of the attempt is ascribed by Knox to two distinguished adherents of the Reformation —Earl Marischal and Henry Drummond of Rickarton in West Lothian, who had been listening just before to one of his "exhortations." The promptness, however, with which he appears to have accepted the proposal, and the extreme care with which he carried it out, indicate that the idea

---

[1] Laing, *W. of K.*, iv., 218.

had already occurred to himself, and had probably been put into the minds of these two noblemen through some pulpit reference to the Regent.[1]

He wrote a long and elaborate letter "to the excellent Lady Mary, Regent of Scotland," and caused it to be delivered by the friendly hand of Glencairn. His *First Blast against the Monstrous Regiment of Women* had not yet been blown or even prepared for issue; the Reformer, so far as we know, was still in his attitude of an enquirer as to "whether a female can preside over and rule a kingdom." The epistle, coming from a plain-spoken man like Knox, is a marvel of moderation and gentleness, yet without any palpable deviation from sincerity. Compared with his usual trenchant style of writing, the composition is like the coo of the dove after the roar of the lion. He calls himself the Regent's "humble subject," and wishes "mercy and peace" for her. He blesses God "who by the dew of his heavenly grace hath so quenched the fire of displeasure in your Grace's heart, which is to my heart no small comfort"; and he rejoices in the "moderation and clemency that your Grace hath begun toward me and my most desperate cause." He assures her, if she "continue in like moderation and clemency toward others, and by godly wisdom bridle the fury and rage of them who regard not the cruel murdering of simple innocents," that "then shall He who

---

[1] Knox, *H. of R.*, i., 252.

pronounceth mercy to appertain to the merciful
first cause your happy government to be praised
in this present age and the posterities to come,
and last, recompense your godly pains and study
with that joy and glory which the eye hath not
seen, nor yet can enter into the heart of mortal
creature." It may "appear foolish to many," he
continues, that he, "a worm most wretched, a
man of base state and condition, dare enterprise
or admonish a Princess so honourable, endowed
with wisdom and graces singularly." But he has
"thought it some discharge of a part of my duty,
if I of very love admonish your Grace of danger,"
"preferring your Grace's salvation and the salvation of the people now committed to your care
before any corporal benefit to myself"; and feeling "if I should hide it from your Grace, I committed no less treason than if I saw you by
imprudency take a cup which I knew to be poisoned, and yet would not admonish you to abstain
from drinking the same." He then proceeds to
emphasise the responsibility of rulers as well as
bishops for the maintenance of true and pure
religion; and shows that a form of "religion universally received" may none the less be "damn-
able and corrupted." Knox cordially admits that
her Grace "cannot hastily abolish all superstition,
neither yet remove from office unprofitable pastors
which only feed themselves"; but this need not
prevent her from "doing what" she "may"; from

"studying with all careful diligence how the true
worshipping of God may be promoted," and how
"the tyranny of ungodly men may be repressed."
With that view he warns the Regent not to be "led
away with that vain opinion that your Kirk and
your prelates cannot err"; and he bids her rather
"lay the book of God before your eyes, and let it
be a judge to their lives, doctrine, and manners,
as also to that doctrine which by fire and sword
most cruelly they persecute." [1]

Knox had not correctly diagnosed the disposition and policy of Mary of Guise. Her benevolent
patronage, meanwhile, of Protestants was due, not
to any real sympathy with their position, but to
that statecraft which (along with some "graces"
of character, as Knox avows) she shared with
other members of her distinguished family. She
read the letter,—so Knox was assured,—but it
produced no impression either in the way of
conviction or of irritation; for a day or two
afterwards she handed it to Archbishop Beaton
with the remark, "Please you, my Lord, to read a
pasquil." [2] Knox, like most other men, disliked
to be laughed at even more than to be persecuted.
He printed his letter soon after it was sent, just
as it reached the Regent's hands; and neither
friend nor foe at the time informed him of the
scornful reception which it had met; but two years

---

[1] The letter is contained in Laing, *W. of K.*, iv., 73–84.

[2] Knox, *H. of R.*, i., 252.

later, when the Regent's "supercilious mockery" had been reported to him, he showed his natural irritation by a reprint of the letter "now augmented and explained." Never did the second edition of a publication differ so widely from the first. The original matter is all retained, but its marked moderation serves only, by sharp contrast, to emphasise the plain-spoken severity of the "additions" and explanations. "My duty to God," he now writes, "has compelled me to say that if no more ye esteem the admonition of God than the Cardinals do the scoffing of pasquils, then He shall shortly send you messengers with whom ye shall not be able in that manner to jest." He now denounces the Regent's own "avarice and cruelty," as well as the "superstition and idolatry which she had maintained." The *First Blast* had in the interval been sent forth. Knox does not hesitate to apply to Mary of Guise some passages in that work which had been originally intended for Mary Tudor; and with a presumption, it must be admitted, which strength of conviction and the provocation of a recent martyrdom [1] may account for, but cannot justify, he attributes the Regent's loss of husband and of sons to her "maintenance and defence of most horrible idolatry, with the shedding of the blood of the saints of God." [2]

VI.   The letter to Mary of Guise was not the only

---

[1] That of Walter Milne in April, 1558. See pp. 183–185.
[2] Laing, *W. of K.*, iv., 450, 453, 454, 458.

instance of Knox's literary activity during this visit to Scotland; although his evangelistic labours were so multiplied and (as he expresses it) "Satan did so hunt me," that "small space was granted to writing." [1] At the request of some who being "before in great anguish did confess themselves somewhat reclaimed by the doctrine," he committed to writing the substance of a discourse on the "Temptation of Christ in the Wilderness." [2] The most notable point in this treatise is his argument against the forty days' fast of our Lord being regarded as an authority for the institution of Lent, which he calls a "superstitious fasting." Even if we knew the exact time of the year when Christ fasted, "Am I, or [is] any Christian bound," he asks, "to counterfeit His actions, as the ape counterfeiteth the act of man?" Christ fasted forty days when He was about to "take upon Him openly" His ministry, not to constrain us to follow literally His example, but "to teach us with what fear, carefulness, and reverence ought the messengers of the Word to enter on the vocation."

To this period also belong, apparently, the Reformer's *Answers to some Questions concerning Baptism*.[3] The small number of Reformed ministers in Scotland had caused many Protestants to

---

[1] Letter to Mrs. Locke, in Laing, iv., 240.
[2] Laing, iv., 87–114.
[3] *Ibid.*, iv., 116–140.

ask whether they might "offer their children to the papistical baptism." Knox answers without hesitation, No. The ceremonial of baptism "now used in the papistry is an adulteration and a profanation," and "whosoever communicateth with the papistical sacraments approveth before the world whatsoever doctrine and religion they [the Romanists] profess." On the other hand, he gives a negative reply with equal distinctness to the further question, "Shall we be baptised again that in our infancy were polluted with that adulterous sign?" "The fire of the Holy Ghost," he declares, "hath burnt away whatsoever we received besides Christ Jesus' simple institution"; and "the Spirit of Christ, illuminating our hearts, maketh the effect of that sacrament to work in us without any iteration of the external sign."

About midsummer, 1556, Knox received from his congregation at Geneva a letter, somewhat inconsiderately yet not unnaturally peremptory, "commanding him in God's name, as their chosen pastor to repair unto them for their comfort." Knox discerned in this summons a providential call and before the end of July he had left Scotland for Geneva.[1] Tytler, followed by some other historians,[2] charges Knox with "want of courage" in thus "retreating" before danger. But surely his bold defiance of the hierarchy in Edinburgh,

[1] Knox, *H. of R.*, i., 252, 253.

[2] Tytler, *H. of Sc.*, vi., 94; Comp. Bellesheim, *Cath. Ch. of Sc.*, ii., 227–228; Stephen, *H. of Sc. Ch.*, i., 548.

only two months before, indicates that cowardice
could not have caused his departure. Apart from
the claim which the congregation of Geneva had
upon his services, there was some reason for believing that in existing circumstances the absence
of Knox for a season from Scotland might be of
more service to the Protestant cause than his
presence. His visit of nine months had, indeed,
been a conspicuous success, especially as a stimu-
lating tonic to those who favoured the Reformation; but the excessive administration of tonics
is not wholesome in the moral any more than in
the physical sphere. A period, of quiet natural
development, under the consolidating influence
of Knox's recent ministration, and amid the
practical toleration of the Regent's government,
probably appeared at this stage to be desirable.
With that view it was not expedient to drive the
hierarchy, as Knox's continued presence was likely
to do, into an attempted renewal of sharp persecution. Such an attempt would force upon the
Regent the alternative of alliance with the prelates
or of more active resistance to their policy; and
in the probable event of her adopting the former
course as on the whole less dangerous and less
disagreeable, a premature conflict would be precipi-
tated which the Protestant party were not yet
strong enough to face. In any case Knox's withdrawal from Scotland was in no sense a flight.
It was neither secret nor hurried: the hierarchy

had abundant time for renewing their citation and
arresting the Reformer.   Before his departure he
paid a farewell visit to almost every district where
he had preached, and on the 7th of July he issued
what he calls a "Letter of Wholesome Counsel to
his Brethren in Scotland"; "not so much," he
declares, "to instruct you, as to leave with you
some testimony of my love."   He admonishes his
"beloved brethren" to meet regularly for congregational worship, "which I would were once a week";
and he sketches for them an Order of Service,
similar to that which he had adopted at Frankfort, Geneva, and also, doubtless, recently in
Scotland.   In the absence of a specially ordained
ministry, he recommends that after some portion
of Scripture has been read, "if any brother have
exhortation, question, or doubt, let him not fear
to speak or move the same, so that he do it with
moderation."   He adds considerately that "if
anything occur within the text, or else arise in
reasoning, which your judgment cannot resolve or
your capacities apprehend   .   .   .   I will more
gladly spend fifteen hours in explaining [*i. e.*, by
letter], as God pleases to open to me, any place
of Scripture, than half an hour in any matter
beside." [1]

Knox had not long left Scotland when the hierarchy resumed proceedings against him.   The
huntsmen who had retired when the lion appeared

----

[1] The letter is contained in Laing, *W. of K.*, iv., 133–140.

now became bold when their intended prey had retired. He was summoned *in absentia* before the Provincial Council; but no written citation ever reached him; and he declares that when a copy of the summons was demanded (presumably by his friends in Scotland) it was refused. For the Reformer's non-appearance, as well as for other offences, sentence of excommunication appears to have been pronounced against him followed by the nominal surrender of his person to the civil power with a view to the penalty of death; for his body was "burnt in effigy at the Cross of Edinburgh." [1]

[1] Laing, *W. of K.*, i., 254; iv., 471.

CHAPTER VII

THE SCOTTISH REFORMATION MOVEMENT BETWEEN
KNOX'S DEPARTURE FROM SCOTLAND IN 1556
AND HIS FINAL RETURN IN 1559—THE RE-
FORMER'S CONTRIBUTIONS IN HIS ABSENCE TO
THE PROGRESS OF THE CAUSE

1556–1559.

DURING the interval between the departure
of Knox from Scotland in July, 1556, and
his return in May, 1559, the way was gradually
prepared for the final conflict in which he was to
take the leading part.   The Reform party became
more numerous and consolidated, more self-reliant
and aggressive: the Regent's demeanour towards
Protestants became less amicable and at length
openly hostile: the hierarchy, encouraged by the
altered attitude of the Court, and stimulated by
the conviction that the Church was in peril, resumed their policy of persecution; the alliance
with France, although it appeared to be sealed by
the marriage of Mary Stuart and the Dauphin,
declined in popularity; and Romanism in consequence lost the benefit which Henry VIII.'s

unwise policy had conferred upon it, of association with patriotism in the minds of the Scottish people. Each of these developments hastened the ecclesiastical crisis, and contributed, directly or indirectly, to the ultimate triumph of Protestantism.

I. In March, 1557, as we have already seen, a letter was despatched to Knox by a section of the Scottish nobility, craving his return to Scotland. His acceptance of the invitation and his detention at Dieppe, owing to discouraging letters from home, have already been related.[1] "Confounded and pierced with anguish," he wrote to the Lords, upbraiding them for having "fainted in their former purpose through fear of danger" and suggesting that they "preferred the friendship of the wicked to the salvation of Brethren."[2] His words, written in natural irritation, may have been, to use his own expression, "somewhat sharp and indiscreetly spoken." Moreover, subsequent reflection led him also to "suspect my own wickedness," and to admit that along with the "doubts and cauld writings of some brethren" were the "cogitations" of what he calls elsewhere his "natural fearfulness."[3] His letter, however,

---

[1] See page 144.

[2] Knox, *H. of R.*, i., 271.

[3] See letter to "sisters in Edinburgh sent from Geneva in April, 1558." With a *naïveté* which disarms criticism, Knox confesses that the "cause of my stop do I not to this day clearly understand." Apparently he had been from the first of two minds as to what he should do. A chivalrous and

proved to be a salutary stimulus to Reforming
zeal; while a recent attempt by the Regent, at
the instigation of France, to involve Scotland in
a needless and unprovoked war with England [1]
had cooled Scottish favour for the French alliance,
and thus weakened so far the cause of Romanism.
" New consultation," accordingly, " was had, what
was best to be done "; and on the 3rd December,
1557, there was drawn up at Edinburgh what was
called a " Common Band," generally known as the
first Scottish " COVENANT." It marks a fresh
stage in the Reformation movement. By absent-
ing themselves from mass and celebrating the
Communion with a Reformed ritual, the Protestants had already organised themselves into a
church for united worship and mutual edification;
by the adoption of this Covenant they took the
further step of organising themselves into a league
for common action and mutual defence.

---

dutiful desire to stand by his Scottish friends conflicted with
reluctance not only to risk his own life but to cause "tumults
to rise" in Scotland, without real benefit to the cause. He
left Geneva, however, resolved to act what he felt to be the
nobler and bolder part. The discouraging letters received at
Dieppe reawakened his doubts; in his vexation at having
his courage thus undermined by those who had urged him
on, he threw the whole blame on the lords; but in calmer
mood he honestly shared the discredit, and could not understand how he had allowed himself to be dissuaded from proceeding to Scotland, except that to "punish my former
unthankfulness, it may be, God . . . permitted Satan
to put in my mind sic cogitations as did impede my journey."

[1] Lesley, *H. of Sc.* (Scott. Text Soc. ed.), ii., 368–372.

"We do promise before the Majesty of God and this congregation"—so ran the terms of the Band—"that we by His grace shall with all diligence apply our whole power, substance, and our very lives, to maintain, set forward, and establish the most blessed Word of God and His congregation; and shall labour at our possibility to have faithful ministers purely and truly to minister Christ's Evangel and Sacraments. We shall maintain them, nourish them, and defend them, the whole congregation of Christ and every member thereof, at our whole power and waring [*i. e.*, sacrifice] of our lives, against Satan and all wicked power that does intend tyranny or trouble against the foresaid congregation." [1]

The Covenant was signed by a large number of nobles and gentry, including the Earls of Argyle, Glencairn, and Morton, Lord Lorne, and Erskine of Dun. The subscribers became known as the "Lords of the Congregation," and constituted themselves into a national Protestant council. Their aims were far-reaching: but their early procedure was moderate. In accordance, substantially, with Knox's "Wholesome Counsel" of July, 1556, regarding stated weekly public worship, it was "ordained that in all parishes of this realm the Common Prayers be read on Sunday and other festival days, publicly, in the parish Kirks, with the lessons of the Old and New Testaments, conform to the order of the Book of

---

[1] Knox, *H. of R.*, i., 273.

Common Prayers" [1]; the curates to be asked to
discharge the office, if qualified and willing; failing these, the most qualified persons available.
"Preaching and interpretation of Scripture," as
distinguished from worship, were meanwhile to
be held in private houses, "until God move the

---

[1] Knox, *H. of R.*, i., 270. It has been disputed whether the
Second Prayer-book of Edward VI or the *Book of Geneva*,
published in the preceding year, be here intended. One might
have supposed that Knox's influence would secure the use of
the latter rather than of a liturgy of which he partly disapproved; yet evidence exists that even in June, 1559, the
Prayer-book set forth by "godly King Edward" was read
in parish churches (Laing, vi., 34); and this testimony is confirmed by an extant summons raised in 1560 by the Vicar of
Lintrathen for payment of teinds on this ground (among
others) that he "has caused the Common Prayers and Homilies to be read weekly to the parishioners," referring apparently to the *Book of Homilies* associated with the Prayer-book
of Edward (*Spalding Miscell.*, iv., 120). Moreover, the men-
tion (in the injunction) of the "*Lessons* conform to the order
of the Book of Common Prayers" does not suit the *Book of
Geneva*, which has no stated lectionary. The probable explanation of the sanction of the English instead of the
Genevan Liturgy at this time is that more copies of the
former, being the older book, existed in Scotland; that
the Service-book of Edward had come into considerable use
before the *Book of Geneva* had been issued; and that Knox
although disapproving of portions of the English liturgy, refrained from protesting against its use in Scotland, just as he
had refrained from such protest while he was in England, so
long as his direct sanction was not required. When the arrangements of worship came afterwards under his own charge,
the English liturgy was superseded by the Genevan Order
(McCrie, *Life of Knox*, note DD; Laing, vi., 227; A. F.
Mitchell, *Scot. Ref.*, 128).

Prince to grant public preaching by faithful and true ministers." [1]

The Protestant leaders had apparently in contemplation not merely reformed worship in every parish alongside of the Romish ritual, but the eventual supersession of the latter by the former. This, however, did not mean necessarily the supersession of the old by a new Church. There was still a widespread hope that, through the action of the State, supported by sympathetic churchmen who realised the need of reform, the existing organisation might be transformed without being demolished. The Lords of the Congregation, accordingly, followed up their enactments by a petition addressed to the Regent and presented in the spring of 1558 by the aged Sir James Sandilands of Calder. The petition craved, on the one hand, full liberty both of preaching and of public worship, including administration of the sacraments "in the vulgar tongue," with Communion "in both kinds"; on the other hand, stringent ecclesiastical discipline, "that the wicked, scandalous, and detestable life of prelates and of the State Ecclesiastical may be so reformed that the people have not occasion to contemn their ministry." The Reformers at this stage appear to have hoped that if a riddance were obtained of ill-living bishops and clergy, those who remained would acquiesce in a Reformed ritual and doctrine,

---

[1] Knox, *H. of R.*, i., 276.

and "the grave and godly face of the primitive Church" would be restored.[1] The Regent gave the petitioners a conciliatory answer. On condition that they refrained from holding "public assemblies" in Edinburgh and Leith, she "promised her assistance to the preachers" of the Congregation "until some uniform order might be established by a Parliament." By this time, however, as will presently be seen, she was on the eve, as she believed, of emancipation from dependence on Protestant support; and subsequent events appear to corroborate the assertion of Knox that simultaneously "she gave signification of her mind to the clergy, promising that how soon any opportunity should serve, she should so put order in their matters, that after they should not be troubled." [2]

II. While the leaders of the Congregation were carrying out, with due caution, the terms of the Covenant, the Regent was bringing to maturity that matrimonial alliance between Scotland and France to secure which she was obliged to court for a time the support of the Protestant nobility. In December, 1557, the Scottish Estates were induced to fulfil the agreement made with France nine years before; and eight commissioners, including Lord James Stewart and Erskine of Dun, proceeded to Paris to make the final arrangements

---

[1] Knox, *H. of R.*, pp. 302–306.
[2] *Ibid.*, p. 307.

for the marriage of Mary Stuart with the Dauphin. On the 19th April, 1558, the treaty of marriage was signed; the contract including an agreement according to which the Dauphin was to bear the title of "King of Scotland." Five days later the marriage was celebrated in the Church of *Notre Dame.*[1] The Regent's policy had thus apparently succeeded. Her son-in-law and her daughter seemed destined to become King and Queen of France and of Scotland; the latter, as the smaller country, would become eventually, under their heirs, an appanage of France; the maintenance of the Roman Church in Scotland would be secured by French support and, if necessary, armed intervention; while France would be effectively fortified in any future conflict with England. At once the motherly ambition, the Catholic aspirations, and the patriotic sentiment of the daughter of Guise were fully satisfied. From this time, accordingly, the relations between the Regent and the Reformers began to cool.[2] Having

---

[1] *Diur. of Occur.*, p. 52; Tytler, *H. of Sc.*, vi., 80, 81.

[2] It was necessary, however, for the Regent to temporise meanwhile and to conceal her change of attitude, owing to her anxiety to comply with the request of the French Court that the Scottish crown should be sent to Paris for the coronation of the Dauphin. Parliament gave its consent, in Nov., 1558. Had the Scots become aware that three weeks before the marriage Mary Stuart had been induced to sign a secret contract, making over Scotland to the King of France in the event of her dying without offspring, the significance of this use of the crown would have been realised, and the insidious

availed herself of the Protestant party to overcome the rivalry of the House of Hamilton, she was now prepared, at first with reserve, but ere long openly, to co-operate with Primate Hamilton in suppressing Protestantism. She failed, however, to estimate aright the strength of the Reformers whom she was about to force into conflict; and her love of France blinded her to the fact that ten years of French alliance had taught to many Scots the lesson that, apart from the religious conflict altogether, the friendship of France involved for Scotland present trouble, with the possibility of eventual annexation.[1]

III. The policy of the Reformers and of the Regent affected the procedure of the Primate. The more aggressive action of the Congregation goaded him, the recently altered attitude of the Regent emboldened him, the failure of his own endeavours to stem, through internal reform, the progress of Protestantism constrained him— to try the effect of renewed persecution. The victim selected to inaugurate the new policy was an aged priest of eighty-two years, Walter Milne, who in his earlier life had travelled in

---

request would, doubtless, have been refused. The Scots never intended that the Dauphin should be recognised as King of Scotland, except as husband of their Queen; and the Estates stipulated that if Mary died without issue the Dauphin was to renounce all claim to the throne (*Diur.*, 52; Tytler, *H. of Sc.*, vi., 83, 84; Hume Brown, *H. of Sc.*, ii., 45.

[1] *Hamilton Papers*, ii., 616; Teulet, i., 414.

Germany and had there imbibed Reformed opinions. During the primacy of Cardinal Beaton he
had become parish minister of Lunan in Forfarshire: but his religious views became known, and,
in order to escape a trial, he had abandoned his
cure and lived in privacy, continuing, however,
to preach secretly Reformed doctrine. He was
at length discovered at Dysart, in Fife, by two
priests in the employment of the Primate, and
was brought to trial at St. Andrews in April, 1558,
before a numerous assemblage of bishops, abbots,
and theologians. His "heresies" included the denial of seven sacraments, of transubstantiation,
and of the obligation of priestly celibacy, which
he had practically repudiated by marriage. When
the old man entered the cathedral where the trial
took place, he appeared so feeble that his judges
doubted whether he could make himself heard.
"But when he began to speak"—so Foxe testifies
—"he made the Church ring and sound again with
so great courage and stoutness that the Christians present were no less rejoiced than the adversaries were confounded and ashamed." When
he was required to retract his "erroneous opinions," "I will not recant the truth," was his brave
reply, "for I am corn and no chaff; and I will not
be blown away with the wind, nor burst with the
flail, but I will abide both." He was handed over
accordingly, as an obdurate heretic, to the secular
power. With the Regent's tacit acquiescence,

although she afterwards disclaimed responsibility,[1] he was burned at the stake on the 28th April, two days after that marriage at *Notre Dame* with which his exposure to hierarchical vengeance was, without his knowing it, indirectly connected. "As for me," were his last words "I am fourscore and two years old, and cannot live long but a hundred better shall rise out of the ashes of my bones. I trust to God I shall be the hindmost that shall suffer for this cause." [2]   The hope of the dying martyr was fulfilled,—he *was* the last victim of Roman persecution in Scotland.

IV.   The burning of Milne was a blunder as well as a crime. It was already too late to terrify Protestants into submission: the martyrdom served only to discredit Romanism and to incite Reformers to more open defiance. The sufferings of an emaciated old man awakened general sympathy; and the resumption of persecution unto death, after an interval of eight years, appeared to show that the comparative toleration recently enjoyed, instead of being the prelude to entire

---

[1] Knox, *H. of R.*, i., 308, 309; Tytler, *H. of Sc.*, vi., 102; Mathieson, *Polit. and Rel. in Sc.* i., 56. The Regent could hardly be ignorant of the proceedings against Walter Milne, for he appears to have been detained for a considerable time in prison, with a view to recantation. Among his judges were the Bishops of Moray and Caithness, who must have received long notice of the trial, and eight days intervened between the sentence and its execution.

[2] Knox, *l. c.*; Foxe, ii., 623–626; Pitscottie, ii., 130–136 (Sc. T. S. ed.); Keith, *Ch. and St.*, i., 156.

freedom of doctrine and worship, was only the temporary interruption, for strategic reasons, of a policy of oppression and bloodshed.

Three significant indications of the growth of popular sentiment against the Roman Church were given during the year 1558. The first was in connection with the martyrdom of Milne. After his condemnation by the ecclesiastical court in St. Andrews, it was found difficult to obtain any competent secular authority to execute the sentence. The Provost of the town and the Bishop's chamberlain successively declined the odious office; it was at length undertaken by an official of lower standing, whom Buchanan describes as an "infamous man," and Pitscottie as a "crapinell [*i. e.*, knave] of the devil." The merchants refused to sell any materials—wood or cord, tar or powder —for the burning; and "the people showed the intensity of their indignation by heaping up a great pile of stones in the place where the martyr suffered, so that the memory of his death might not perish with his life." [1] The second incident related to a summons which, at the instigation of the hierarchy, the Regent had issued, ordering certain Protestant evangelists—including Harlaw, Douglas, and Methven [2]—to appear at Edinburgh on the 18th of July. The citation was probably

---

[1] Buchanan, 189; Pitscottie, ii., 135; Foxe, ii., 626.

[2] Harlaw had been exercising his gifts mainly in Edinburgh, Douglas in Leith, Methven in Dundee (Knox, *H. of R.*, i., 256).

regarded as the easiest method of getting rid of the preachers, who might be expected to flee rather than to "compear." Following Knox's example, however, two years before, they responded to the summons. But they did not appear alone. "Many faithful men" from the West, headed by James Chalmers of Gadgirth in Ayrshire, penetrated into the room where the Regent and the bishops had assembled. They charged the Primate and his fellow-prelates with this fresh outbreak of oppression; plainly intimated to the Regent that they "would suffer this no longer"; and in token of their determination to add force, if required, to remonstrance, "every man put on his steel bonnet." The Queen Dowager perceived at once the necessity of timely concession; declared that she "meant no evil" to them or to their preachers; called the intruders her "loving subjects"; and then, turning to the bishops at her side, forbade them to trouble either the preachers or their champions. "And so,"—writes Knox,—"the day of summons being discharged, began the brethren universally to be further encouraged." [1] The third incident was of a different character, yet equally suggestive, in another way, of the growth of anti-Roman sentiment. It occurred in September, on the occasion of the annual commemoration of St. Giles. When the image of the saint was borne, as usual, in solemn procession

---

[1] Knox, i., 257, 258; Pitscottie, ii., 137.

along the High Street of Edinburgh, "the hearts
of the brethren"—so Knox records—"were wonderfully inflamed" on "seeing such abomination
so manifestly maintained." "Down with the
idol!" was the cry. One of the onlookers "took
him by the heels, and dadding [knocking] his head
to the causeway, left 'Dagon' without head or
hands." "The priests and friars fled faster than
they did at Pinkie Cleucht." "Down go the
crosses, off goes the surplice"; while "a merry
Englishman" who stood by exclaims in jeering
tone, "Why fly ye, villains, now, without order?
Turn, and strike every one a stroke for the honour
of his god!" Knox significantly concludes his
account of the incident with the remark, "After
that Baal had broken his neck, there was no comfort to his confused army." [1]

V. On the 14th July, 1558, a few days prior
to the citation of the preachers, Knox printed at
Geneva, for circulation in Scotland, two tracts
which had an important bearing on the ecclesiastical situation. One of these was his "Appellation
to the Nobility and the Estates of Scotland" from
the sentence pronounced against him by the hierarchy two years before. In form this appeal was
somewhat belated: in substance, it was timely in
a high degree. To Knox personally the sentence
of the bishops was of little account: and evidently he had bided his time until the renewal

---

[1] Knox, i., 259–261.

of persecution, in April 1558, provided an appropriate opportunity for his testimony. The real occasion of the "Appellation" was the martyrdom of Milne and the policy which it appeared to inaugurate. He exposes the injustice of churchmen who are at once accusers and accused, being also allowed to assume the position of judges: he declares that the issues raised by himself and others could be properly tried only by a "general Council of the Church"; he claims, meanwhile, that "until the controversies be lawfully decided" he and other victims of persecution ought to be protected by the civil power, and that when a trial takes place, the standard of judgment must be "the plain Word of God." [1]   He maintains, further, the right of preachers "to appeal from the judgment of the visible Church to the knowledge of the temporal Magistrate, who by God's law is bound to hear their causes, and to defend them from tyranny." It was lawful in their case, to "appeal unto Cæsar." [2]   If the visible Church, God's chosen organ for the diffusion of religious truth, flagrantly failed to fulfil its appointed function, and disregarded that Word of God which is its divine directory, there was no alternative except to appeal to that other "Minister of God," the civil power, to accomplish the work which the Church had egregiously failed to perform. We shall see

[1] Laing, *W. of K.*, iv., 469, 470.
[2] *Ibid.*, p. 472–476.

presently the effect of the "Appellation" on the
Protestant leaders who were also members of the
Scottish Parliament.

Knox had a further appeal to his countrymen.
It was possible that the Scottish Estates would
be unfaithful to their responsibilities equally
with the Church. Accordingly, from his watch-
tower at Geneva he addresses a message, not
merely to the nobility and Estates, but to the people at large, in his "Letter to the Commonalty of
Scotland." He bids them remember that they—
the people—shared with their rulers the responsibility for the religious condition of the nation;
for "in the hope of the life to come God hath
made all equal." "You may lawfully," he continues, "require of your superiors that they provide for you true preachers, and expel such as
under the name of your pastors devour and destroy the flock." If, however, "your superiors
be negligent, most justly ye may provide true
teachers for yourselves," and with a view to their
maintenance "withhold the fruits and profits
which your false bishops and clergy most unjustly
receive of you, unto such time as they be compelled faithfully to do their charge and duties;
which is to preach unto you Jesus Christ truly, to
minister His Sacraments according to His own
institution, and to watch for the salvation of your
souls." "Nay, further," he adds, in a closing
word of warning, "as your rulers are criminal,

with your bishops, of all idolatry committed, and of the innocent blood that is shed, because they [the rulers] maintain them [the prelates] in their tyranny"; "so are you criminal and guilty of the same crimes, so many of you as give no plain confession to the contrary, because ye assist and maintain your rulers." [1]   It was a bold declaration in that age.   "This doctrine, I know," writes Knox himself, "is strange to the blind world." [2] Fortunately, as regards the Reformation, the Scottish Estates fulfilled, so far at least, their obligations, in 1560; and the drastic intervention of the "Commonalty" was not required.   But Knox, after all, in this letter only anticipated, of necessity vaguely and crudely, the great principle embodied in popular representative government, viz., that the real fountain of power in the State, along with the ultimate responsibility for national policy, belongs, or ought to belong, not to any privileged section of the community, but to the citizenship at large.

VI.   Knox's "Appellation," the recent renewal of persecution, and the popular sympathy with Protestantism thereby evoked, led to the Lords of the Congregation taking another step forward in realising the aims of the Covenant.   In accordance with the terms of the "Appellation," they prepared a statement of grievances and a

---

[1] Laing, *W. of K.*, iv., 524, 525, 527, 528, 533, 534.

[2] *Ibid.*, p. 535.

demand for redress, to be laid formally before the Estates in November, 1558. They "require" that Acts of Parliament giving " power to the Churchmen to proceed against so-called heretics" be suspended till a "General Council [of the Church] have decided all controversies in religion"; that "the prelates be removed from the place of judges," and be allowed to act only as "accusers" before a temporal tribunal; and that no condemnation for heresy be valid unless "the heretics be convicted" "by the manifest Word of God." [1]   This "Petition of Rights" was presented beforehand to the Regent, "because we were determined to enterprise nothing without her knowledge." [2]

Mary of Guise, although now resolved to proceed against the Protestants, was unwilling at this stage to lose their support; for the question of giving the "Crown Matrimonial" to the Dauphin was to come before the approaching Parliament. She put off the petitioners with "amiable looks and good words," keeping, however, "their bill close in her pocket." The Reform leaders accordingly, on the 29th of November, went direct to the Estates with a trenchant manifesto, to which they gave the suggestive title of "Protestation." After referring to their previous petition, presented to the Regent for transmission, they

[1] Knox, H. of R., i., 309–311.
[2] Ibid., i., 312.

protest "against that most unjust tyranny which we heretofore most patiently have sustained"; solemnly testify that they are not to be held guilty "for violating such rites as man without God's Word hath commanded"; and significantly add that "if any tumult shall arise among the members of this realm" on account of the "diversity of religion," "the crime thereof be not imputed to us, who most humbly do now seek all things to be reformed by an Order." [1] It was an emphatic warning that unless the constituted authorities took in hand the needful measures of reformation, the policy of "passive resistance" might at any moment be exchanged for active and, it might prove, violent conflict.

VII. The death of Mary Tudor, and the accession of Elizabeth, in November 1558, a few days before the Scottish Parliament assembled, helped to precipitate the ecclesiastical crisis, and constrained the Regent to terminate the policy of friendly toleration. If Scotland was to be delivered from Protestant heresy and to be preserved for the Catholic Church, the object must be accomplished now, before a Protestant English Government had time to assist the Scottish Reformers. From this Parliament, accordingly, may be dated the final struggle, in which the Regent, hence forward in open alliance with the hierarchy and under the stimulus of the house of

---

[1] Knox, H. of R., pp. 313, 314.

13

Guise, endeavoured to suppress the Reformation in Scotland.[1]   In the spring of 1559, a fresh order was issued by the Privy Council prohibiting all preaching by unauthorised persons.   The Regent resumed the repressive citations which the men with the "steel bonnets" had constrained her to cancel about nine months before.   When four notable Reformed preachers,—Harlaw, Willock, Christison, and Methven,—supported by influential laymen, continued their "unauthorised" ministrations, they were summoned to appear at Stirling on the 10th of May, to answer the charge of rebellious conduct.[2]

There is evidence that the Regent entered with some misgiving [3] on a conflict the outcome of which must have appeared at least doubtful. But French influence and policy combined with her own Catholic convictions and family ambition to urge her onward.   France was at this time negotiating a treaty [4] with Spain and with the

---

[1] The hierarchy realised at this crisis that reform must accompany repression; and a Provincial Council, held early in March 1559, enacted numerous reforming canons. Fresh provision, also was made for the instruction of the people, including a short manual of the mass, nicknamed the "Twopenny Faith."   But such "measures of reform" as Catholic writers admit, "came too late."   Robertson, *Statuta*, ii., 142; Bellesheim, ii., 244–252; Lesley, ii., 397–399 (Sc. T. S.).

[2] Knox, *H. of R.*, i., 317.   Tumults also were stated to have been occasioned by their preaching.   (See citation in McCrie, Note GG; A. Lang, *Scot. Hist. Rev.*, Jan. 1905, p. 116).

[3] Sir James Melville's *Memoirs*, pp. 76, 77.

[4] The Peace of Cambrai, concluded on 2nd April, 1559.

Empire. The main objects of that treaty were to crush Protestantism in Europe, and, as a means to that end, to depose the "illegitimate" Elizabeth from her throne in favour of the next heir, Mary Stuart, who had already assumed the arms of England. The persecution of the Huguenots was resumed; and a special ambassador was sent to Mary of Guise to communicate the policy of the French Court, and to induce her to suppress Protestantism in Scotland "before the heretics should spread any farther." The triumph of Romanism in Scotland would be the prelude to the conquest of England (where Protestantism was not firmly established) for the Catholic Church, and for the future King and Queen of France and Scotland.[1] Before the conflict, however, thus inaugurated, actually began, the protagonist of Scottish Protestantism had reappeared on the scene.

[1] Sir James Melville's *Memoirs*, as above; Tytler, *H. of Sc.*, vi., 109, 110.

CHAPTER VIII

FINAL RETURN OF KNOX TO SCOTLAND—THE CLOSING CONFLICT AND THE ESTABLISHMENT OF THE REFORMATION

1559-1560

KNOX arrived in Edinburgh from Dieppe on the 2nd May, 1559, eight days before the date at which the Reformed preachers were summoned to appear at Stirling. He was at once informed of the ecclesiastical crisis, and resolved to stand by his four fellow-preachers "in the brunt of the battle." [1] By this time a large company of Reformers had been convened at Dundee to support the cited preachers. On the 5th of May, Knox hastened to the meeting-place and accompanied the assembly thence to Perth, where the Reformed Book of Common Prayer was already in use. [2] There the Protestant host, already over five thousand in number, but mostly unarmed, remained; while "one of the most grave and most wise barons"—Erskine

---

[1] Letter of Knox to Mrs. Locke (Laing, *W. of K.*, vi., 21).
[2] *Ibid.*, p. 22.

of Dun—proceeded to Stirling, in order to acquaint the Regent with their proceedings, and to persuade her, if possible, to withdraw the citation. Disconcerted by the prompt demonstration of the Reformers before she had assembled her own forces, the Regent temporised. Without expressly agreeing to postpone the summons, she "solicited Erskine to stay the multitude" from coming to Stirling, and promised to "take some better order." Erskine understood this promise to mean that if the Reformers refrained from advancing in force, she would refrain, meanwhile at least, from further proceedings against the preachers. At his advice, accordingly, the latter, along with their adherents, remained at Perth, and the Regent was saved from an unwelcome incursion. Soon afterwards, with what was regarded as a breach of faith, she proclaimed the preachers outlaws for non-appearance.[1] The proclamation was a virtual declaration of war. It was now indicated that Protestant preachers were to be treated not as mere heretics, to be tried and (if

---

[1] Knox (*H. of R.*, i., 317, and *W. of K.*, vi., 23), Buchanan (191), Spottisw. (i., 271), Tytler (vi., 115), Burton (iv., 65), and Hume Brown (*H. of Sc.*, ii., 57), all represent the Regent as guilty of a breach of faith in this matter. Andrew Lang (*H. of Sc.*, ii., 48–50), relying mainly on Buchanan's statement that the Regent demanded of Erskine "that he should send the multitude home," holds that her promise was "conditional" as well as "vague." " She probably amused Erskine by some promise of 'taking better order'" (*Sc. H. R.*, Jan. 1905, p. 118).

found guilty) condemned after a judicial process, but as rebels, to be summarily crushed, along with their open adherents, by military force. With the help of the hierarchy and the French Government, the Regent had now raised a considerable army. It was ere long increased to eight thousand men,[1] partly Scots, partly Frenchmen; and her manifest policy was to suppress Protestantism.

II. Meanwhile, a further development of the conflict took place at Perth. A sermon "vehement against idolatry," *i. e.*, against the mass, had been preached by Knox on the 11th of May in the ancient Church of St. John the Baptist,[2] immediately after the news of the outlawry had been received. The congregation had not dispersed when a priest proceeded to celebrate mass at the high altar. A youth, who expressed the sentiments of persons older than himself,—Knox describes him as standing "among certain godly men,"—exclaimed, "This is intolerable that, when God by His Word has plainly damned idolatry, we shall stand and see it used in despite." The irritated priest struck the boy, who retaliated by throwing a stone. The stone missed the priest, but broke an image. It was as if a lighted match

---

[1] Hume Brown, *H. of Sc.*, ii., 58.

[2] The Church was divided into the East and the West Church early in the seventeenth century, and in the eighteenth century a third or " Mid " Church was formed.

St. John's Church, Perth, where Knox preached in May, 1559. (Now divided into East, West, and Mid Churches.)

had been applied to a heap of combustibles. "The whole multitude that was about began to cast stones," and to destroy with their hands "other monuments of idolatry." The report of the disorder brought many more on the scene— not "gentlemen" or "earnest professors" of Reformed doctrine, as Knox is careful to record, but a "rascal multitude." These undisciplined supporters of the cause, finding the work of destruction sufficiently accomplished in the Church of St. John, proceeded to deal similarly, and even more violently, with the Franciscan, Dominican, and Carthusian monasteries, until only the walls of the buildings remained.[1]

Knox and those associated with him were conscious that the doings of the "rascal multitude" were not creditable, and might alienate influential sympathy from the Reform cause. He remained, accordingly, in Perth, as he himself naïvely expresses it, to "instruct" and, presumably, to restrain "those who were young and rude in Christ."[2] His hand is easily recognised in various missives or manifestos addressed at this juncture to the Regent, to the French ambassador (D'Oysel), to the Scottish nobility, and to the "pestilent

---

[1] Knox, *H. of R.*, i., 321–323; Lesley, *Vernac. Hist.*, p. 272. Knox gives in the *History* his deliberate opinion of those who took part in the work of destruction. In a letter written soon after the events related, he had unadvisedly included them among the "brethren" (Laing. vi., 23.)

[2] Knox, i., 324.

prelates and their shavelings." In these epistles all rebellious intentions are expressly repudiated; the claim for liberty of preaching and worship is emphasised as what the Protestants are bound at all hazards to maintain; and the organisation of the Congregation is declared to be intended not for offence but for defence. So long, however, as open "idolatry" was preached and imposed, and cruel persecution continued, "just vengeance" would be executed, and a "contract of peace never be made." [1]

It was manifest to both parties that a conflict was inevitable: yet neither side was prepared to precipitate hostilities. Lord James Stewart, moreover, and the Earl of Argyle, although recognised as Reformers, remained in the Regent's camp; and their position there exerted over both parties a restraining influence. Through the mediation of these two leaders a treaty was arranged, by which Perth was surrendered to the Regent's forces: while its Protestant citizens were to have freedom of worship, and the city was to be exempt "from the garrison of French soldiers." [2]

III. The truce was only temporary: the conflict was soon resumed elsewhere. From Perth the Protestant centre of consultation and operation was transferred to St. Andrews: and again Knox is in the forefront. At this stage—in the

---

[1] Knox, i., 326–336.
[2] *Ibid.*, i., 340–342.

Interior of West Church, Perth, being part of the Church of St. John's, where Knox preached on 11th May, 1559. The pulpit no longer exists, but its site is marked by the white cross in photograph.

end of May—the Earl of Argyle, Lord James
Stewart, and other notable Reformers departed
from the Regent, on the ground that she had
failed to fulfil the terms of the treaty. Soldiers
in the pay of France, although of Scottish na-
tionality, were retained in Perth and allowed
to assault members of the congregation.[1]   An
assembly of Protestant leaders was convened at
St. Andrews on the 3rd of June.   Among those
who responded to the summons was Knox.   He
preached on the way at Anstruther and at Crail:
he was resolved also to preach in the city of the
Primate, and to realise his "assured hope" when
he lay ill in a French galley more than ten years
before.   The Archbishop heard of his intentions,
and threatened to have him saluted with a dozen
"culverins" (firelocks).   Many of the Reforming
leaders counselled that "the preaching should be
delayed for that day"; but Knox pleaded the
requirement of conscience and disregarded the
menace.   He preached in the parish church on
the "Cleansing of the Temple," not only without
molestation, but with so much effect that the
magistrates, supported by the majority of the
citizens, proceeded "with expedition" to remove
"all monuments of idolatry" from the Cathedral
and other churches of the city.[2]

---

[1] Knox, i., 346; Spottisw., i., 274, 275.

[2] Knox, H. of R., i., 348, 349.   Simultaneously the monasteries of the Greyfriars and Blackfriars were destroyed, only
the walls being left standing; but this appears to have been

The Primate could hardly have been expected
to submit tamely to such a defiance of his authority. He repaired to the Regent, who by this
time had reached Falkland with an army led by
D'Oysel and Châtelherault. She proceeded towards St. Andrews to attack the Reformers,
and actual warfare again appeared imminent; but
when a force of three thousand men under Argyle
and Lord James Stewart barred the way at Cupar,
a second truce or "assurance" for eight days was
concluded, nominally with a view to a friendly
conference, but really in order to cover a withdrawal of the Regent to the south of the Forth.
During this interval the "purging" of churches
and monasteries continued; among other buildings dealt with was the Abbey of Lindores.[1]

IV. At the expiry of the truce on the 1st of
June, the Reformers took possession of Perth,
which surrendered after a brief resistance [2]; the
citizens being for the most part in sympathy with
the Protestant movement. A few days afterwards, against the will of Knox and many others,
the Abbey of Scone was destroyed by fire [3]; Stir-

the work neither of the Reformers nor of the magistrates,
but of the "rascal multitude" (see Hume Brown, H. of Sc.,
ii., 60). "There is no contemporary evidence to prove that
the Cathedral was demolished at the Reformation" (Hay
Fleming, St. Andrews, p. 51).

[1] Knox, H. of R., i., 353; Laing, W. of K., vi., 26.
[2] Knox, H. of R., i., 357–359.
[3] Ibid., i., 359–362. "Whereat [writes Knox] no small
number of us were offended." He and other Protestant

The Town Church, St. Andrew's, where Knox preached in 1547, 1559, and 1571-72. (From an eighteenth-century print).

ling was occupied by a military force, and all "monuments of idolatry" were removed from its churches; Linlithgow Abbey was similarly purged. Before the end of the month the main body of armed Protestants, under Argyle and Lord James Stewart, entered Edinburgh, where a mob had already assailed the Blackfriars' and Greyfriars' monasteries, and "had left nothing but bare walls, yea, not so much as door or window." [1] Within a few days the Reformed forces, after the arrival of contingents, amounted to six thousand.[2] It was a critical juncture. The destructive doings of excited and irresponsible multitudes tended to alienate influential sympathy from the Reform cause; while the Regent and her partisans charged the Protestants with cloaking political revolution under so-called religious reformation.[3] To Knox was committed the task of publicly explaining and vindicating the Reformers' position. On the very day of their arrival in Edinburgh, he preached in

leaders appear to have done "what in them lay to have stayed the fury of the multitude." The notorious profligacy of Bishop Hepburn of Moray, who also held the abbacy of Scone, and was there at the time; the belief that "by his counsel was Walter Milne put to death"; and the evil reputation of the abbey as regards tolerance of immorality, combined to stimulate popular violence. An old woman, who lived in the neighbourhood declared the burning to be a judgment of God, and testified that "since my remembrance this place hath been nothing else but a den of whore-mongers."

[1] Knox, *H. of R.*, i., 362, 363; Calderwood, *H. of the Kirk*, i., 474, 475.

[2] Laing, *W. of K.*, vi., 35.   [3] Knox, *H. of R.*, i., 363.

St. Giles', and, as the Regent herself declared,
"took the greatest pains to defend the chief supporters of the religion from the charge of aiming
at the Crown, and of having any other object in
view, except the advancement of the Gospel." [1]
In a private letter, written prior to the delivery
of the sermon, Knox states "that we mean no
tumult, no alteration of authority, but only the
reformation of religion and suppression of idolatry." [2]   The discourse, accordingly, was followed
up by a public manifesto, declaring that "in all
civil and political matters" the Reformers will be
"obedient subjects"; and that the entire object
they had in view was liberty of conscience, the
right ministration of Word and sacraments, deliverance from persecution, and—here the patriotic element comes into view—removal of the
"burthen intolerable of the French soldiery." [3]

The Regent continued to treat the Protestants
as rebels; and after receiving assurance that
Lord Erskine,[4] the governor of Edinburgh Castle,

---

[1] Teulet, *Papiers de l'état relatifs à l'histoire de l'Ecosse*,
i., 325; P. Forbes, *Pub. Transact. in Reign of Elizabeth*, i.,
180.   At a later stage the Protestant lords contemplated the
propriety of electing the Earl of Arran or Lord James Stewart
as regent in the room of Mary of Guise (*St. Pap. Eliz. Foreign*,
i., 446).

[2] Letter to Mrs. Locke (Laing, *W. of K.*, vi., 30).

[3] Knox, *H. of R.*, i., 365–367.

[4] Lord Erskine (afterwards Regent Mar) was one of those
who "repaired" to Knox in 1556 (*ibid.*, p. 249), and who
invited the Reformer to return to Scotland in 1557.   While

would not be antagonistic to her, she advanced on the city with an increased force.   The Reformers at first resolved to offer resistance; but the attitude of Lord Erskine, along with the diminution of their ranks at the approach of harvest, led, on the 24th of July, to an agreement between the two parties to be valid until the 10th of January. The army of the Congregation consented to evacuate the capital, and to refrain from injury to " Kirks" or " Kirkmen," on the understanding that the Protestant citizenship and their preachers were unmolested in their worship.   On neither side, however, was this " appointment" regarded as other than a temporary pacification.   The Regent waited for French reinforcements, and the Reformers for assurance of more effective support from their countrymen or from England, before continuing the conflict and bringing it to a decisive conclusion.[1]

favourable to the Reformation from the ecclesiastical standpoint, he was among those who were afraid of civil war.   He refused to let either Regent or Reformers obtain possession of the Castle of Edinburgh; but his attitude during this period, although nominally neutral, was more friendly towards the Regent than towards the Protestants.   See "History of the Estate of Scotland from 1559–1666," in *Wodrow Misc.*, p. 64; Knox, *H. of R.*, i., 375.

[1] Knox, *H. of R.*, i., 378–382; Tytler, *H. of Sc.*, vi., 145. The agreement of the 24th of July, which Knox gives in full, contains no clause about the dismissal of French soldiers from the country: but the Reformers appear to have alleged that the Regent, on this occasion, promised to dispense with such foreign service; and when, instead of this, she received

V. By this time Knox had been appointed
minister of St. Giles'; but his counsel and service
were too valuable for the leaders of the Reform
movement to lose, and on the 26th of July he
departed from Edinburgh with the Protestant
host, leaving John Willock in his room.[1] During

fresh reinforcements from France, they accused her of break-
ing an engagement which she denied having made (Knox,
H. of R., i., 397, 398, 413; *St. Pap. Eliz. For.*, i., 409, 446;
Sadler, *St. Pap.*, i., 430, 431). Andrew Lang (*Sc. Hist. R.*,
Jan., 1905, p. 128) charges Knox with making "statements
false and deliberately misleading about the agreement, particularly at an interview with Croft, Governor of Berwick,
who certainly understood Knox to mean that a promise to
dismiss the French was *connected* with the compact (*St. Pap.*,
Eliz., i., 446; Bain, *Cal.*, i., 237). But, assuming that Croft
understood Knox rightly, (1) if the latter deliberately mis-
informed the former, it is strange that he should have
supplied so carefully in his *History* the proof of his own false-
hood. (2) Knox's view of the significance of the agreement
was shared by other Reformers. Was there a general conspiracy of mendacity? (3) There is a possible solution of the
difficulty without impugning the honesty of either the Regent or the Reformers. Châtelherault, who then still adhered to the Queen-dowager, acted as intermediary between
her and the Protestant lords. In his anxiety to effect an
agreement, he may have assured the Reformers rather too
confidently that if they accepted loyally the terms of the
compact, the Regent would be able to send away the unpopular French auxiliaries; and this assurance may have been
interpreted as involving a promise by Mary such as she never
intended to give.

[1] Knox was publicly elected by "the congregation of Edinburgh" on 7th July (*Wodrow Miscellany*, p. 63). Willock
had arrived in Scotland from Friesland in October, 1558, and
had preached in the interval at Edinburgh, Dundee, Ayr, and
other places (Knox, *H. of R.*, i., 256; note, 388).

the autumn of 1559, Knox takes the leading
part on the Reform side in religion and even
in politics. His chief task was to enlighten
the people as to the real nature and importance of the conflict on which the Protestants
had been constrained to enter. In a letter
written from St. Andrews on the 2nd of September, he speaks of having "travelled through the
most part of this realm"; he declares with thank-
fulness that "men of all sorts and conditions embrace the truth"; that "the trumpet soundeth
over all the land"; and that a "ministry is established" in Edinburgh, St. Andrews, Dundee,
Perth, Brechin, Stirling, and Ayr.[1] About the
same date, Sadler, the English ambassador, testifies that "the preachers have so won the people to
their devotion, their power is now double that
[which] it was in the cause of religion."[2]

Knox had other work, less congenial, on hand
during this period of truce. The substantial support, in the form both of money and military force,
which the Regent and the Catholics were receiving
from France, must—so it was considered—be
balanced by like support being secured for the
Reformers from England: and Knox was regarded
as, on the whole, the fittest person to conduct the
necessary negotiations.   He had served effectively the cause of the English Reformation; he

---

[1] Letter to Mrs. Locke, in Laing, *W. of K.*, vi., 78.
[2] *State Papers*, i., 431.

had undergone peril and endured exile among English churchmen during Mary Tudor's reign; and although his " First Blast " had prejudiced him in the eyes of Elizabeth, her Prime Minister, Cecil, and the ambassadors to the French and Scottish Courts, Throgmorton and Sadler, were fully aware of his integrity and influence.[1]   The Reformer accordingly was instructed to propose to the English Government a league for the deliverance of Scotland from the double incubus of Roman superstition and French interference.[2]   In the beginning of August, he conferred at Berwick with Sir James Croft, governor of that town, and was prepared to proceed to Stamford in Lincolnshire, where an interview between Cecil and himself had been arranged. But his arrival in Berwick had been observed by spies and reported to the Regent; the Government of England did not yet see its way to an avowed alliance with Scottish Protestants which would have affected prejudicially English relations with France and Spain; and Knox returned home with no more than a letter from Cecil, in which the latter offered moral support to the Scottish Reformers, but refrained from committing his country to actual intervention.

---

[1] See letter from Throgmorton to Cecil, 7th June, 1559, in Forbes's *Public Transactions*, i., 119. "Forasmuch as Knox is now in Scotland in as great credit as ever man was there, it were well done not to use him otherwise than may be for the advancement of the Queen's Majesty's service."

[2] Laing, *W. of K.*, vi., 56: Teulet, i., 326.

It was due, however, partly to Knox's plain speaking in connection with these negotiations that England eventually took the step which the interests of both nations demanded. He set before Queen Elizabeth, through her ministers, the real aim of France in its endeavour to establish a paramount influence in Scotland. That influence was not an end but a means—a means of strengthening the position of France as regards England. Now (so Knox contended), while there was no reason to question the sincerity of the Reformed and of the anti-French party in Scotland, still French subsidies on the one side and Scottish impoverishment on the other were likely to issue in the triumph of the Regent unless help arrived from England for the Protestants.[1]   By the middle of August, as the outcome of the negotiations conducted by Knox, the English Government resolved to enter privately into the alliance for which the Scottish Reform party pleaded, and it inaugurated the league with a subsidy of £3000.[2]   The assistance was comparatively small; but it convinced the Protestant leaders that England had

---

[1] Laing, W. of K., vi., 60–69. Cecil was doubtless well aware of the designs of France, but it strengthened his hands, in his communications with Elizabeth, to have the French policy plainly declared by other testimony.

[2] Sadler, St. Pap., i., 387.   The resolution was come to, indeed, before the letter of Knox to Cecil was received; but what the Reformer wrote to the Prime Minister was, in effect, what had previously been set forth by him at Berwick to Sir James Croft, and transmitted to headquarters.

at length recognised their cause as also hers; and it encouraged them to maintain a conflict in which England could not afford to allow them to be worsted.

VI. In one other sphere the judgment and courage of Knox advanced the Protestant cause. Hitherto the Reformers had refrained from any formal renunciation of the Regent's authority; they had taken up the position of men who had been driven into armed opposition on religious grounds because freedom of preaching and of worship had been withheld. Mary's own procedure at this juncture supplied an adequate occasion for the Protestant leaders throwing off, or at least suspending, their allegiance on patriotic grounds. We have seen that, not without good reason, the fear of actual or virtual annexation by France had been awakened in Scotland. On the 10th of July, the Dauphin, on whom the Scottish Crown Matrimonial had been bestowed, became King of France. He bore also the title of King of Scotland; and in the event of Mary Stuart's death, especially if she left no issue, then, with a French Regent on the throne and a French army in the country, the danger to Scottish independence would obviously be real and imminent. On the 19th of September, accordingly, the Lords of the Congregation, with whom, by this time, Châtelherault had allied himself, demanded the dismissal of foreign troops. The Regent declined to comply;

and when the demand was repeated a month later, the refusal was renewed. At a convention of nobles and representatives of burghs, the propriety of renouncing allegiance was discussed. " It was thought expedient that the judgment of the preachers should be required." Knox and Willock were summoned to the meeting. They gave it as their opinion that as the Regent had "denied her chief duty to the subjects of this Realm, which was to minister justice to them indifferently, to preserve their liberties from invasion of strangers, and to suffer them to have God's Word freely and openly preached among them," therefore "for the preservation of the Commonwealth," the " born counsellors, nobility, and barons of the Realm" might "justly deprive her of all regiment and authority." Knox took care, however, to require that "no such sentence be pronounced against her, but that, upon her known and open repentance, and upon her conversion to the Commonwealth, place should be granted to her of regress to the same honours from which she justly might be deprived." [1] Allegiance was to be suspended, not permanently withdrawn. The advice of the preachers commended itself to the Lords who, on the 23rd of October, resolved to suspend Mary of Guise from the regency. They emphasised in their protestation her "planting of strangers" in the realm, her "sending continually [to France] for

---

[1] Knox, *H. of R.*, i., 442, 443.

greater forces," and her evident purpose to "suppress the liberty of our native country," and "to make us and our posterity slaves to strangers for ever." Such a policy, it was declared, "is intolerable in free countries," and "prejudicial to our Sovereign Lady [Mary Stuart] and her heirs."[1] It was a straightforward and patriotic policy; and if it deprived the Reformers of the support of some who shrank from the peril of civil war, it won the sympathy of others who were determined to prevent Scotland from becoming a province of France. It helped, apparently, to decide at least one distinguished waverer. A week after the withdrawal of allegiance had been declared, Maitland of Lethington left the service of the Regent and rejoined the ranks of his former associates in the Reformation movement.[2]

Knox, of course, had other reasons for resisting Mary of Guise than the fear of French encroachment on Scottish liberty. In his eyes the despotism of Rome was a greater evil than the domination of France. But the national sentiment by which, from the outset, he was characterised never departed from him. He was a Scot to the core; and we have no reason to believe that the patriotic element which had entered into the Protestant policy was regarded by him with indifference. When national independence appeared

[1] Knox, *H. of R.*, i., 444, 445.
[2] *Ibid.*, i., 463.

to be at stake, the religious Reformer became also the Scottish patriot. Knox's solicitude for his country at this time is attested by three private letters written soon after the 5th of November, when the Protestants were defeated in a skirmish near Holyrood by the Regent's troops, newly re-inforced by a fresh contingent from France. To Sir William Cecil, on the 18th of November, he describes the gloomy outlook "unless greater force remove the Frenchmen." [1] To Sir James Croft, a month later, he writes anxiously that "the French have on hand some hasty and great enterprise"; "for they have shipped much ordnance." [2] To Mrs. Locke, a few days afterwards, he declares that "one day of trouble since my last arrival in Scot-land [referring to the 5th of November] hath more pierced my heart than all the torment of the galleys." [3] Amid heavy burdens of public anxiety at this period, Knox had the alleviation of domestic comfort. In September 1559 his wife and children arrived in Scotland. In spite of poor health, she appears to have supported him not only with her sympathy, but with practical help as his amanuensis. [4]

---

[1] Laing, *W. of K.*, vi., 99.

[2] *Ibid.*, vi., 102.

[3] *Ibid.*, vi., 104.

[4] *Ibid.* In his letter to Mrs. Locke, above quoted, Knox mentions incidentally that his wife was unable to find some extract; and he states in explanation that "her rest hath been so unrestful since her arriving here, that scarcely could she tell on the morrow what she wrote at night."

VII. The defeat of the Congregation by the French forces, the attitude of the Governor of the Castle, who "would promise unto us no favours," and the desertion of many of the rank and file in the Protestant host, who "did so steal away that the wit of man could not stay them," led to a pause in the conflict. The apparent lukewarmness at this crisis of many who, as the event proved, sympathised with the Reformation movement, was the result probably of various causes. Knox mentions the "impoverishment" of the leaders who were unable on that account to maintain an army. It is not unlikely, also, that the covetous motives of some lay promoters of the Reformation may already have become manifest, and thus have cooled popular sympathy. Many, moreover, who were Protestants by conviction, may have clung to the hope of a pacific Reformation, or have shrunk from a conflict in which men might have to fight against kinsmen and friends. Dispirited, accordingly, through defeat, and still more through inadequate national support, the Reformers retired from Edinburgh immediately after the engagement at Holyrood and took up their quarters in Stirling.[1] It was "a dolorous departure," writes Knox: the situation seemed desperate; but he was not the man to despair of what he believed to be a righteous cause. On the day after the arrival in Stirling

---

[1] Knox, *H. of R.*, i., 464, 465; ii., 3.

he preached in the Greyfriars' Church a sermon
(from Psalm lxxx.) in which he confesses char-
acteristically that some of them had good reason
to humble themselves before God for trusting in
"their own strength and an arm of flesh"; while
others of them had been, up till recent days, "a
great comfort to their enemies, and a great discourage" to themselves.[1] Nevertheless, he declares emphatically his conviction that their
"cause, in spite of Satan, shall prevail, for it is
the eternal truth of the Eternal God."[2] Knox
himself states that after that sermon "the minds
of men began wondrously to be erected"; and
that this idea was no mere outcome of self-esteem
is indicated by the testimony of contemporaries,[3]
and by the resolution of the Council of the Congregation that very afternoon to continue the
conflict, and to apply again to the English Government for assistance.[4] The fresh application
to England, especially when a sovereign like

---

[1] On the 18th November (Laing, W. of K., vi., 100),
Knox had already discovered that "amongst us were such
as more sought the purse than Christ's glory."

[2] Knox, H. of R., i., 471, 472.

[3] Buchanan (H. of Sc., xvi., 196) writes Knox's "bright
and clear discourse" (luculentam concionem), and of "his raising the minds of many into a sure hope of speedy deliverance." The Historie of the Estate of Scotland from 1559 to
1566 represents the lords at Stirling as "taking new courage,
partly being persuaded by a godly sermon made by John
Knox" (Wodrow Misc., p. 72).

[4] Knox, H. of R., i., 473.

Elizabeth had to be approached, required a high degree of diplomatic sagacity. Diplomacy was not Knox's strong point: he was better fitted for bold testimony than for skilful manœuvre: and he regarded not as a disappointment, but as a relief, the supersession of himself on this occasion by Maitland as ambassador from the Congregation to the English Government. For such an office Maitland was specially qualified both by natural gifts and by experience; while Knox had little aptitude for it, and less inclination.[1]

VIII. During Maitland's absence in England, Knox made St. Andrews his headquarters. He writes from there on the 18th of November with mingled feelings; they "hope deliverance" but "stand universally in great fear."[2] The fear was well founded. Fresh reinforcements were arriving from France. On Christmas Eve a strong detachment was sent to surprise and overwhelm the Reformers at Stirling, and these escaped capture only by hasty flight.[3] St. Andrews was the centre next threatened; and although the Protestants, with a little army of six hundred,

---

[1] Diplomacy without dissimulation is difficult: and even the straightforward Knox once deflected from strict honesty in his negotiations with England. He met the plea of English statesmen, that military support of Scottish Protestants would lead to war with France, by suggesting that they might send a thousand men to Scotland and then "declare them rebels!" (Laing, *W. of K.*, vi., 90, 94).

[2] *Ibid.*, vi., 101.

[3] "Hist. of the Estate of Scot.," in *Wodrow Misc.*, 74, 75.

valiantly withstood the advance of four thousand
Frenchmen at Kinghorn, at Kirkcaldy, at Cupar
(where Knox inspirited them with a "comfortable
service"),[1] and finally at Dysart, the annihilation
of the Reformed forces in Fife appeared imminent.   At this crisis, however, the first-fruits of
Maitland's embassy were reaped.   On the 25th
of January an English squadron appeared in the
Forth, seized two French vessels which carried
provisions for the Regent's army, and blocked the
estuary against the advance of ships from France
with additional reinforcements.   The tide had
turned.   The French army, which had approached
within six miles of St. Andrews, "retired more
in one day than they had advanced in ten."[2]
Queen Elizabeth and her Government had at
length fully realised the danger to England of
French predominance in Scotland: and this
timely appearance of the English fleet was followed up, in the end of February, at Berwick, by
a "contract" between the two countries.   It was
agreed that a "convenient aid of men of war on
horse and foot" should be despatched without
delay from England to assist the Scots in driving out the French; the Scots, on the other hand,

---

[1] He preached appropriately from John vi., on the disci-
ples in the midst of the sea while Jesus was on the mountain.
"The fourth watch," he said, "is not yet come"; they
"must abide a little"; but he was "assuredly persuaded
that God shall deliver us" (Knox, *H. of R.*, ii., 8).

[2] Laing, *W. of K.*, vi., 108.

undertaking to perform a like service for Elizabeth in the event of an invasion of England.[1]

IX. The Regent and her party became now defenders instead of assailants. Her army, on tidings being received of the approach of the English, retired within the fortifications of Leith. She herself, along with the Primate and other dignitaries, civil and ecclesiastical, was admitted by Lord Erskine into the Castle of Edinburgh.[2] Meanwhile, on the 2nd of April, 1560, the English army, under the command of Lord Gray de Wilton, had crossed the Border and was met two days later at Prestonpans by the Scottish forces under Châtelherault, Lord James Stewart, and other leaders of the Congregation.[3] Such a sight had never before been witnessed. The ancient alliance between Scotland and France had been broken, through the selfish policy of the latter to make Scotland a tool for the promotion of French interests; the alliance was destined never to be renewed until modern times. The ancient quarrel with England, although not forgotten (for the English army received no warm reception from the people), was subordinated to

---

[1] Knox, *H. of R.*, ii., 47–49; *Wodrow Misc.*, pp. 79, 80. The English contingent amounted to ten thousand; and the Scots bound themselves to furnish England, if invaded, with "two thousand horsemen and two thousand footmen."

[2] *Ibid.*, ii., 58; Lesley, *H. of Sc.* (Sc. Text Soc. ed.), ii., 432–435.

[3] Knox, *H. of R.*, ii., 57, 58.

patriotic as well as religious considerations,—a prelude to the more cordial and permanent union of later days.

Before the united army left Prestonpans to lay siege to Leith, a final appeal was addressed to the Regent. She was asked to render the armed co-operation of England unnecessary by the dismissal of those French soldiers whose continued presence, it was declared, constrained the Reformers to seek and obtain English assistance.[1]   No satisfactory answer, however, at this stage was expected; and on the 27th of April a " Band " was signed by lead-ing Scottish nobles and gentry. In accordance with the patriotic character which the Protest-ant movement had now assumed, they pledged themselves not only, as they had formerly done, to "set forward the Reformation of religion, that the truth of God's Word may have free passage within the realm, with due adminis-tration of the sacraments"; but to "take part with the Queen of England's army for the expul-sion of the [French] strangers, oppressors of our liberty," and for the government of the country "under obedience of the King and Queen, our Sovereigns, by the laws and customs of the coun-try and born men of the land." [2]

[1] Buchanan, xvi., 197.

[2] Knox, _H. of R._, ii., 61, 62. This Band, which Knox gives in full, was probably drawn up by himself; the putting of the religious aim of the conflict in the forefront betokens his hand. The signatures include forty-nine leading nobles

X. The siege of Leith proved to be an arduous
undertaking. The "ordnance of the town" gave
great annoyance to the assailants; whereas the
breaches made in the walls during the day were
promptly repaired by the French soldiery during
the night. In the skirmishes outside the walls,
on the occasion of sudden sallies, the Frenchmen
had, on the whole, the advantage.[1] Amid the ineffectiveness of the Scottish military forces, on
both sides, the issue appeared to depend mainly
on whether France or England would be the
more ready to despatch reinforcements. But
at this time the French Government, owing
to the unsettled condition of affairs at home,[2]
grudged men, while Queen Elizabeth, as on
former occasions, grudged money. England
and France both desired a termination of the
conflict; and accordingly commissioners were appointed by the Governments of each nation to
meet in Edinburgh and to treat for peace. Before
they met on the 16th of June, two hindrances in
the way of pacification had been removed. On
the one hand, the false position into which the

---

and gentry, among whom were Lord James Stewart, Châtelherault, Argyle, Glencairn, and Rothes. The adhesion of several prominent Catholics, as Lords Huntly and Somerville,
notwithstanding the Protestant character of the document,
indicates the strength of the patriotic and anti-French sentiment which the Regent's policy of dependence on France
(apart from the religious question) had fostered.

[1] Knox, *H. of R.*, ii., 59, 60, 66, 67.

[2] The conspiracy at Amboise had intervened.

Regent had drifted by her subservience to French policy and her employment of French forces; on the other hand, the attitude of rebellion which the Reformers had been constrained to adopt through the necessity of suspending, on patriotic as well as religious grounds, their allegiance to the Regent—these two causes of strife had been terminated by the death of Mary of Guise on the 10th of June. When her end approached, she sent for Argyle, Lord James Stewart, and other Protestant nobles. Her dying counsel was to procure the withdrawal both of English and of French soldiers from the land.[1]

Within a month of the Regent's death a treaty was signed in which England and France were nominally the contracting parties, but Scottish affairs were the main subject determined. The French and English armies were both to depart; an Act of Oblivion was to be passed by the Estates, to be afterwards confirmed by Queen Mary and her Consort; and the government of the country, in the royal absence, was to be in the hands of a Council of Twelve,—five to be chosen by the Estates and seven by the Queen, —out of twenty-four persons selected by Parliament. The subject of religion, out of which the whole conflict had arisen, was by common consent ignored. France could not afford to endorse Protestantism; England, or at least Elizabeth, was

---

[1] Knox, *H. of R.*, ii., 70, 71.

not prepared to be a party to the establishment of Calvinism or Puritanism; the settlement of ecclesiastical questions was left to the Scottish Estates.[1] To Knox, the issue so far was satisfactory; and to his suggestion, we may presume, was due the solemn thanksgiving on the 19th of July in St. Giles' Church. In his discourse on that occasion he gives thanks to God for "setting this perishing realm at a reasonable liberty"; and for having "partly removed our darkness, suppressed idolatry, and taken from above our heads the devouring sword of merciless strangers."[2]

XI. The Estates assembled on the 1st August, 1560. From the strictly legal standpoint this Parliament was informal; for the Sovereign was neither present in person nor represented by a commissioner. A minority, accordingly, of the membership objected to the validity of the procedure; but the unusually large attendance gave to the convention an authority which at a national crisis no informality could invalidate.[3] While a portion of the clergy and laymen present were opposed to the Reforma-

---

[1] Knox, *H. of R.*, ii., 85, 86.

[2] *Ibid.*

[3] The attendance included one duke, thirteen earls, and nineteen other lords, the Primate, five other bishops, and twenty abbots and priors; one hundred and ten barons; and the representatives of twenty-two burghs (Teulet, i., 614).

tion, the Parliament as a whole was strongly Protestant. Knox did his utmost, in his own sphere, to secure due consideration for the religious needs of the time. From his pulpit in St. Giles' he applied to existing circumstances the prophecies of Haggai, and enforced the national duty of rebuilding the house of God and of preferring divine honour to selfish advantage.[1] The "mockage" of some, indeed (even among those friendly to the Reformation), foreshadowed coming disappointment; but the prevailing evangelical sentiments were embodied in a largely signed and trenchant supplication to Parliament by the barons, gentlemen, burgesses, and others, "true subjects of this realm, professing the Lord Jesus Christ." In this supplication are recounted the erroneous doctrines of Romanism; the unfounded pretensions of the papacy; the (idolatrous) ministration of the sacraments; the immorality, rapacity, and persecuting cruelty of leading clergy; and the petitioners crave a remedy for a "burden intolerable upon the Kirk of God within the realm." [2]

It was indicated at the outset on which side the sympathies of the Estates lay by the resolution to ask from those who objected to Roman doctrine a detailed statement of their own belief. The drawing up of this Confession of Faith was

---

[1] Knox, *H. of R.*, ii., 88.
[2] *Ibid.*, ii., 89–92.

intrusted to six ministers—Knox, Row, and Willock, who belonged to the more advanced section
of the Reformers; Wynram, Spottiswoode, and
Douglas, who represented the more moderate
party.[1] The first draft was composed by one
man, presumably Knox himself [2]; but Wynram,
and also Lethington, to whom the document was
committed for examination, while approving the
doctrine, are stated to have "mitigated the
austerity of many words and sentences."[3] Knox
states that "within four days" of the parliamentary order, the Confession (consisting of
twenty-five chapters) was presented; but we
need not infer that the work was prepared within this brief interval.[4] It bears no marks of
hasty production. Knox had doubtless spent
many days upon its composition, in anticipation
of the task which devolved upon him; and the
four days were occupied, presumably, in revision.
Like other Reformed Confessions, this product of
Scottish Protestantism emphasised the suprem-

---

[1] Knox, *H. of R.*, ii., 128. By a coincidence all the six
bore the name of John.

[2] Randolph, letter to Cecil, in Laing, *W. of K.*, vi., 120.

[3] *Ibid.*, p. 121. Wynram and Maitland appear also, from
Randolph's letter, to have recommended the omission of the
strongly worded chapter on the Civil Magistrate; but apparently the commission did not endorse that recommendation, unless Prof. A. F. Mitchell's conjecture be adopted
(*Scott. Ref.*, p. 101), that they objected only to a particular
sentence regarding the limits of obedience.

[4] A. F. Mitchell, *Scott. Ref.*, p. 99.

acy and sufficiency of Holy Scripture as the rule
of faith; the worthlessness of human works as
the ground of a sinner's pardon; and the determination of the true Church not by antiquity,
succession, or general prevalence, but by the
faithful preaching of the Word, the right administration of the sacraments, and the fidelity of
ecclesiastical discipline. The Church as a divine
institution is firmly upheld; but there is no shrink-
ing from the investiture of the civil magistrate
with the power of "dealing" with a corrupt ecclesiastical organisation. We have seen how, at
an early period of his career as a Reformer, Knox
appears to have been influenced by the first Helvetic Confession, which George Wishart translated and brought back with him to Scotland; and
the strong statement of that manifesto, that they
who "bring in strange or ungodly opinions should
be constrained and punished by the magistrates,"[1]
finds its echo in the declaration of this Scottish
standard of doctrine that to the civil magistrate
belong the power and duty of "suppressing all
idolatry and superstition." [2]

The Confession of the early Scottish Reformers
is, in most particulars, conspicuously broader than
that of the Westminster divines [3]: and it is signalised by three other admirable features.   (1)

---

[1] Chapter xxiv. of "Helvetic Conf.," *Wodrow Misc.*, 21.

[2] The *Confession of Faith professed and believed by the Protestants within the realm of Scotland*, chap. xxiv.

[3] See Additional Note at the end of this Chapter.

15

Amid the general backwardness of early Protestant Christendom in recognising its evangelistic responsibility it is refreshing to find on the title-page of the Confession the grand missionary motto: "This glad tidings of the Kingdom shall be preached through the whole world for a witness to all nations." (2) Amid arrogant claims at various periods to a *jus divinum* both by Episcopalians and by Presbyterians, and amid the narrow views at once of Ritualists and of Puritans as to forms of worship, the testimony of this old Confession of 1560 is significantly liberal: "Not that we think that one policy and one order of ceremonies can be appointed for all ages, times, and places." (3) Once more: in no Confession of any age is the fallibility of its own testimony so expressly and so finely set forth:

"Protesting that if any man will note in this our Confession any article or sentence repugning to God's Holy Word, it would please him, of his gentleness, and for Christian charity's sake, to admonish us of the same in writing: and we of our honour and fidelity, do promise unto him satisfaction from the mouth of God (*i. e.*, from His Holy Scriptures), or else reformation of that which he shall prove to be amiss."[1]

The promptness with which the Confession was presented is equalled by the expedition with which it was sanctioned. We have two accounts

---

[1] Knox, *H. of R.*, ii., 94, 96, 113.

of the proceedings in Parliament from men who
were present—that of Knox, and the one given
by the English ambassador, Randolph. To the
former, strong in the conviction that the declaration of faith contained "the truth, the whole
truth, and nothing but the truth," it occasioned,
apparently, no surprise that although numerous
adversaries of the Reformation were members of
the Estates, there was little expressed dissent
and still less disputation. "The Confession," he
writes, "was willingly accepted, without alteration of any one sentence." [1] But the English onlooker records his astonishment. "I never heard
matters of so great importance neither sooner dis-
patched nor with better will agreed to." [2]

Reformed ministers were in attendance, "*standing upon their feet*, ready to have answered in case
any would have defended the papistry"; but their
services were not required. The Primate and two
other bishops —Crighton of Dunkeld and Chis-
holm of Dunblane—contented themselves with
giving an adverse vote on the ground that
"they had not sufficient time to examine" the
document [3]: otherwise they "spake nothing." [4]
They were joined in their dissent by five temporal lords who gave no further reason for their
vote than the ultra-conservative maxim, "We

---

[1] Knox, *H. of R.*, ii., 92, 121.
[2] Randolph, letter to Cecil, in Laing, *W. of K.*, vi., 116.
[3] *Ibid.*, p. 117.
[4] Knox, *H. of R.*, ii., 122.

will believe as our fathers believed." [1]   The
oldest peer of the realm, Lord Lindsay, whom
the English ambassador designates "as grave
and goodly a man as I ever saw," uttered a
Nunc Dimittis : rejoicing that it "hath pleased
God to let me see this day"; while the Earl
Marischal—grandfather of the founder, on Protestant lines, of Marischal College and University at Aberdeen—declared that seeing the
"pillars of the Pope's Church here present speak
nothing to the contrary of the doctrine proposed,
I cannot but hold it to be the very truth of God." [2]
How much the attitude of the Romanists, and
especially of the prelates, was due to fear, to lack
of thorough conviction, to argumentative inability, to apathy engendered by hopelessness—it is
impossible to estimate; but the significant absence
or ineffective presence of the leaders of the Roman
Church, and their apparent acquiescence in the
ruin of their cause, was an "imbecile attitude," [3]
which must have helped to determine the course
of waverers and time-servers, and thus to turn this

---

[1] The Earl of Athol and Lords Somerville and Borthwick
are mentioned by Knox; the Earls of Caithness and Cassilis
by Randolph.   Athol was at first a strong adherent of Mary
Stuart, but afterwards signed the warrant for her custody in
Lochleven.   Borthwick was a staunch supporter of Mary of
Guise; he died in 1565.   Somerville, as we have seen, had
signed the "Band" of April, 1560.   The Earl of Cassilis
subsequently became a Protestant (Knox, *H. of R.*, ii., 533).

[2] Randolph, letter to Cecil; Knox, *H. of R.*, as above.

[3] Andrew Lang, *H. of Sc.*, ii., 78.

parliamentary victory of the Reformation into a permanent ascendency.

The adoption of the Confession of Faith was followed by other ecclesiastical procedure. All former Acts of Parliament inconsistent with the Confession were annulled; all doctrines and usages contrary to it were declared illegal. A fresh statute formally abolished the "jurisdiction and authority of the Pope in this Realm," and interdicted under pain of exile and civil disability the solicitation of any title or privilege from him. Another Act rendered it penal to celebrate or even to hear mass: the penalty for a first offence being confiscation of property; for a second, banishment; for a third, death.[1] It is impossible, of course, to defend this policy of intolerance and threatened persecution. The principle of religious toleration was not then understood in Scotland any more than in other parts of Christendom.[2] It is fair to remember, however, that the intolerance of the Scottish Reformers in 1560 was consistent with their previous remonstrances against persecution. The complaint of Scottish Protestants against their persecutors had been founded on Roman intolerance, not of religious dissent, but of divine truth; on the infliction of pains and

---

[1] *Acts of Parl. of Scot.*, ii., 24th Aug., 1560; Knox, *H. of R.*, ii., 123, 124.

[2] Cranmer the martyr had been also Cranmer the persecutor; and the endorsement of the burning of Servetus the Unitarian by Calvin and other divines is well known.

penalties not in itself, but through illegal and unjust procedure,[1] and because of wholesome testimony against noxious error.

Three circumstances, moreover, in connection
with this persecuting enactment against Roman
Catholics deserve to be noted: (1) What Parliament now made penal was not Roman doctrine as a whole, but one particular external
manifestation of Romanism, viz., saying or hearing mass: and this on account of the blasphemous
idolatry which was believed to be involved. From
the Reformers' standpoint, penal statutes against
the mass were so far parallel to the laws still in
force against scandalously blasphemous repre-
sentations of things sacred, such as shock the
religious sentiments of the nation at large. (2)
The severe measures which the Reformers approved against "mass-mongers," as they were
called, must be judged in the light of the fact
that adultery, perjury, and blasphemy were also
offences whose appropriate punishment was considered to be death.[2] The stern policy of early
Scottish Protestants regarding the mass was thus
due, not to pure ecclesiastical intolerance, but
to severe principles regarding the punishment of

---

[1] The Reformers complained: (1) that the standard of
judgment was not the Word of God, but the mere traditions
of the Church; (2) that the accusers were also the judges;
(3) that in particular cases, like that of Wishart, the death
penalty was exacted without the sanction of the civil power.

[2] Book of Disc., vii. (Knox, *H. of R.*, ii., 227).

what they regarded as moral offences, and to the theocratic identification of sin with crime. (3) While the penalty of death was ordained by Scottish Parliament (in the event of a third offence) and endorsed by our early Reformers,[1] in no single instance is that extreme penalty known to have been actually imposed in the lifetime of Knox. Primate Hamilton, indeed, after enjoying a considerable portion of his former revenues for eleven years, was executed in 1571; not, however, for saying mass, but for complicity in the assassination of the Regent Moray.[2] There is also a case of four priests, who were condemned to death in 1569 for taking part in a mass at Dunblane; but the pillory and exile were substituted for the scaffold.[3] The only authenticated cases of the death penalty being actually exacted are those of two priests who were hanged for saying mass in 1573 and 1574 respectively.[4] No record remains of the special circumstances which led to such exceptional severity: and it is significant that both cases took place in the interval between the

---

[1] "We dare not prescribe unto you [*i. e.*, the Privy Council] what penalties shall be required of such [referring to those who profaned the sacraments either with the idolatry of the mass or through unauthorised ministration]; but this we fear not to affirm that the one and the other deserve death," Book of Disc., (Knox, *H. of R.*, ii., 254; comp. 441, 446.)

[2] Richard Bannatyne's *Memorials*, p. 104. The Bishop "confessed the Regent's murder."

[3] Bellesh., *Cath. Ch. of Sc.*, iii., 205.

[4] Buchan., *Hist.*, 242; *Diur. of Occ.*, 341.

death of Knox and the return of Andrew Melville to Scotland, while the Church was without any eminent leader. The Reformers' hearts were on this question sounder than their heads: and while they maintained that the "idolatry of the mass" was a crime which deserved death, they refrained from urging the civil power to enforce the extreme penalty.

ADDITIONAL NOTE ON THE SCOTTISH CONFESSION OF 1560 COMPARED WITH THE WESTMINSTER CONFESSION

1. The earlier document is only three-fifths of the length of the later; and as the style is much less concise, it contains a considerably less proportion of theological material.

2. Nine of the chapters have the same titles in both documents—God, Creation, Holy Scripture, Sin, Good Works, the Church, Church Councils, Sacraments, the Civil Magistrate. In the old Scottish Confession an article is devoted to each of the great objective facts of Christianity—the Incarnation, Passion, Resurrection, and Ascension of Christ: while there is a conspicuous absence of such articles as appear in the Westminster Confession on various acts and operations of divine grace—Effectual Calling, Justification, Adoption, Sanctification.

3. There is a warmth of sentiment and diction in the earlier document such as one misses in the more precise and logical Confession of the subsequent century. The former "breathes the spirit of true confessors." "Long have we thirsted, brethren,"—

so the preface begins—"to have notified unto the
world the sum of that doctrine which we profess.
.   .   .   To our weak brethren we would communicate
the bottom of our hearts, lest that they be troubled
or carried away"; and the preface closes with an
expression of firm "purpose to abide to the end in the
Confession of this our Faith."

4. As regards doctrinal details; (a) while the
equality of the three persons of the Godhead is distinctly enunciated in both documents, the older Con
fession, unlike the later, is silent as to the procession
of the Spirit from Son as well as from Father; thereby
testifying to the non-essential character of one of the
main questions which led to the schism between
Eastern and Western Christendom. (b) The omission
of the word "Predestination," and the broad statement about election have already been noted (p. 154).
(c) In the chapter on Original Sin, while the image
of God is said to be "utterly defaced" through Adam's
transgression, there is nothing corresponding to the
statement of the Westminster Divines that the guilt
of Adam's sin was *imputed* to all his posterity (vi. 3.).
(d) Similarly there is no express reference to that im-
putation of Christ's righteousness which the Westminster Confession emphasises. (e) There is in the
Confession of 1560 (ch. ix.) no such limitation of the
purpose of the Atonement to any particular section
of mankind as is made by the Westminster Divines
(C. of F., iii. 6.). (f) The older Confession, while
repudiating transubstantiation as emphatically as that
of Westminster, goes further than the latter in the
direction of declaring that the bread and wine become, after consecration, the channel for genuine

believers, of spiritual participation in and nourishment by Christ's body and blood. The authors of the older Confession "confess and undoubtedly believe that the faithful do so eat the body and drink the blood of the Lord Jesus Christ, that He remaineth in them and they in Him: yea, they are so made flesh of His flesh, and bone of His bones, that as the Eternal Godhead has given to the flesh of Jesus Christ life and immortality; so doth Christ Jesus' flesh and blood, eaten and drunk by us, give unto us the same prerogatives" (ch. xxi.). (*g*) Polemical as the older Confession is against Roman error, it exhibits no parallel to the extreme anti-papal invective of the Westminster Divines, who describe the Pope as "anti-Christ," the "man of sin," and the "son of perdition" (ch. xxv.). (*h*) The duty assigned by the earlier document to the civil magistrate of "the maintenance of the true religion," and "the suppressing of idolatry and superstition" (xxiv.), is substantially re-imposed by the later Confession, when it enjoins the magistrate to "take order that all heresies be suppressed; all corruptions and abuses in worship and discipline prevented or reformed" (xxiii). (*i*) While in most particulars the Confession of Knox and his colleagues is broader than its successor, it is narrower as regards salvation outside the visible Church. "There shall none be participant thereof but such as . . . in time come unto Him [Christ], avow His doctrine, and believe into Him" (chap. xvi.). With greater caution the Westminster standard refers to the visible Church "out of which there is no *ordinary* possibility of salvation" (chap. xxv.).

CHAPTER IX

KNOX AND THE ORGANISATION OF THE REFORMED SCOTTISH CHURCH

1560–1561

BY the Parliament of 1560 the doctrine, worship, and government of the Roman Church in Scotland had been overthrown; Romanism had been disestablished, and Protestantism had been established as the national religion. Acts of Parliament, however, can neither make nor unmake churches, although they may contribute to the process; and the work of Knox and his colleagues, lay and clerical, had only begun. There were little more than a dozen recognised and effective Reformed preachers to instruct the nation [1]; and while the majority of the people probably sympathised with the Reformation, the Protestant congregations were few and devoid of ecclesiastical cohesion. A Reformed Creed had been recognised:

---

[1] These included, besides Knox himself and his five associates in the production of the Confession (see p. 224): David Lyndsay, at Leith; Christopher Goodman, at St. Andrews; John Christison, at Dundee; Adam Herriot, at Aberdeen; David Ferguson, at Dunfermline; Paul Methven, at Jedburgh; and John Carswell, in Argyle.

a Protestant Church had still to be organised, with an orderly ministry and government, an authorised ritual and discipline, an adequate and reliable temporal provision. To secure these objects, a church polity had to be framed.

I. So early as April, 1560, the Lords of the Congregation, probably at Knox's own suggestion, had anticipated future requirements, and had intrusted the task of drawing up a constitution to the Reformer himself, and to the other five ministers associated with him in the composition of the Confession of Faith.[1] The outcome of their labours was the Book of Discipline, which had been presented as a draft to the Council of the Congregation in May, 1560.[2] It was kept, apparently, *in retentis* until after the dissolution of Parliament in August, when the commission to Knox and his colleagues was formally renewed.[3] Subsequently it was submitted, in the form of a Latin translation, to Calvin, Beza, Bullinger, and other Swiss Reformers,[4] prior to its being laid before the Privy Council in January, 1561.[5]

This remarkable document was never accepted by the Estates; but it was adopted by the Church

---

[1] Knox, *H. of R.*, ii., 128, 183.

[2] *Ibid.*, ii., 257. The document was afterwards called the First Book of Discipline, to distinguish it from the later polity drawn up by Andrew Melville.

[3] *Ibid.*, ii., 128.

[4] Laing, *W. of K.*, vi., 119.

[5] Knox, *H. of R.*, ii., 257.

as of ecclesiastical authority; and not the least
interesting portions are those which remained a
dead letter through lack of civil sanction.   They
embody the ideal church constitution which the
Reformers, and particularly John Knox, the chief
author of the work, endeavoured, although in part
ineffectually, to realise.[1]

II. The Book of Discipline recognised five class-
es of church office-bearers, three of which were
certainly designed to be permanent—the minister,
elder, and deacon.   The additional office of reader
was apparently intended to be temporary; regarding that of superintendent there is room for
divergent opinions.   To the minister belonged the
public preaching of the Word, the ministration of
the sacraments, and, along with the elders, the
exercise of ecclesiastical jurisdiction and discipline.   He was to be elected by the people, but
examined and (in the event of approval) admitted
by the superintendent and other ministers of the
province or district.   The admission was to be
without imposition of hands; this ceremony, it
was considered, might appear to signify not only
the transmission of ecclesiastical authority, which
the Reformers acknowledged, but also the communication of supernatural gifts, which they disavowed.[2]   The elders were to be men of "best

[1] See A. F. Mitchell, *Scot. Ref.*, pp. 144–183.

[2] Knox, *H. of R.*, 189–193.   The Second Book of Discipline (followed by the Westminster Form of Church Government), restored the "laying on of hands."

knowledge in God's Word and cleanest life." It
was their function to assist the minister in the
government of the Church, and in the discipline
and supervision of the congregation. They were
also to take heed to the doctrine, diligence, and
demeanour of the minister, to admonish him if
necessary, and to bring any case of flagrant delinquency before the superintendent and ministers
of the district.[1] To the deacons belonged the duty
of receiving and administering congregational revenue; of collecting and distributing alms; and of
"assisting in judgment" the minister and elders.
Elders and deacons were to be elected by the
congregation, and only for one year at a time,
"lest by long continuance of such officers men
presume upon the liberty of the Church."[2]   The
readers were intended to supply, so far, the place
of the ministry until sufficient qualified ministers
were obtained. Their duty was restricted to the
reading of Scripture and of the Common Prayers;
but they were encouraged to aspire to the higher
office; and those who were found qualified meanwhile to address the congregation received the
further designation of "exhorters."[3]   To the superintendents (who were to be "ten or twelve,"

---

[1] Knox, *H. of R.*, ii., 192–194, 233–235. The Presbytery,
to which this responsibility afterwards belonged, had not
yet been constituted.

[2] *Ibid.*, 234. The Second Book of Discipline enacted that
election should be for life.

[3] *Ibid.*, 199, 200.

although this number was never actually attained) the "charge and commandment" were to be given "to plant and erect Churches, to set, order, and appoint ministers," and meanwhile to "travel in such provinces as to them shall be assigned," so that "Christ Jesus may be universally preached throughout this realm."

The superintendent resembled a bishop in so far as he held an office superior in authority to that of an ordinary minister, and exercised territorial supervision over a province. But he differed from a bishop in so far as his office was not a new order; no additional rite of consecration being required. Ordinary ministers of the province, moreover, took part in his admission, and he was subject to their admonition as well as to the jurisdiction of the General Assembly.[1] It is commonly supposed that the office of superintendent, like that of reader, was from the first designed to be temporary; and, as a matter of fact, it erelong disappeared. There appears to be ground, however, for believing that the institution was rather a *tentative* arrangement, the result, perhaps, of a compromise between divergent views in the Church as to the retention of the episcopate in modified form; so that the continuance or discontinuance of the office might be intended to depend on its effectiveness or ineffectiveness after a fair trial.[2]

---

[1] Knox, *H. of R.*, ii., 201–208.

[2] That the superintendentship was intended from the first to be only a temporary provision is maintained by

The Book of Discipline contains no formal
regulations as to church courts; but the existence
of Kirk Session, Synod or Provincial Court, and
General Assembly is throughout implied. The

McCrie (*L. of Knox*, Chap. vii.); Lee, *Constit. H. of Ch. of
Sc.*, i., 169); Cunningham (*Ch. of Sc.*, i., 283), and others;
somewhat hesitatingly by Grub (*Eccles. H. of Sc.*, ii., 99) and
Rankine (Story's *Ch. of Sc.*, ii., 440). The language of the
Book of Discipline in two places is regarded as supporting
this contention. "We have thought it good to signify such
reasons as moved us to make difference between preachers
at this time," "We have thought it a thing most expedient
for this time, etc." The reasons given, moreover, viz., the
small number of ministers and the limited number of congregations, are circumstances which were expected to pass
away. On the other hand, (1) there is no hint in the Book
of Discipline either of Presbyteries or of any other kind of
executive which might afterwards supersede the superintendentship; (2) express provision is made for filling
vacancies in the office, without any suggestion that successors might not be required; (3) the two reasons given for
the institution of superintendents are reasons rather for the
appointment of (*a*) "exhorters" or readers to supply for a
time the place of ministers, (*b*) special commissioners with
the limited function of "planting" new congregations.
These various considerations suggest that the institution of
the superintendentship was intended to be experimental
rather than of necessity temporary. The compilers of the
Book may have come to no final decision as to the continuance or discontinuance of the office; and the cautious
phrases "at this time" and "for this time," as well as the
adducing of reasons which might erelong cease to exist,
may indicate merely that, amid some doubt as to the success of the experiment, it was deemed expedient to avoid
committing the Church at that stage to any permanent
arrangement. Archbishop Spottiswoode, who must have
received the information from his father, states that "divers"
of the six compilers of the Book favoured "the retaining of

Presbytery as a court was afterwards developed under Andrew Melville. In the time of Knox it existed only in germ as a weekly meeting of neighbouring ministers and elders for the study of Holy Scripture.[1] The Kirk Session consisted, as at present, of the minister and elders of the parish; the Synod, of the ministers and elders of a province, presided over by the superintendent; the General Assembly, of all the ministers (including superintendents, without official precedence) and of lay commissioners from churches which chose thus to be represented. In the renunciation of a hierarchy; in the institution of an eldership without the function of preaching; and in the recognition of the right of the laity to share in the Church's government, the Scottish Reformers and their Book of Discipline exemplified the influence of Calvin and Geneva.

III. For the public Worship of the Church, the Reformers adopted the *Book of Geneva* used by the congregation of English refugees in that city. It was now revised and issued in Scotland, with a view to Scottish use, under the name of the *Book*

---

the ancient policy," *i. e.*, the episcopate (see Keith, *Ch. and St.*, iii., 15, who quotes an unpublished note in Spottiswoode's MS.); and the elder Spottiswoode, two years before his death in 1585, declared his regret that the episcopate had been abolished (Spottisw., *H. of Ch.*, ii., 337). Such divergence of view among the leaders of the Reformation might very well have led to the adoption of a compromise which left both parties free as to ultimate arrangements.

[1] A. F. Mitchell, *Scott. Ref.*, 159; Knox, *H. of R.*, ii., 242.

16

of Common Order.[1] This Book contains forms
of prayer and praise for ordinary public worship
and for the ministration of the sacraments and
other religious ordinances; but, unlike most other
liturgies, it leaves to the officiating minister considerable freedom both of modification of and
supplement.[2] Among its notable features are (1)
the absence of a lectionary; although the Book
of Discipline enjoins continuous reading of the
Bible at divine service, without "skipping and
divagation"[3]; (2) the omission, as in Calvin's
liturgy, of congregational responses[4]; (3) the
inclusion not only of Psalms in metre and of
metrical versions of other parts of Scripture,
but of doxologies and "human hymns," including the "Veni Creator"; (4) the exclusion of
any prayer for the sanctification of the elements in the Holy Communion, in order to
avoid the appearance of transubstantiation doctrine[5]; (5) the celebration of marriage in church,

---

[1] See Ch. V., p. 142. In the Book of Discipline the *Com-
mon Order* is said to be already " used in some of our Kirks "
(Knox, *H. of R.*, ii., 186); by 1564 its use was enjoined in
ordinary church worship as well as in the special services
(Cald., *H. of K.*, ii., 284. Sprott and Leishman (*Book of
Common Order*, etc., 240, 241, 253) described in detail the
" Pedigree of the Book of C. O."

[2] *Book of Common Order*, pp. 22, 31, 86, 125.

[3] Book of Disc., ch. ix., Knox, *H. of R.*, ii., 240.

[4] This omission was due perhaps, in part, to Knox's experience of responses at Frankfort.

[5] The prayer of sanctification was restored in the Westminster Directory of Worship.

"in open face and public audience" of the congregation, the most convenient time being "Sunday before sermon" [1]; (6) the strong discouragement of prayer at burials, and the absence of all provision for it, in order to guard against prayers for the dead [2]; and (7) the non-observance of church festivals and commemoration of saints, chiefly, as it appears, "because in God's Scriptures they have neither commandment nor assurance," but also on account of the prevalent abuses and superstitions connected with such "holidays." [3]

IV. As regards ecclesiastical discipline, in the more special sense, provision is made in the Book of Discipline for the private admonition of those whose offences are "secret or known only to a few"; and if the offender promise amendment and fulfil his promise, this "secret admonition" is deemed sufficient. For open and flagrant offences a profession of penitence before the congregation

---

[1] Book of Disc., ch. ix. in Knox, *H. of R.*, pp. 247, 248.

[2] *Ibid.*, 249–251; Sprott and Leishman, *B. of C. O.*, 78, 243. The authors of the Book of Discipline do not absolutely prohibit a burial service; they only "judge it best" that there be "neither singing nor reading" (*i. e.*, of prayers); and, as if conscious that in guarding against superstition, they might discourage religion, they add; "Yet notwithstanding we are content that particular kirks use them [singing and prayers], with the consent of the ministers, as they shall answer to God, and to the Assembly of the Universal Kirk gathered within the realm."

[3] Knox, *H. of R.*, ii., 185, 186. Somewhat inconsistently, however, the days are inserted in the ecclesiastical calendar prefixed to the *Book of Common Order*.

is required: and what this involved is illustrated by references, in early kirk session records, to the "pillar of repentance" at which the offender stood, clad in sackcloth, with bare feet, and neck encircled by the iron ring attached to a pillar or to the wall of the Church. After such discipline had been undergone, however, and tokens of repentance had been shewn, the Church was to receive back the offender into fellowship: she "ought to be no more severe than God." On the persistently impenitent person excommunication is to be pronounced; and all, except members of his family, are prohibited from intercourse with him, except from what is necessary or expedient for his conversion. Yet his case is not to be treated as hopeless; his "most discreet and nearest friends" are to "travail with him, to bring him to knowledge of himself"; and "all are to call to God" on his behalf. Various offences in addition to murder, viz., blasphemy, idolatry, perjury, and adultery, are declared to be beyond the sphere of the Church's discipline, because those who commit such transgressions ought to be "taken away by the civil sword." With a fine inconsistency, however, the Book provides that, "in case" such offenders "be permitted to live," and do afterwards give evidence of repentance, the minister, elders, and chief men of the Church are, in the name of the congregation, to "receive that penitent brother into their favour, as they require

God to receive themselves when they have offended"; and "one or two, in name of the whole, shall kiss and embrace him with all reverence and gravity, as a member of Christ Jesus." [1]

The Book of Discipline makes it clear that the congregation, and not merely the minister and elders, excommunicate and absolve. The minister's duty is to *move* the offender to penitence, and the congregation to excommunication or absolution. The elders' function is to assist the minister in such offices, and to offer the right hand of restored fellowship to the penitent. But with the congregation the administration of discipline is held really to lie. It was this conception of congregational power and responsibility which made public confession of, and satisfaction for, heinous sin appropriate. When the Reformed Church afterwards went back to the pre-Reformation standpoint regarding discipline, so far, at least, as to transfer the exercise of it from the congregation to office-bearers, the publicity of the ordeal ceased to have the old significance. Public exposure became purely punitive instead of being, as originally intended, restorative; and so, slowly but steadily, it passed away.

V. The Book of Discipline emphasises the necessity of the "virtuous education and godly up-bringing of the youth of this realm." If Scotland owes to enlightened Roman prelates three

---

[1] Book of Disc., Head VII., Knox, *H. of R.*, ii., 227–233.

out of her four universities, she is indebted
mainly to Knox and the early Reformers for her
parochial-school system; and if adequate provision for secondary education, as the link between parish school and university, has been left
to modern times, this postponement has been due
to the fact that the counsels of the Reformers
were, on this point, in great measure ignored.
The Book lays down that in every parish there
should be not only a church, but a school, at
which secular and religious instruction were to be
given; and, "further, that in every notable town"
an academy or "college" should be erected, at
which suitable preparation [1] might be supplied to
promising youth for future study at the "great
schools called Universities."

The authors of the Book of Discipline anticipated our legislature by more than three centuries in advocating compulsory education; the
children of the well-to-do, were to be educated
at their parents' expense; but "the children of
the poor on the charge of the Church." The encouragement of university training was to be
secured by the establishment of bursaries on a
liberal scale, viz., seventy-two for St. Andrews,
as the oldest and at that time the largest university, and forty-eight each for Glasgow and
Aberdeen. "If God shall move your hearts," so

---

[1] Among the subjects mentioned as requiring to be taught
in these "colleges" were "Logic and Rhetoric."

the authors of the Book address the Privy Council, "to establish and execute this order, and put these things in practice, your whole realm, within few years, will serve itself of true preachers, and of other officers necessary for your Commonwealth." [1]

VI. Of special importance are the proposals of the Book of Discipline regarding the Church's patrimony. At the dawn of the Reformation, as we have seen, the possessions of the Church, including landed property or "temporalities," and ecclesiastical teinds or "spiritualities," amounted nominally to about one-half of the wealth of the kingdom: but during the generation preceding the fall of Romanism, the revenues had been largely diminished through actual or virtual alienation. Still, much remained; and the compilers of the Book set forth how it might be used. They proposed to revert to the spirit of the usage which prevailed in the best days of the Roman Church. Support of monks and beneficed clergy; establishment and endowment of schools and universities; maintenance of hospitals and distribution of alms—ministry, that is, for the soul, culture for the mind, relief for the body,—these had been the three channels in which the wealth of the old Church had run, before accumulated abuses had diverted it into lay and clerical

---

[1] Knox, *H. of R.*, ii., 209–220; A. F. Mitchell, *Scot. Ref.*, pp. 174–178.

aggrandisement. Knox endeavoured to secure substantially similar arrangements. While vexatious ecclesiastical exactions, such as "the uppermost cloth," funeral perquisites, Easter offerings, etc., were to be abrogated, the legitimate property of the Church, he maintained, ought to be devoted entirely to the sustenance of the ministry, the education of youth, and the relief of the poor by kirk sessions. The provision proposed for the ministry was by no means excessive. "We require it to be such that ministers may have occasion neither of solicitude nor of insolence and wantonness." [1] For the ordinary pastor is indicated a stipend equal probably in purchasing power to the recognised minimum of £200 (not, however, yet universally realised) at the present day [2]; and the rational principle is laid down that pastors having families should have a somewhat larger stipend than those who have none. For superintendents, whose duties involved much costly travel, the stipend proposed was probably equal in real value to that of the present livings of leading city charges. In a time anterior to the establishment of funds for widows and children of the clergy, the Book of Discipline strongly advocates the sustentation of the families of deceased ministers who "did faithfully serve the Kirk of

[1] Book of Disc., Head V., Knox, *H. of R.*, ii., 197.

[2] For a detailed calculation of the value of ministers' stipends as proposed by the Book of Discipline, see Principal Lee, *Constitutional Hist. of Ch. of Sc.*, i., 162.

God." The proposed destination of ecclesiastical revenue to education has already been indicated. As regards relief of the poor, the authors are careful to state that they would be no "patrons of stubborn and idle beggars, who make a craft of begging: those must be compelled to work, or else be punished by the magistrate." But "for the widow and fatherless, the aged, impotent or maimed, who neither can nor may travail for their sustentation: for such, as also for persons of honesty fallen into decay and penury, ought provision to be made," and "their indigence relieved." [1]

VII. In the development and expansion of the Scottish Reformed Church, a main factor, at once of consolidation and of progress, was the General Assembly. The Assembly, unlike the hierarchy which it superseded, was the exponent of the lay as well as of the clerical opinion of the Church; a bond of union for all the Reformed congregations of the country; a national institution which rivalled Parliament in its influence: an agency for enactments affecting the religious life of the nation; the directress of popular sentiment in spiritual concerns. The General Assembly was intended to be the great "Living Epistle" of the Church of Scotland—the Confession of Faith and the Book of Discipline embodied together in the personalities of living men. The first General

---

[1] Book of Disc., Heads V. and VI., Knox, *H. of R.*, ii., 197, 198, 200, 201, 221–225.

Assembly of the Church met in Magdalen Chapel,
in the Cowgate of Edinburgh, on the 20th December, 1560. It consisted of only forty-two
members,[1] who assembled as "ministers and commissioners of the particular kirks of Scotland,
convened upon the things which are to set forward
God's glory and the weal of His Kirk in this
realm." [2] The main business of this first Assembly was to sanction the appointment of such as
were "best qualified for the preaching the Word,
ministering of the Sacraments, and reading of the
Common Prayers." [3] We cannot doubt, however,
that the Book of Discipline was carefully considered by the members of the court, prior to its
presentation in the following month to the Lords
of the Council, with a view to ratification by the
Estates. The Assembly adjourned till the 15th of
January,[4] the date on which Parliament also was
to meet; and although no record of this adjourned
meeting now remains, it may be assumed that the
Book of Discipline then received the Church's
approval; for at the ensuing Assembly of May,

---

[1] Only six out of the forty-two were ministers, viz.: Knox,
Lyndsay, Goodman, Row, Christison, and Harlaw (Calderwood, *Hist. of the Kirk*, ii., 44).

[2] *Book of the Universal Kirk*, p. 1.

[3] Calderwood, *Hist. of the Kirk*, ii., 45–46. Thirty-five
ministers and eight readers were appointed. Among those
ordained to the ministry was Erskine, the Laird of Dun,
who was thereafter appointed Superintendent of Angus and
Mearns.

[4] *Ibid.*, p. 47.

1561, the document is twice referred to as an ecclesiastical authority.[1]

Very different was the reception of the Reformers' polity by the Estates. The Book was subscribed, indeed, by over thirty members of the Privy Council, with a reasonable provision that the life-interests of beneficed men should be respected, on condition of the maintenance of a Reformed ministry in their respective benefices.[2] If the document had consisted merely of regulations for the worship, organisation, and government of the Church, it would probably have been endorsed by the Estates; for the Reformed Church, during this earliest period of its existence, was allowed by the State, in such matters, to have a pretty free hand. But the recommendations of the Book regarding the ecclesiastical patrimony, and the assumption that the Reformed Church was eventually to inherit the entire property of its predecessor, could find no favour with landowners who (themselves or their fathers) had already "greedily gripped to the possessions of

---

[1] Calderwood, *Hist. of the Kirk*, ii., p. 127.

[2] Knox, *H. of R.*, ii., 257, 258. The list of signatures includes the names of the Duke of Châtelherault, Lord James Stuart, Earl Marischal, and the Earls of Argyll, Menteith, and Morton. Maitland of Lethington afterwards declared, however, that "many subscribed *in fide parentum*, as the bairns are baptised" (Calderwood, *H. of K.*, ii., 160); and his sneers at the signatures suggest that some subscribed in the full knowledge that there was no prospect of the Book ever being ratified by Parliament.

the Kirk," or looked on her remanent wealth with covetous eyes.[1] Knox now fully realised the mercenary motives of a portion of those who had zealously joined in the attack on the old Church. "Everything," he writes, "that repugned to their corrupt affections was termed, in their mockage, devout imaginations." He "wondered how men that profess godliness could of so long continuance hear the threatenings of God against themselves," yet "never have had remorse of conscience," nor have "intended to restore anything of that which they had stolen"; and he recalls the ancient proverb, "The belly hath no ears." [2]

The claim of Knox and his colleagues on behalf of the Reformed Church to the whole ecclesiastical patrimony was undoubtedly a large one; but in view of the national duties which the Church undertook to discharge,—charitable and educational as well as religious,—it could not be stigmatised as selfish: and a substantial assessment on ecclesiastical as well as secular wealth might have sufficed for the maintenance of other national objects. If the claim had been conceded, not only would the provision for national religion, popular education, and relief of the sick and poor have

---

[1] It must in fairness be stated, however, that such landowners pleaded that the church property had been bestowed by their own forefathers largely in return for the promise of masses for the dead, which they were *now* taught to regard as profitless and blasphemous services (see p. 13).

[2] Knox, *H. of R.*, ii., 128, 129.

been permanently adequate without the imposition of national burdens, but, as an incidental
benefit, the bitter conflict which lasted for a
century between Presbyterianism and Episcopacy
might have been avoided. For the covetous
policy of misappropriating church property,
adopted by leading landowners, led, as we shall
find, to the earliest movement for the restoration of the episcopate, and thus inaugurated a
protracted strife which was terminated only by
the Revolution Settlement of 1690.[1]

VIII. If the Scottish Parliament gave scant
encouragement to the claims· of Knox and the
Reformed ministers as regards the Church's
patrimony, it supplied them with a fresh opportunity of vindicating the Church's doctrine.
A discussion was arranged in presence of the
Estates between representatives of the old faith
and of the new. On the Romanist side were
Principal Anderson of King's College, Aberdeen; John Lesley, the historian, afterwards
Roman Catholic Bishop of Ross; and two other
ecclesiastics of less note. On the Protestant side
were Knox, Willock, and Goodman. Two accounts
of the disputation are extant—one by Lesley, the

[1] See p. 350. The lack of adequate sustentation was also
one cause of the superintendentship failing, at least in part,
to fulfil the purposes of its institution; and this office, with
its subordination to the General Assembly, might have been
accepted as a convenient compromise between the episcopate and the presbyterate.

other by Knox. Each narrator, as was to be expected, maintains that the opposite party was discomfited and silenced.[1] According to both historians the "Sacrifice of the Altar" occupied the attention of the controversialists[2]; and apparently the chief point of interest in the discussion was an apparent disavowal by the Romanists of the propitiatory efficacy of the mass. Anderson is represented as declaring "Christ offered the propitiatory: and that could none do but He: but we offer the remembrance." If the Principal has been correctly reported, we can imagine (in view of the Protestant claim for the conservation of the Church's patrimony) the mingled feelings with which Knox would listen to the interpolation of some nobles who were acute enough to discern the bearing of the question on their own reappropriation of church lands—"If the mass may not obtain remission of sins to the quick and to the dead, wherefore were all the abbacies so richly endowed with our temporal lands?"

IX. The twelve months which followed the establishment of the Reformation were for Knox

---

[1] Lesley, ii., 448–450; Knox, *H. of R.*, ii., 138–141.

[2] Lesley states that the Protestants asked of "the verity and manner of the blessed sacrament and sacrifice of the altar"; and Knox declares "we required of the Papists principally that the mass, and the opinion thereof by them taught unto the people, be laid to the square-rule of God's Word."

a year not only of public activity, but of literary labour and of domestic trouble. During
the autumn of 1560, while the Book of Discipline was being revised by the Swiss Reformers,
Knox occupied himself with that portion of his
History of the Reformation which was originally
intended to be the whole, viz., the narrative
of the final conflict in which he and his fellow-
Reformers had just been engaged.[1] He designates this part of the *History* as a "Confession";
and the original motive of its composition was
fully as much apologetic as historical. It is a
vindication of the Scottish religious revolution
and of its chief promoters before their fellow-
countrymen and before the world.

"In this our Confession," he writes, "we shall faithfully declare what moved us to put our hands to the
reformation of religion; to the end that as well our
enemies and our brethren in all realms may understand how falsely we are accused of tumult and rebellion: as also that our brethren, natural Scotsmen,
of whatever religion they be, may have occasion to
examine themselves if they may with safe conscience
oppose themselves to us who seek nothing but Jesus
Christ's Evangel to be preached; His holy sacraments to be truly ministered; superstition, tyranny
and idolatry to be suppressed; and finally our
native country to remain free from the bondage
of strangers." [2]

---

[1] This is the portion of the *History* now contained in Book
II. and part of III.   [2] Pref. to Book II. in *H. of R.*, i., 278.

The first express reference to the work as in progress is found in a letter of Knox, dated 23rd October, 1559 [1]; but it must have been commenced at a considerably earlier date.[2] By the end of September, 1560, one Book (what is now the Second) had been completed, bringing the *History* down to November, 1559 [3]; and the Reformer had probably written part of what is now Book III. before the close of the year, in a brief interval of comparative exemption from public work and worry.[4] One cannot but marvel at the diligence with which Knox, amid pulpit and pastoral work, "care of all the Churches," and constant employment in ecclesiastical business and negotiations, nevertheless occupied his few leisure hours with the composition of a *History* for which he himself was largely providing the materials. He undertook the task with a view to no immediate controversial advantage (for he declined to let the work be published in his lifetime [5]), but

---

[1] Laing, *W. of K.*, vi., 87.

[2] Knox, *H. of R.*, i., 383. In October, 1559, he was writing about events which took place so late as August of that year.

[3] Letter of Randolph, in Laing, *W. of K.*, vi., 121.

[4] The other Books, viz., what is now Book I. (containing a narrative of earlier struggles after Reformation), and Book IV., bringing the record down to June, 1564, were completed in 1566 (Laing, i., p. xxviii.). Book V., which continues the *History* to Queen Mary's abdication, was afterwards added by an unknown hand, on the basis, probably, of documents found among Knox's papers after his death.

[5] Laing, *W. of K.*, vi., 558.

in order to supply an effective vindication of himself and of his colleagues after his removal from the world. It is not the manner of fanatics, among whom Knox has sometimes been classed, thus to look beyond the turbid judgment of contemporaries to the calmer verdict of posterity. That Knox's *History* should be one-sided was inevitable; that his language is sometimes intemperate is undeniable; his chronology is sometimes inaccurate; but the honesty of the writer and the substantial trustworthiness of his record of events within his own experience have been generally admitted. As a literary work the *History* holds a notable place on account of its vivid descriptions, its trenchant diction, and its dramatic union of grim earnestness with bright humour.

Along with literary labour this first year of the Scottish Reformed Church brought to Knox heavy domestic trouble. In December, 1560, the wife for whose arrival in Scotland he had longed,[1] and to whose self-denying helpfulness during a period of labour and anxiety he bears, as we have seen, incidental testimony, was taken away; and the Reformer was left a widower with the two boys born at Geneva, who had scarcely yet emerged from infancy. A brief but pathetic parenthesis in his *History* describes the "no small heaviness" which he suffered "by reason of the late death of his dear bed-fellow, Marjorie Bowes"[2]; and her

---

[1] Laing, *W. of K.*, vi., 27.   [2] Knox, *H. of R.*, ii., 138.

place in his household was but imperfectly supplied by a mother-in-law who continued to vex
her own and her son-in-law's soul with her
"troubled conscience." [1]   Among those who wrote
to comfort Knox in his sorrow was John Calvin,
to whom the bereavement of "his most excellent
brother, . . . deprived of the most delightful
of wives," was "grief and bitterness." [2]

This domestic grief came to Knox amid political
anxiety. The French Government had not ratified the Treaty of Leith, entered into by its
own representatives. The Queen of Scots and her
Consort, King Francis, had declined to confirm the
recent Acts of the Estates. The powerful house
of Guise was impelled at once by religious
and by personal considerations to promote a
policy of French intervention. The Scottish
Catholics, accordingly, had reason to hope, and
the Scottish Protestants to fear, a French invasion; while the Queen of England, who grudged
the cost of the expedition of 1559, was in no mood
to promise a renewal of assistance. "When all
these things came to our ears," writes Knox,
"many were effrayed"; and it required all the
power of himself and of other Reformed preachers
to assure the people that God would "perform in
all perfection that work which was not ours but
His own." [3]   What was regarded as a "wonder-

---

[1] Laing, *W. of K.*, vi., 513.

[2] Letter of Calvin, in Laing, vi., 124, 125.

[3] Knox, *H. of R.*, ii., 131, 132.

ful deliverance" unexpectedly took place. By
the death of King Francis, on 5th December,
1560, "the pride of the Papists in Scotland began
to be abated." "They perceived God to fight for
us." The danger of Scotland becoming an appanage of France, and of French policy and religion
being imposed by force on the Scottish people,
was removed. Mary might or might not conform to the faith of the majority of her subjects; but at any rate she would no longer be
supported in her policy by the power of a French
husband and sovereign who claimed to be King
of Scotland.[1] Still, as the Queen's widowhood
practically involved her return to Scotland, the
deliverance in which the Reformer rejoiced
was accompanied by a peril which he had good
cause to fear. If, however, as appears to be the
case, he was the confidant of the Protestant
Earl of Arran in the latter's aspirations at this
time after Mary's hand,[2] he may have hoped,

[1] Knox, *H. of R.*, ii., 137. Incidental testimony is borne to
the personal importance of Knox, and to his intimacy with
well-informed and influential friends on the Continent, by the
fact that he appears to have had the earliest intimation in
Scotland of the French King's mortal illness.

[2] Knox records the fact of Arran's letter to Mary with the
significant accompaniment of a ring, and also the receipt by
the Earl of a discouraging answer. He adds that the Earl
"bare it more heavily than many would have wist" (Knox,
H. of R., ii., 137); as if he (Knox) knew more of the circumstances than others; and Randolph, on the same subject,
declares (January, 1561) that "of all these matters there is
no man privy except Knox" (Laing, *W. of K.*, vi., 122),

not unnaturally, that a young widow of eighteen, under the guidance of a Protestant husband as well as a Protestant brother, and removed from the immediate influence of a Catholic Court and kindred, would not give serious trouble to the Scottish Reformed Church. He was destined erelong to discover that Mary Stuart, as Queen of France, was in reality much less a cause for Protestant anxiety than Mary as resident Queen of Scotland.

CHAPTER X

1561–1563

THE encounter between John Knox and Mary Stuart not only constitutes one of the most interesting episodes in the biographies of the Reformer and of the Queen, but occupies a conspicuous place in Scottish history. No two personalities could be more dissimilar than the Puritan Protestant who revered Calvin as master, and the bright young Queen who had presided over the gayest Court in Christendom. No two standpoints could be more divergent than those of the man whose life-work was to build up a strong and independent Reformed Church, and of the woman who had been educated in the belief that absolute submission to princes was a religious duty, and that her own mission was to restore the Roman Church in Scotland. A keen encounter between the two was predetermined: unpleasant personal relations were almost inevitable.

I. The leaders of the Scottish Reformation do not appear to have questioned the propriety, however some of them might anticipate the danger of the Queen of Scots living and reigning, after the death of her husband, the King of France, henceforth in her native land. Their attention in the early part of 1561 was devoted to the best means of preventing her presence from injuring the Protestant cause. There was reason for vigilance and consideration. Three hundred letters had been despatched by Mary to various Scots of standing in the prospect of her early return. The Catholic bishops assembled at Stirling in the spring of 1561 to take counsel in view of the changed and (from their point of view) more hopeful circumstances. The Catholic lords were credited with a design to seize the capital. In the month of April, Bishop Lesley was in France with authority to propose, on their behalf, that the Queen should land somewhere in the north of Scotland, where Romanism was strong, and be received by an army of 10,000. "The Papists," writes Knox, "began to brag as if they would have defaced the Protestants." [1]

1. The first object of the Reformers was to strengthen the new edifice of the Protestant Church, in order to increase the difficulty of undermining its stability and of interfering with its polity. Here the General Assembly took the initiative. The Church had failed, as we have seen, to secure the transference to herself of

---

[1] Knox, *H. of R.*, ii., 156–161; Lesley, *H. of Sc.*, ii., 450.

PALATIVM REGIVM EDINENSE,
quod & Cænobium S. Crucis.
The royal palace of holy rood-hous, by J. G.

Holyrood Palace as it was prior to 1650.

the ancient ecclesiastical patrimony; but much, nevertheless, had been accomplished. A Reformed Confession had been adopted; the mass had been proscribed as idolatry; the General Assembly, as a supreme ecclesiastical court, had been constituted; a Reformed Order of Worship had been instituted; the ranks of the Reformed ministry had been largely supplemented; and five out of ten proposed superintendents had been appointed for the completion of the Church's organisation and for the supervision of her work.[1] The General Assembly which met in May, 1561, endeavoured to fortify yet further the position of the Reformed Church. It addressed a Supplication to the Privy Council demanding the suppression of the already prohibited mass, the removal from churches of all remaining monuments of idolatry, and the further "plantation" as well as adequate sustenance of Reformed superintendents, ministers, exhorters, and readers. These requirements were approved by the Privy Council; and thus, according to Knox, whose influence in framing the petition and securing its favourable reception is apparent, "gat Satan the second fall." [2]

2. The next point was to make it clear to the Queen that French interference with Scottish

---

[1] These superintendents, although nominated on 20th December, 1560 (*Universal Kirk*, 1–3), were not actually set apart until March, 1561 (Knox, *H. of R.*, iii., 144).

[2] Knox, *H. of R.*, ii., 161, 164.

policy would not be tolerated. Here the Estates
appropriately intervened. An opportunity for effective testimony in this direction arrived on the
18th of February, when ambassadors came from
Mary to Scotland, followed by a similar embassy
from Catherine de' Medici, the Regent of France.[1]
The main object of both legations was to obtain
a renewal of the ancient French alliance; and an
attempt also appears to have been made to secure for the Roman episcopate and priesthood the
continued possession of the ecclesiastical patrimony. The Estates, at their meeting in May,
made it sufficiently clear that they would enter
into no such alliance with a nation which had
"helped to persecute them" as would involve a
breach of the existing league with those who had
helped to deliver them; and "as Scotland had for-
saken the Pope and papistry," Scotsmen "could
not be debtors to his foresworn vassals." [2]

3. The third object was to ensure that the Queen,
on her return, should abstain from overturning
the new ecclesiastical settlement; and should retain as her advisers those who were the recognised
leaders of the nation. For the attainment of this
end, Lord James Stewart, at the request of the
Estates, although without any definite commission, visited Queen Mary in April. He had little
difficulty in convincing his sister that, even from

[1] *Diur. of Occ.,* p 64; Labanoff, *Letters of Mary Stuart,* i., 80.
[2] Knox, *H. of R.,* ii., 166, 167.

her own religious standpoint, it would be unwise
to attempt any reversal, meanwhile at least, of
the Scottish ecclesiastical policy, or even to effect
any substantial change in the *personnel* of her
ministers of State. The same counsel appears to
have been given to the Queen by her French advisers.[1] Mary was a zealous Catholic, and her
kinsmen in France were hopeful that through her
instrumentality not only Scotland, but England,
would eventually be regained for Rome. But the
proposal of the more sanguine Scottish Romanists to attempt at this juncture a political and
ecclesiastical counter-revolution was regarded
even in France as impracticable. It was necessary (they considered) for Mary to temporise in
order ultimately to triumph; and for the present,
accordingly, it was advised that "two should
walk together" even although not "agreed."

The danger to the Reformed cause from the return of Queen Mary was thus lessened; but it was
not removed. She resolutely declined, and was
not constrained, to ratify the Treaty of Leith,
according to which foreign troops were to be
permanently withdrawn from Scotland; the possibility, therefore, of subsequent French intervention, with the Queen's sanction, was not
foreclosed.[2] She continued to refrain from

---

[1] Sir James Melville, *Memoirs*, 31; Nau, *Mary Stuart*, 116.

[2] See Throgmorton to Queen Elizabeth in Knox, *H. of R.*,
ii., 169–174. The chief reason of Mary's "refusal" to confirm the treaty was, doubtless, the acknowledgment which

confirming the Parliament or Convention of 1560, by which Protestantism had been established; and thus a door was left open for repudiation when opportunity might arrive.[1] She held out no hope of changing her religion, as Henry IV. afterwards did in somewhat analogous circumstances; and her Romanism could not fail to foster a Catholic party both at the Court and in the country. Finally, her personal antagonism to John Knox had even then been manifested, and was known in Reformed circles. "The Queen of Scotland"—so the English ambassador in France, Throgmorton, wrote to Queen Elizabeth in July, 1561—"is thoroughly persuaded that the most dangerous man in all her realm of Scotland is Knox." [2]

II. At the time of Mary's arrival in Scotland, on the 19th August, 1561, the attitude of Knox as well as of other Reformers was one of anxiety and suspicion. On the day of her landing at Leith he saw a "forewarning" in the "very face of Heaven, which did manifestly speak of dolour, darkness and all impiety." There was "corruption of the air"; "the mist was thick and dark . . . the sun was not seen to shine two days before, nor two days after." [3] The safe

---

it contained of Elizabeth as legitimate Queen of England; but the exclusion of French soldiers was also, presumably, in the Scottish Queen's mind.

[1] *Diur. of Occ.*, pp. 62, 280, 281.
[2] Tytler, *H. of Sc.*, vi., 467.
[3] Knox, *H. of R.*, ii., 269.

arrival of the Queen, moreover, was signalised by
the pardon of some criminals, riotous craftsmen
of Edinburgh; and Knox discerned beneath this
act of grace a sinister purpose, as the culprits (so
he held) had committed their offence "in despite
of the religion." [1]

With more reason the preparations made for
"that idol, the mass, to be said in the Chapel" of
Holyrood, "pierced the heart of the Reformer."
The service, indeed, was stated to be for the benefit of the Queen's uncles and other Frenchmen
who had accompanied her on the journey; but
Knox was not deceived by this plea of the over-
complacent (as the Reformer considered) Lord
James Stewart, who stood as guard at the chapel
door, in order, as he said, to stop all Scotsmen
from taking part in the idolatry.[2]   The Queen's
personal participation in the mass was tacitly admitted; and the Reformer was not pacified by the
proclamation issued that morning by the Privy
Council in the Queen's name.   The proclamation
began by threatening with death those who might
"attempt any thing against the form [of religion]
which her Majesty found publicly standing at her

---

[1] Knox, *H. of R.*, ii., 270.   They had violently rescued the
deacon of the butchers, who had been accused of bigamy;
but who pleaded that he had been "lawfully parted" from his
first wife " after the manner of the papistical religion" (*ibid.,*
155).

[2] *Ibid.*, ii., 271.   The chapel in which the mass was celebrated was not the Church of Holyrood Abbey, but a private
chapel in the Palace (see Hay Fleming, *Mary Q. of S.,* 257).

arrival in this her realm"; but it proceeded to warn all not to "molest any of her domestic servants, or persons whosoever came forth of France, for any cause whatsoever." [1]

On the following Sunday Knox relieved his conscience. From the pulpit of St. Giles' he testified that "one mass was more fearful to him than if 10,000 armed enemies were landed in any part of the realm, of purpose to suppress the whole religion." Four years later he acknowledged that he had "done most wickedly" that day; not because he had spoken too strongly, but because he had not gone further, and "done what in him lay to have suppressed that idol in the beginning." [2] Our modern principles of religious toleration render it difficult for us to sympathise with Knox's Protestant thoroughness; yet, after all, he was only anticipating the provision made at the Revolution of 1689, by which to this day "Papists" are "debarred from the British Crown," and the Sovereign of Great Britain renounces the doctrine of transubstantiation. The Catholics of Scotland, moreover, had not yet given up the hope of a counter-revolution; Scottish Protestantism was still in danger, and the event proved that Knox's fears were far from groundless. In any case the allowance of mass in Holyrood Chapel, after it had been proscribed by statute,

---

[1] Knox, *H. of R.*, ii., 273.
[2] *Ibid.*, ii., 277; comp. Laing, *W. of K.*, vi., 131.

was an obvious inconsistency, justifiable only as a necessary compromise adopted to prevent civil war. The Reformer received little encouragement in his protest. The only man of high rank, apparently, who supported him publicly was the Earl of Arran; and within a year this nobleman became insane. "As the Lords of the Congregation," writes Knox, "repaired unto the town, at the first coming they shewed themselves wonderfully offended that the mass was permitted; so that every man, as he came, accused them that were before him; but after they had remained a certain space, they were as quiet as were the former." He quotes with evident gusto a sarcastic saying of Robert Campbell of Kinyeancleuch, that the "holy water of the Court sprinkled on them took away all their fervency"; and he adds that men were blinded to the peril of toleration, on the one hand, by the Queen's constant outcry against the attempt "to constrain the conscience"; on the other hand, by the subtle suggestion of some that, if gently dealt with, she might be won to the Reformed side.[1] It is not likely that Lord James Stewart and Maitland of Lethington, who became the chief ministers of State, were either fascinated or deceived; but they considered, doubtless, as men of the world, that the toleration of a single private mass in the Palace chapel was a moderate price to be paid for the practical endorsement

[1] Knox, *H. of R.*, ii., 274–276.

which Mary had given to the establishment of the Reformed faith.

III. A few days after his sermon in St. Giles', Knox was invited by the Queen to a private colloquy at Holyrood. The interview was presumably approved and probably suggested by her brother and Maitland. They could have little expectation that Knox would persuade Mary to renounce the mass; but they may have had some hope that the Reformer might be won over by the Queen to their own moderate standpoint.[1] For a detailed account of the conference we are dependent on Knox's narrative alone,[2] although Lord James was present; but the record bears internal marks of truth. Mary was no unworthy antagonist, intellectually, at least, of the Reformer. In a letter to Cecil, written six weeks after the interview, Knox admits that he observed in her a "shrewdness beyond her years"[3]; and the report of the interview discloses no little acuteness in the Queen's reasoning. It is probable that Mary, at the outset, did not omit an endeavour to exert over the Reformer that fasci-

---

[1] In a letter to Throgmorton, written on the day of the interview, Randolph testifies to the great influence of Knox at this time, and indicates the need which must have been felt of securing his concurrence in the policy of moderation. "I fear nothing so much as that one day he will mar all. . . . He ruleth the roost and of him all men stand in fear" (Laing, *W. of K.*, vi., 129).

[2] Knox, *H. of R.*, ii., 277–286.

[3] Laing, *W. of K.*, vi., 132; comp. Knox, *H. of R.*, ii., 286.

nating influence which had been successful in the
case of others; she declared afterwards that she
had "sought" his "favours by all possible
means,"[1] but the conversation apparently soon
drifted into a discussion of various grounds
of complaint against him. Two charges against
the Reformer were stated, which referred chiefly
to his ministry in England. On one of these, however, little stress seems to have been laid. It was
his alleged "necromancy" practised in England
—a fatuous invention of Romanists which simply
attests the Reformer's acknowledged power. The
reference to it by the Queen gave Knox an opportunity of saying that he, "wretched sinner," must
patiently bear an accusation which had also been
made against Christ Himself; and that so far from
being guilty of the offence, he could bring numerous witnesses to his having "spoken against such
arts, and against those that had used such impiety." The other charge, connected with his
ministry in England, was that he had been "the
cause of great sedition and slaughter there"—a
charge which rested, presumably, on his continuing to preach Protestant doctrine after Mary
Tudor's accession, and on his writings circulated
in that country during her reign. From his own
standpoint, Knox had no difficulty in answering
that the charge was without foundation, unless
"to teach the truth of God in sincerity, to rebuke

[1] *H. of R.*, ii., 387.

idolatry, and to will a people to worship God according to His Word be to raise subjects against their princes." The charge of causing sedition, however, was based chiefly on the *Monstrous Regiment of Women*, and the publication of this work formed the third count in the Queen's indictment. This unfortunate treatise could not be disowned; but Knox explains that the work had been composed with special reference, not to her Majesty, but to Queen Mary of England; and he adds that "if the realm [of Scotland] finds no inconvenience from the regiment of a woman . . . neither I nor that book shall hurt you or your authority." With characteristic plain-spokenness, however, even when wishing to be conciliatory, he designates Mary Tudor a "wicked Jezebel," and introduces with quite unconscious offensiveness, the assurance that he would be "as well content to live under your Grace as Paul under Nero"!

The interview between the Queen and the Reformer culminated in the important question of subjects resisting their princes and rejecting their princes' religion. "Ye have taught the people," said Mary "to receive another religion than that which their princes can allow, and how can that doctrine be of God, seeing that God commandeth subjects to obey their princes?" Knox quoted, in reply, the example of Daniel and his fellows under Nebuchadnezzar and Darius, in the

Old Testament, and of the Apostles under the Roman Emperors, in the New. "But none of these," aptly interposed the Queen, "raised the sword against their princes." "God," rejoined Knox, "had not given to them the power and the means." "But, think ye," persisted Mary, "that subjects having power may thus resist?" Knox, in his illustrations from Scripture had evaded this crucial point; but the Queen's acuteness in reasoning constrained him now to avow a conviction in direct antagonism to the famous compromise of Augsburg in 1555—*cujus regio ejus religio*. He boldly proclaimed the doctrine which is now (at least in most civilised countries) a truism, but was then a paradox, and which the British nation learned only through the fiery ordeals of the seventeenth century—the principle of limited and constitutional monarchy. This doctrine, received by Knox and Buchanan long before from John Major,[1] was now enunciated with great plainness before Mary. "If princes exceed their bounds, and do against that wherefore they should be obeyed, there is no doubt that they may be resisted even with power." Knox illustrates the duty of subject to prince by that of child to parent. A frenzied father might attempt the life of

---

[1] See p. 23. Buchanan afterwards unfolded the doctrine in his *De Jure Regni* (1579)—the possession of which book was declared penal by the Scottish Parliament in 1584; while, a century later, the University of Oxford committed it to the flames. See Hume Brown. *George Buchanan*, 269, 270.

his own children; if the children bound and imprisoned him till the frenzy was passed, would they be doing wrong?

"It is even so with princes that would murder the children of God that are subject to them. Their blind zeal is nothing but a very mad frenzy; and therefore, to take their sword from them, to bind their hands, and to cast themselves into prison till they be brought to a more sober mind, is no disobedience against princes but just obedience, because it agreeth with the Will of God."

Mary was not accustomed to such plain speaking. "She stood as it were amazed"; and at length answered somewhat pettishly, "I perceive my subjects shall obey you and not me." "My travail," said Knox, "is that both princes and subjects obey God." Afterwards, in reply to Knox's reminder that God "craves of kings that they be, as it were, foster-fathers to His Church, and commands queens to be nurses to His people," Mary declared readily, "Yes, but ye are not the Kirk that I will nourish: I will defend the Kirk of Rome; for I think it is the true Kirk of God." Thereupon Knox, after the manner of the polemics of the time, roughly denounced the Roman "harlot." Mary pleaded "conscience"; and when Knox responded that conscience must be enlightened by the Word of God, and proceeded to demonstrate that the mass was unscriptural, Mary dexterously referred to diverse interpretations by different doctors, adding, "Whom shall I believe?" "Ye are owre sair for me," she continued; "but if they were here that I have heard, they would answer you." Knox replied that the "Papists never would come to conference, unless they themselves were admitted for judges"; and that he "would to God the learnedest Papist in Europe were present to sustain the argument." But the Queen, having already heard probably of Ninian Winzet's forthcoming controversial *Tractates*,[1] was able to tell her visitor, "Well, ye may perchance get that sooner than ye believe." The discussion was interrupted by the dinner hour; and Knox who, in spite of roughness of speech, begotten by constant controversy, had the heart of a gentleman, closed the interview with the loyal wish and prayer, in which a virtual surrender of the extreme doctrine of the *Monstrous Regiment* was implied, that the Queen might be "as blessed within the Commonwealth of Scotland as ever Deborah was in the Commonwealth of Israel." His hopelessness, however, as to any change in Mary's attitude to the Reformed Faith was expressed in his emphatic answer to some "familiars" who asked him what he thought of the Queen. "If there be not in her a proud mind, a crafty wit, and an indurate

---

[1] The earliest of these was issued in February, 1562 See Additional Note at the end of this Chapter.

heart against God and His truth, my judgment faileth me." [1]

IV. This first encounter between Queen Mary and Knox is a fair specimen of the relations which existed between them. Four other private interviews are recorded; each, like the first, being on Mary's own invitation, not at Knox's request. The earliest of these was in December, 1562, after a sermon at St. Giles', in which the Reformer had referred to princes that were "more exercised in fiddling and flinging than in reading or hearing of God's most blessed Word." Mary had evidently heard an exaggerated report of the sermon, and was so far appeased by Knox's assurance that he did not "utterly damn" dancing, provided "the principal vocation of those who use that exercise" be not neglected, and the occasion of the dance be not unseasonable.[2] But when she requested that if he heard anything about her that "misliked" him, he would come to herself and tell her; and when she received the rather ungracious answer, that neither his "conscience nor the vocation whereto God hath called" him, permitted him to "wait upon your chamber door or elsewhere, and then to have no further liberty but to whisper my mind in your Grace's ear," Mary "turned her back upon him," offended. Knox overheard, as he left the room, some remark of

---

[1] Knox, *H. of R.*, ii., 286.

[2] News had recently arrived of fresh persecution in France. *Ibid.*, ii., 330.

surprise that he was "not effrayed"; and replied,
with mingled gallantry and scornful unconcern,
"Why should the pleasing face of a gentlewoman
effray me? I have looked on the faces of many
angry men, and yet have not been effrayed above
measure." [1]

The next interview took place four months
afterwards, in April, 1563, in that Castle of Lochleven where, a few years later, Mary was to have
so bitter an experience. At the preceding Easter,
mass had been publicly celebrated, contrary to
law, in various places. When the Government
took no steps to vindicate the statute, some
priests in the south-west country had been appre-
hended by ardent Protestants, who declared that
they would "complain neither to Queen nor to
Council," but would punish the "idolaters by such
means as they might." Mary probably suspected
that Knox was the source of this Protestant ebul-
lition; but she prudently sent for the Reformer
and asked him to assist in its suppression. "She
travailed with him earnestly two hours before supper," he writes, urging him "to persuade the
gentlemen of the west" to leave the priests alone
and not to take "her sword in their hand." Knox
was ready with Old Testament precedents, from
Phineas downwards, for private persons in special
emergencies undertaking magisterial duty; and he
plainly told her Majesty that the remedy lay with

---

[1] Knox, *H. of R.*, ii., 331–335.

herself, viz., to "punish mass-mongers according
to the law." The Queen received his advice in no
good temper; but after a night's reflection, and
some converse probably with her brother (who by
this time had been created Earl of Moray), she
looked at matters, or professed to look at them,
in a different light. She sent for Knox early in
the morning, when she was out hawking. After
"long talk" on various topics, including the offer
of a ring to herself by Lord Ruthven, "whom I
cannot love," and an appeal to Knox for help in
reconciling the Earl and Countess of Argyle, "for
my sake," she reverted to the subject of the previous evening, and dismissed the Reformer with
a promise that she would cause all offenders to
be summoned for trial. He was courteous enough
to assure her that by so doing she would "please
God, and enjoy rest and tranquillity." The Queen
kept her promise. Within about a month forty-
eight "mass-mongers" were tried for breach of the
law, and the majority of these (including Archbishop Hamilton) were "committed to ward."
But Knox became convinced afterwards that this
loyal compliance with the law was "done of a
most deep craft" to allay the suspicion of Protestants, and to dissuade them from trying to
"press the Queen with any other thing concerning matters of religion at the Parliament which
began within two days thereafter." [1]

---

[1] Knox, *H. of R.*, ii., 371–380. Knox candidly records that
at the Lochleven interview the Queen warned him against

The fourth interview between Queen and preacher was the least agreeable of all. It took place in the early summer of 1563, during the sitting of Parliament. Knox had referred in a sermon to a rumour of the Queen's marriage to Don Carlos of Spain. The proposal was seriously entertained by Mary herself, and was believed at the time to be favoured even by some of her Protestant counsellors. The possibility of such a marriage between the Queen of Scots and the son of the arch-persecutor, Philip II., was too much for the Reformer, whose English experience had taught him to dread the issue of a matrimonial alliance with Spain. He declared from the pulpit that "whensoever the nobility of Scotland consent that an 'infidel' shall be head to your sovereign," they will "bring God's vengeance upon the country." Had the Queen been aware at the time of the character of Don Carlos, who appears to have been half imbecile and half monster, she might perhaps have excused Knox's intervention, even although she disliked his reasons. But to one who, amid other more personal aims, had never lost sight of her mission as a prop of the Papacy, the prospect afforded by the Spanish

---

Gordon, ex-Bishop of Galloway (who wished to be made a superintendent) as a "dangerous man." "Therein," writes Knox, "was not the Queen deceived"; and whether he was influenced by Mary's counsel or not, at any rate Gordon, although "the man most familiar with" Knox, was "frustrated of his purpose."

alliance was attractive: and apart from this consideration, Knox's interference with her matrimonial affairs appeared to her as the consummation of meddlesomeness. The preacher was summoned to Holyrood, and was conducted into the royal presence by Erskine of Dun. The Queen, "in a vehement fume," amid threats of vengeance mingled with womanly weeping, demanded indignantly, "What have ye to do with my marriage, and who are ye within this commonwealth?" Knox replied, with dignity, that "albeit neither earl, lord, nor baron," yet had God made him "a profitable member within the same," to whom "it appertains to forewarn of such things as may hurt it"; and for the nobility to consent that their Queen should be "subject to an unfaithful husband" was "to do as much as in them lieth to renounce Christ, to banish the truth from them, to betray the freedom of this realm, and perchance in the end do small comfort to" the Queen herself. Mary's answer, according to Knox, was "inordinate passion" and "tears in abundance." Her emotion was apparently sincere, and Knox was touched. He declared that he had "never delighted in the weeping of any of God's creatures." "I can scarcely well abide the tears of my own boys," he continued, "whom my own hand correcteth, much less can I rejoice in your Majesty's weeping." But "I must sustain, albeit unwillingly," he added, "your Majesty's tears rather than I dare hurt my conscience, or betray my Commonwealth through my silence." The Queen was not appeased. The Reformer was asked to withdraw to the antechamber, where he entertained the "fair ladies of the Court" with discourse upon the transitory character of all earthly things, and upon "that knave death, that will come whether we will or not." After the expiry of an hour, Erskine of Dun came from the Queen to bid him depart to his house until new "advertisement."[1]

V. The last occasion, so far as is certainly known, on which Queen and Reformer met, was of a semi-public character. The meeting took place in December, 1563, when Knox was put on his trial for treason before the Privy Council. Two months previously he had been practically forced to take a bold step, which to timid Protestants appeared dangerous, but was dictated not by rash impulse, but by deliberate policy. During the Queen's absence from Edinburgh, in the summer of 1563, the existing arrangement that mass should be said in Holyrood only in her presence was notoriously disregarded. Two zealous Reformers —Patrick Cranstoun and Andrew Armstrong— openly protested at one of the celebrations against the breach of the law, and on the 24th of October were cited to trial on the charge of violent invasion of the Queen's palace. If these two men

---

[1] Knox, *H. of R.*, ii., 386–389.

were to be punished, the law restricting the celebration of mass would evidently become a dead
letter. Knox, accordingly, wrote and circulated
an epistle to the brethren, asking their "presence,
comfort, and assistance" at Edinburgh on the day
of trial, not only for the protection of the accused, but lest "a door be opened to execute
cruelty on a greater multitude." [1] The case was
postponed until the 13th of November, and no
record of subsequent proceedings appears to have
been preserved. A copy of Knox's letter, however, came under the royal eyes; and amid the
eagerness of the Queen to strike the arch-enemy
of the mass, the trial of the original protesters
was, possibly, departed from. Moray and Maitland, anxious to avoid a rupture with the Queen,
sent for Knox, and endeavoured to persuade him
to humble himself before her for his alleged offence
of "convoking the Queen's lieges" without her
authority. But Knox, firm in the conviction that
he had only done his duty, and fortified by the
private assurance of the Queen's Advocate (John
Spens of Condie) that he had been guilty of no
misdemeanour, replied to the two statesmen that
he had a just defence for all he had done. The
trial, accordingly, proceeded. As Mary entered the
Council chamber, Knox observed her laughing,
and overheard her say to some of her "placebos"
(as he calls them), "Yon man gart me greet, and

---

[1] Knox, *H. of R.*, ii., 393–395.

grat never tear himself; I will see gif I can gar
him greet." She was doomed to disappointment.
"I am in the place where I am demanded of conscience to speak the truth," Knox declared, in the
course of the proceedings, "and therefore the
truth I speak, impugn it whoso list." He was
able to plead numerous precedents for "convocation of the lieges" during the Reformation
struggle: and, indeed, every Sunday he con-
voked them to his preaching. The real and only
question was whether the purpose of convocation
were lawful. The Queen endeavoured to shew
the treasonable character of Knox's action by
quoting the warning in his letter about a door
being opened to execute cruelty, and by suggesting that the Reformer had ascribed such cruelty
to herself. But the accused had no difficulty in
showing that the warning was intended to refer
not to the Queen, but to those "pestilent papists"
who desired the extermination of "all such as
profess the Evangel of Jesus Christ," and who had
inflamed without cause her Majesty "against
those poor men." The trial ended in the discomfiture of the Queen. Knox was acquitted by almost all the members of the Council, including
even a personal enemy, Henry Sinclair, Catholic
Bishop of Ross, and President of the Court of
Session. On being sarcastically upbraided by the
Queen, Sinclair replied that "neither affection to
the man nor love to his profession moved" him

"to absolve him, but the simple truth which appeared in his defence." Had the Council condemned Knox on this occasion, the majority would have condemned themselves.[1]

The antagonism of the Queen to Knox was intensified by his marriage, in March, 1564, to Margaret Stewart, daughter of Lord Ochiltree, a maiden of seventeen. The young bride seems to have been warmly attached to her husband, who was thrice as old as herself [2]: and there is no reason to believe that the union, although out of accord with general sentiment, was other than a happy one. Mary's indignation was excited, not by the disparity of age, but by what she regarded as the Reformer's presumption in allying himself, even remotely, with the royal family. "The Queen" —so the English ambassador reported—"stormeth wonderfully; for that she [Margaret Stewart] is of the blood and name."[3]

VI. In reviewing the earlier relations of Knox with Mary, we must not lose sight of the constant

---

[1] Knox, *H. of R.*, ii., 398–412; Calderw., *H. of the K.*, ii., 233. The later relations between the Queen and Knox will be referred to in Chapter XII.

[2] "By sorcery and witchcraft," writes Nicol Burne, a Catholic detractor of Knox, "he did so allure that poor gentlewoman that *she could not live without him*" (T. Graves Law, *Cath. Tractates*, p. 162). We hear little of Margaret Stewart's wedded life with Knox except her ministration to him on his death-bed. Three daughters were born of the marriage.

[3] Laing, *W. of K.*, vi., 533.

danger which overhung the Reformation during
the period of her personal reign in Scotland. That
peril, always existing, became manifest, as we
shall find, at the time of the Queen's marriage
with Darnley, when the power of the Protestant
leaders, both lay and clerical, was for a time
paralysed: and this temporary paralysis, which,
but for Mary's own folly, might have been permanent, justified Knox in his attitude of persistent
and unbending opposition to the Queen. This
opposition could not but manifest itself in
unpalatable testimony. The issues at stake required a plain-spoken prophet, not a smooth-
tongued courtier. It may be admitted, however,
that the Reformer, even on his own shewing,
while rendering due respect to his Sovereign in
personal intercourse, sometimes failed in consideration for her difficult position, as well as
conscientious convictions, and was needlessly as
well as unwisely repellent and unsympathetic.
Did he thus miss the chance of removing the
young Queen's prejudice, and even of influencing
her character and policy? That long interview
at Lochleven, when he was "oft willing to tack
his leave," but when she detained him with
confidential converse about a domestic trouble
in which she asked his aid, and even about a
love-affair connected with herself, suggests that
although Mary regarded Knox as her chief antagonist, she was not insensible to that underlying

sympathy which, in spite of superficial hardness, attracted to the Reformer the confiding regard both of men and of women. What, then, prevented Knox, in his earlier intercourse with the Queen, from seeking to win, rather than merely to withstand? To a man who believed in the grace of God and in his own power as God's minister, her "indurate heart" could, at the outset have been no adequate deterrent. May not his demeanour towards Mary be accounted for, to some extent, by the supposition that in the earlier part, at least, of her reign, he was not without some fear of her power of fascination, and that he steeled himself against it by adopting an aspect of unsympathetic harshness, which misrepresented his true nature? We know from the Reformer's intercourse and correspondence with Mrs. Bowes and Mrs. Locke, that he was far from being impervious to womanly influence; and his courtship of Margaret Stewart shows, what he himself once indicated, that he had a full appreciation of "the pleasing face of a gentlewoman." The occasional relaxation, moreover, of his attitude to the Queen, even at interviews when he was, on the whole, stern, points to a kindlier, gentler, and more real self behind the demeanour of rough severity which, for his own protection, he felt himself constrained to assume. Eventually, however, Knox's heart became wholly hardened against her: and towards the adulterous accomplice, as he believed, of her husband's murderer, his feeling was that of deep detestation.

ADDITIONAL NOTE TO CHAPTER X

John Knox and Roman Catholic Controversialists

1. Knox's encounter with Principal Anderson and (the future) Bishop Lesley has been already related.[1]

2. Ninian Winzet was one of the most estimable of the clergy who adhered at the Reformation to the Roman Church. He was Headmaster of Linlithgow School, and Provost of the Collegiate Church of the town. His significant admission as to the ignorance and vicious lives of the "maist part" of the clergy has already been recorded [2] but he was a strenuous opponent of Protestantism. He appears to have held a public discussion at Linlithgow with Knox regarding the mass, during a visit of the latter to the town in June, 1559. After the Reformation he was ejected for nonconformity. He came under Queen Mary's notice soon after her return to Scotland, and was probably one of her domestic chaplains at Holyrood. In February, 1562, he received permission from the Queen to address the Protestant leaders. He did so in a series of controversial Letters and Tractates, in which, among other subjects, he raises the question whether John Knox were a lawful minister, seeing that he had renounced and declared to be null his Roman ordination. Knox published no reply, contenting himself with pulpit references, in

---

[1] See page 253.

[2] See page 15.

which he declared that, like John the Baptist, he had been "extraordinarily called." Winzet's attacks upon Protestantism culminated in his "Last Blast of the Trumpet of God's Word against the usurped authority of John Knox and his Calvinian brethren," printed in July, 1562. The work was seized by the authorities as seditious, and Winzet had to flee to the Continent, where he renewed the controversy with his "Four Score Three Questions." Eventually he became Abbot of the ancient Scoto-Irish monastery at Ratisbon.[1]

3. On the occasion of a visit of Knox to Ayrshire in September, 1562, a disputation was arranged between the Reformer and Quintin Kennedy, Abbot of Crossraguel in that county, and a son of the Earl of Cassilis. The Abbot had previously signalised himself as a champion of the Roman Church by the issue, in 1558, of a "Compendious Tractive" in which Scripture is described as only the witness, and the Church (represented by Council or Pope) as the judge in all questions regarding the Faith. More recently, in 1561, he had published a belated reply to Knox's address at Newcastle before the Council of the North, in 1550. The disputation was held in the house of the Provost of Maybole, before a large company of Catholic and Protestant nobles and gentlemen, and it lasted three days. It was agreed that the first subject of controversy should be the mass: and the discussion began well; for the Abbot, after a preliminary *caveat* that he was not to be held as acknowledging that what General Councils had determined was really disputable, announced, to the

---

[1] Hewison, *Ninian Winzet*, i., Introduction and pp. 35, 47.

Reformer's satisfaction, that he would maintain and
"defend no mass, as concerning the substance, institution, and effect, but that mass only which was
instituted by Christ." He defined the mass to be
"the sacrifice and oblation of the Lord's Body and
Blood"; and promised that his arguments would be
grounded "upon the Scripture of Almighty God as
his warrant." But when he insisted on discussing, as
his first scriptural testimony, the bread and wine of
Melchizedek as a type of the oblation made by Christ
at the Last Supper, the disputation drifted into the
subordinate question whether Melchizedek's bread
and wine were intended to be a sacrifice offered to
God, as the Abbot contended, or a refreshment offered
to men, as Knox maintained. For the better part of
two days this minor point was discussed. In vain,
on the third day, according to his own account, at
least, the Reformer endeavoured to bring back the
disputation to the main question, viz., whether the
mass, as celebrated in the Roman Church, has or
has not "approbation of the plain Word of God."
The auditors, apparently, had become utterly
wearied, and pleaded that they were "altogether
destitute of all provision both for horse and man."
The Abbot agreed to resume the discussion in Edinburgh if the Queen permitted; but no resumption
actually took place, and within two years Kennedy
died.[1]

4. Ten years after his encounter with Kennedy,
Knox wrote a reply to the letter of a Scottish Jesuit,
James Tyrie. The circumstances and nature of this
controversy will be detailed in Chapter XIII.

---

[1] Laing, *W. of K.*, vi., 151, 220.

19

CHAPTER XI

AMID general agreement between Knox and the lay leaders of the Scottish Reformation upon the vital question of dethroning Romanism and establishing Protestantism, there was serious divergence of opinion on several important points affecting the success of the Protestant movement and the well-being of the Reformed Church.

I. So early as 1555, after Knox's first return from exile, the question of principle against expediency, of thoroughness against compromise in reformation, had been involved in the discussion which then arose as to whether Protestants ought, or ought not, to continue their attendance at mass. The divergence reappeared in 1559, after the Reformer's final return, in the earlier support given to the prosecuted preachers by Knox, along with the Earl of Glencairn and Erskine of Dun, against the more cautious attitude adopted by Lord James Stewart, the Earl of Argyle, and Maitland, who believed that the Reformation of the Church and the liberty of preaching might be obtained by peaceful means, until the duplicity of the Regent united the Reformers in the policy of resistance. The cleavage manifested itself again, at a later stage, during the interval between the establishment of the Reformation and the return of the Queen, in regard to the question of the Church's patrimony.

II. On the return of Queen Mary from France in August, 1561, the divergence between Knox and the statesmen, who were led by Lord James Stewart and Maitland, once more came to the surface. 1. Knox, the man of principle, thoroughly convinced that his cause was that of God, and must ultimately prevail, would have administered consistently the law which made the mass penal. In his view, the Queen's "liberty should be their thraldom ere it was long"; a bold and faithful course was the only true and safe policy. The "principal ministers" supported their leader, but "the votes of the Lords did prevail against" them.[1] The leading Protestant laymen, apart from that fascination which a young and beautiful Queen exerted over some of their number in the earlier years of her reign, had less faith both in their cause and in their countrymen. They believed that if Mary were prevented from worshipping God according to the faith and rites in which she

---

[1] Knox, *H. of R.*, ii., 292.

had been brought up, she would be constrained to ally herself with the reactionary party which aimed at the restoration of Romanism; and this party would be strengthened, while the Protestant cause would be weakened, by the parade which would be made of needless hardship imposed on the Queen. Knox acknowledged no real power save that of God, and believed that if the leaders of the Reformation were faithful to God's truth they would ultimately triumph. The Lords of the Congregation, as men of the world, recognised that, rightly or wrongly, Mary was a power in the land; and they desired by timely concessions to retain her, so far and so long as was possible, on their own side.

2. Statesmen like Moray and Maitland, moreover, were largely influenced by the political purposes associated with their ecclesiastical aims. They discerned in the union of England and Scotland a consummation inevitable as well as desirable; and they were anxious that the union should be accomplished in circumstances as favourable as possible to their native land. Mary Stuart was the nearest heir to the English throne. Her ambition to be Queen of both kingdoms united her policy, so far, with theirs; and they trusted to her gradually realising that, in order to secure her succession to the English realm, it was indispensable for her to relinquish the Roman faith. They could not achieve their purpose without Mary's co-operation; they were

ready, accordingly, meanwhile, to make concessions as to her personal religious profession, in
order to retain her alliance; and they hoped that
the prospect of the double crown, along with a
Protestant marriage, would render those concessions ultimately unnecessary. For men like Knox,
such political scheming had no attraction. He
sympathised, doubtless, with the desire for union
with England as a guarantee for the continuance
of Scottish Protestantism; but to surrender truth
and to countenance "idolatry" for any mere political object, or even for a religious as well as political benefit, could not but appear to so thorough a
Reformer as "traffic with Satan" and doing evil
that good might come.

3. Another occasion of contention between
churchmen and statesmen was supplied by the
powers claimed for the General Assembly. Those
whose policy was to prevent an open rupture between Queen and Church foresaw the peril to
peace which the Assembly involved. When the
time, accordingly, of the half-yearly meeting in
December arrived, after Mary's return, Maitland
denied the power of churchmen "to assemble
themselves, and to keep conventions" without
the allowance of the Queen." "Take from us
the freedom of Assemblies," was Knox's memorable answer, "and you take from us the Evangel.
Without Assemblies, how shall good order and
unity in doctrine be kept?" When complaint was

made that the leading laymen were not taken into
confidence by the clerical members of Assembly,
the latter retorted that the Lords no longer, as
before, " kept convention " with the ministers.[1]

4. The Protestant statesmen differed yet further from Knox as to the proper way of speaking
about the Queen.   Knox did not scruple, after he
had abandoned the hope of Mary's conversion, to
refer to Queen Mary as "the slave of Satan" and
to the divine "vengeance" as hanging over the
realm by reason of her impiety.   From a man
of earnest character, who sincerely believed that
the mass was idolatrous and offensive to God, and
who discerned that the example of the Queen was
drawing many of her subjects into sinful conformity, what else could be expected?   He continued, indeed, to pray for his Sovereign at public
worship; but to the supplication, " Illuminate her
heart," the suggestive condition was added, "Gif
Thy good pleasure be."   To men like Maitland
who, although Protestants by conviction, were not
prepared to stigmatise Romanism as impiety, such
language appeared to be a "rousing of the heart
of her people against her Majesty, and against
them that serve her." [2]

III. The crisis of divergence was reached in the
early summer of 1563, when the first Parliament
after Queen Mary's return was held.[3]   Knox hoped

---

[1] Knox, *H. of R.*, ii., 294–297.

[2] *Ibid.*, ii., 427–431.

[3] Mary's advisers postponed as long as possible the meeting

that advantage would be taken of this occasion to
put the Reformed Church on a firmer constitutional
basis, and to legalise the Book of Discipline; or
at least to secure a more adequate sustenance for
the Protestant clergy[1] and a more faithful administration of the statutes against the mass. To the
Reformer's disappointment and disgust, the Lords
were in no mood to "urge the Queen," in case she
might refuse to hold a Parliament at all. With
what appeared to Knox miserable pusillanimity,
they counselled the postponement of any demands from Mary in the ecclesiastical sphere until
her expected marriage approached. It would
then—so it was argued—be easier to make conditions with her, in return for grants and privileges solicited by her: and the "first thing that
should be established" would be the "Reformed
Religion." [2] Knox showed his disappointment

---

of the Estates, to avoid the inconvenient discussion of
"affairs in Church and State."

[1] Early in 1562, the Privy Council assigned one-third of the
ecclesiastical patrimony to the crown and to the ministers;
the remaining two-thirds being left in the possession of the
Roman clergy until the death of the existing beneficiaries.
The share allocated to the Reformed ministers was about
24,000 pounds Scots, out of which were paid stipends of 100
to 300 merks, ($£5$, 11s, 1d to $£16$, 13s, 4d); the purchasing
power of money, however, being probably twelve times as
great as at present. Poorer ministers complained that
"neither were they able to live on the stipends appointed,
*neither could they get payment of that small thing that was
appointed.*" (Knox, *H. of R.*, ii., 307–311.)

[2] *Ibid.*, ii., 382.

and indignation in a sermon preached at St. Giles' during the session of Parliament. He "poured forth the sorrow of his heart"; plainly declared that the Lords of the Congregation were "betraying God's cause" when they had it "in their own hands to establish it"; and could see in their procedure "nothing but a reculling [relapse] from Christ Jesus."[1]

IV. At the ensuing General Assembly (June, 1564), from which "the lords that depended on the Court" were conspicuously absent, an attempt was made, through a private conference between politicians and preachers, to arrive at a common understanding. Maitland was the chief speaker on the one side, Knox on the other. Two points were discussed. The first was the general question whether a subject could lawfully resist his sovereign. Maitland appealed to Romans xiii., 1 ("Whosoever resisteth the power resisteth the ordinance of God"); and demanded to know how the "person placed in authority may be resisted, and God's ordinance not transgressed." Knox had not forgotten his scholastic training under Major. He drew a distinction between the divine ordinance of government and the individual human administrator. The former was "constant, stable, perpetual," and therefore unalterably binding. But particular "men, clothed with their authority," are "mutable, transitory, sub-

---

[1] Knox, *H. of R.*, ii., 384, 385.

ject to corruption"; therefore the prince who abuses his authority "may be resisted," while "yet the ordinance of God is not violated." Maitland quoted the opinions of Luther and Melanchthon, but was informed that what they opposed was the doctrine of "Anabaptists who deny that Christians should be subject to magistrates" at all; and Knox was able to produce a copy of the famous Apology of Magdeburg, drawn up in 1550 by its clergy in defence of the citizens, when these opposed the Emperor, Charles V. The Apology declared that "to resist a tyrant is not to resist God nor yet his ordinance." Let.1ington glanced over the document and the list of signatures. "Homines obscuri!" was his scornful comment; to which Knox gave the memorable answer, "Dei tamen servi." [1]

The second question discussed at the conference was more specific, viz., whether they might "take the Queen's mass from her." On this point the clergy as well as the laity were divided. Douglas, the Rector of St. Andrews University, and Wynram, Superintendent of Fife, followed by a majority of the nobility, maintained that if the Queen "opposed herself to the only true religion," they might "justly oppose themselves to her." "As concerning her own mass," however, they were "not yet resolved whether by violence we may take it from her, or not." On the other hand,

---

[1] Knox, *H. of R.*, ii., 435, 436, 442, 453, 454.

Knox and his colleague, Craig, led a party which
reasoned that "as the mass was abomination, so
it was just and right that it should be suppressed;
and that in so doing men did no more wrong to
the Queen's Majesty than they that should by
force take from her a poisoned cup when she was
going to drink it." The conference broke up
without any formal decision: the divergence of
view had not been lessened, but rather emphasised; and Knox declares that after that time the
ministers that were called "precise" were "held
of all the courtiers as monsters." [1]

V. Particularly notable and detrimental to
the Reformed Church was the estrangement
between Knox and Moray. Referring to the
period immediately preceding the Parliament of
May, 1563, Knox writes that "the matter fell
so hot between the Earl of Moray and John Knox,
that familiarly after that time they spake not
together more than a year and a half." The Reformer wrote to the statesman a letter, in which
"he gave a discharge to the said Earl of all further intromission or care with his affairs." He
reminds him, not without pathos, "in what
estate he was when first they spake together
in London" ten years before; and he recalls
"how God had promoted him [Moray] and that
above men's judgment," so that now "I leave
you victor of your enemies," advanced "to great

---

[1] Knox, *H. of R.*, ii., 454-461.

honours," and "in credit and authority with your
Sovereign." He had hoped that Moray would
"ever have preferred God " to " his own affection,"
and the "advancement of God's truth" to his own
"commodity." But he, Knox, had been "frustrate in this my expectation." "If after this"—
so the letter concludes—"ye shall decay, as I fear
that ye shall, then call to mind by what means
God exalted you; which was neither by bearing
with impiety neither yet by maintaining of pestilent Papists." [1]   Knox admits that his altered
relations with Moray were an occasion of "triumph" to those who "envied that so great familiarity was between the said Earl" and himself;
and he charges them with ceasing not "to cast
oil on the burning flame." A quarrel between
the chief Protestant noble and the leading Reformed minister must obviously have weakened
the cause to which both were attached.   It helped
to pave the way for a temporary Roman reaction.

VI. The estrangement between Moray and Knox
arose from difference of standpoint and aim. 1.
Both were patriotic politicians and sincere Reformers; but the one was a keen statesman who
attached himself to the Protestant cause; the
other was an ardent Reformer, constrained by
his religious zeal to ally himself with a political
party. Moray's chief aim in the interval between
1561 and 1565 was to strengthen Mary Stuart's

---

[1] Knox, *H. of R.*, ii., 382, 383.

government and her chance of peaceful succession to the English throne. With this view he promoted a policy which would satisfy the more moderate Protestants both of England and of Scotland, without either driving Scottish Romanists into rebellion, or cooling the zeal of English Romanists into political apathy. So long, therefore, as the Protestant ascendency in Scotland did not appear to be imperilled, he wished to be as tolerant towards Catholics as was practicable. He seems, moreover, to have hoped that Mary would be eventually persuaded to conciliate Elizabeth by a Protestant matrimonial alliance, and even to co-operate actively in completing the work of organising the Reformed Church, if not to become a Protestant herself.[1] Knox, on the other hand, was a Reformer first and principally; a politician only in so far as the politics of the time had important bearings on religion. His aim was to make not only the government but the people thoroughly Protestant: and so long as a Catholic

[1] Maitland, with whom at this period Moray was in accord, wrote on 25th October, 1561, to Sir William Cecil about Mary: "I see in her [Mary] a good towardness, and think that the Queen your Sovereign shall be able to do much with her in religion, if they ever enter on a good familiarity (Laing, *W. of K.*, vi., 137). Randolph writes to Cecil (January, 1562) that it was reported that even the Cardinal of Lorraine was content that the Queen (of Scotland) should "embrace the religion of England" (*ibid.*, vi., 138); and Randolph personally was not without hope that Mary "may in time be called to the knowledge of His truth, or at least not have that force to suppress His evangell here" (vi., 147).

Pulpit from which Knox is believed to have preached
in St. Giles's. (Now in the National Museum
of Antiquities, Edinburgh.)

leaven was tolerated, he feared the increase of its influence, and trembled for the spiritual safety of the nation as a whole. He preferred internal conflict with all its hazards, while a Protestant ascendency was maintained, to internal peace which would give Romanists the opportunity of recovering their strength, increasing their numbers, and preparing for a future struggle. 2. On the subject of the Queen's marriage the views of Moray and Knox were less divergent than the latter probably supposed. It is very unlikely that either Moray or Maitland ever approved, any more than Knox himself, of Mary's contemplated marriage to Don Carlos of Spain.[1] They were not unwilling, however, for strategic reasons, to give some diplomatic consideration to the proposal. It was expedient to bring home to Elizabeth that unless a marriage approved both by England and Scotland were speedily contracted by the Scottish Queen, a matrimonial alliance hostile to English interests might be arranged by Mary and her counsellors.[2] Knox either did not understand

---

[1] Knox states that Maitland was "not a little offended that any bruit should have risen of the Queen's marriage with the King [Prince] of Spain."—*H. of R.*, ii., 390.

[2] In a letter of Kirkcaldy to Randolph, of date April, 1654, Maitland is represented as stating that "all that was spoken of the marriage with Spain was done to cause England grant to our desires" (Laing, *W. of K.*, vi., 540). This policy of the Scottish statesmen produced some effect; for, in March, 1564, Elizabeth suggested the Protestant Lord Dudley as a suitable husband for Mary (Keith, *Affairs of Ch. and St.*, ii.,

this diplomacy; or, if he did, condemned a duplicity which accustomed the people to the
thought of their Sovereign marrying a Catholic.
3. Knox appears to have had no such hope as
Moray and other statesmen seem to have cherished,
of the Queen's permanent acquiescence in the ascendency of Protestantism in Scotland as well as
in England. Himself regarding religion as above
politics, he gave Mary Stuart the credit of a
resolution never really to sacrifice the Roman
Church even to her own political aspirations. To
him, accordingly, all humouring of the Queen
with a view to her ultimate surrender of the hope
of re-establishing Romanism was a vain policy
which would issue certainly in disappointment
and, possibly, in disaster.[1]

The breach between Knox and Moray was
closed about the time of the Queen's marriage
with Darnley, when the statesman became an
exile and the Reformer the leader of a depressed

----

224); and this alliance would have satisfied both Knox and
Moray; but Elizabeth would not commit herself (in the event
of the marriage) to the nomination of Mary as her successor;
and this was indispensable to the alliance being approved by
the political advisers of the Scottish Queen.

[1] Randolph wrote to Cecil on the 16th December, 1562,
that Knox "is so full of mistrust in all her [Mary's] doings,
words, and sayings as though he were either of God's privy
council, . . . or that he knew the secrets of her heart so
well that neither she did or could have for ever one good
thought of God or of His true religion."—Laing, W. of K.,
vi., 146.

Church. Common misfortune, apparently, was the means of healing discord. The "burning flame of contention ceased not to burn until God, by water of affliction, began to slocken it." [1] Knox, moreover, on the one side, realised that if Moray had been a lukewarm promoter of Protestantism, he had been an effective protector of Protestant preachers: Moray, on the other hand, had to acknowledge that if Knox's policy of "thorough" might have led to civil war, his own policy of compromise had issued in grave detriment and peril both to Church and State.

---

[1] Knox, *H. of R.*, ii., 303.

CHAPTER XII

1565-1568

THE brief period of two years between Mary
Stuart's marriage to Darnley in July, 1565,
and her abdication at Lochleven in July, 1567,
constitutes the chief crisis not only of the Queen's
life, but of Scottish Protestantism. Mary found
and lost an opportunity of inaugurating, if not of
accomplishing, an ecclesiastical revolution. The
Reformed Church of Scotland, bereft for a while
of its political protectors, owed its safety, under
divine Providence, to Knox's influence over the
people and to the Queen's passion and folly.

I. In 1564, at the suggestion of Elizabeth, the
Earl of Lennox, who had been banished for treason in 1545, was allowed to return to Scotland
and to reclaim his forfeited estates. In the following spring, his son Darnley, a great-grandson,
through his mother, of Henry VII., and next to
Mary herself in the line of the English succession,

was also encouraged by both Queens to return to
his native land.[1]   From the outset it was generally believed that the restoration of Lennox was
connected with a proposed marriage between
Mary and Darnley.   Moray and Maitland were
under the impression that Elizabeth favoured the
union; and they probably reckoned upon Darnley, who was a Catholic, but not particularly zealous, being willing to change his faith if conversion
were eventually to be rewarded with two thrones.
Darnley's first night in Scotland, the 10th of
February, was spent at Lethington, as Maitland's
guest.[2]   Within a fortnight he had "heard Knox
preach, supped with Moray, and danced with the
Queen." [3]   Within a month, Mary Stuart's willingness to consider him as a future husband on
political grounds had been overshadowed by a
personal predilection, which speedily developed
into passion.   Unexpectedly Elizabeth raised
difficulties.   Until she herself married, or had resolved not to marry, the succession to the English throne must remain unsettled; she objected,
moreover, to the marriage with Darnley as prejudicial to "Mary and herself" and "dangerous
to the weal of both countries." [4]   The attitude
of the Queen of England affected the policy of
Moray and Maitland.   The marriage, it now

---

[1] A. Lang, *H. of Sc.*, ii., 136; Bain, *Cal.* ii., 124–127.

[2] Skelton, *Life of Maitland*, ii., 144.

[3] A. Lang, *H. of Sc.*, ii., 137.

[4] Knox, *H. of R.*, ii., 474; Froude, *H. of E.*, vii., 269.
20

appeared, instead of promoting, would hinder the
recognition of Mary as Elizabeth's successor, and
might imperil the alliance of the two realms;
while, as regards Scotland, the motive to Darnley's conversion being now removed, the marriage
would be a cause of offence to the Protestant party.
Moray, accordingly, exerted his influence against
the nuptials: in addition to political and ecclesiastical considerations, he had probably by this
time discerned Darnley's overbearing character and his unfitness for the position of royal
Consort.[1] Maitland, more cautious, endeavoured
to persuade the Queen to "make no haste in the
matter."[2] But Mary had resolved to set personal before political considerations. By this
time, moreover, the influence of David Rizzio,
her private secretary, superseded that of former
counsellors; and Rizzio warmly espoused the
cause of the man who afterwards became his
assassin. A convention of the Scottish nobility
at Stirling on the 15th of May gave its approval
to the proposed marriage, and the nuptials were
celebrated in Holyrood Chapel on the 29th of
July, 1565.[3] Moray, along with other nobles and
gentry, including Châtelherault, Glencairn, Ochiltree, and Kirkcaldy of Grange, trusting to English help which never came, raised an insurrection

---

[1] Tytler, vi., 378, 390.
[2] Ibid., vi., 386 (letter of Randolph to Cecil, 30th March).
[3] Ibid., v., 393, 394.

Greyfriars' Church, Stirling, where Knox preached on the occasion of the Coronation of James VI. in 1567.
(Now East and West Churches.)

first to prevent and then to protest against the marriage, but their enterprise received scant support: they were proclaimed outlaws, and had to flee into England.[1]

II. What was Knox's attitude towards the royal marriage? We have seen that when the alliance with Don Carlos was in contemplation, he declared in St. Giles' that to allow the Queen to wed a Romanist was equivalent to the banishment of Christ from the kingdom. The objection was equally applicable to the case of Darnley; and the opposition of Knox and Moray (even although from different standpoints) to a marriage which both regarded as detrimental to the State and perilous for the Church, contributed, doubtless, at this period to their reconciliation.

While statesman and Reformer, however, were agreed as to the danger which the marriage involved, they differed widely in the steps which they took to meet the emergency. Moray and his friends raised a petty and fruitless insurrection: there is no evidence that it received any actual support from Knox. The Reformer used the opportunity to testify afresh against "papistry," and to warn Church and State against unseasonable toleration. Although his name is not specially mentioned in connexion with the General Assembly of June, 1565, we may with

[1] Continuation of Knox, *H. of R.*, ii., 496; Burton, *H. of Sc.*, ii., 123.

confidence ascribe to Knox's suggestion its main procedure. If the Queen was resolved to marry a Romanist, without parliamentary approval, then let the Church renew her demand for the long-postponed ratification of the Protestant statutes of 1560; and, in accordance therewith, let the "papistical and blasphemous mass be suppressed throughout the realm, and that not only in the subjects, but in the Queen's Majesty's own person." [1] Probably no member of Assembly expected the Queen herself to renounce the mass; but it was regarded as important at this juncture to remind both Court and nation that the rite was illegal; and to the Assembly's testimony may, perhaps, be attributed the withdrawal of Darnley from the chapel, after his marriage, when mass was about to be celebrated. Three weeks later, with a view, presumably, to propitiate Protestants, yet without renouncing Romanism, the young King attended service in St. Giles'. Knox's sermon did not tempt him to return. He heard his own and the Queen's co-religionists repeatedly described as "pestilent Papists." A parallel also appeared to be suggested by the preacher between Darnley and Ahab, between Mary and Jezebel: and a significant reference was made to "boys and women being sent as tyrants and scourges to plague the people for their sins." [2]

[1] Calderw., *H. of Kirk*, ii., 287–289.

[2] The sermon was published, and is contained in Laing, *W. of K.*, vi., 233–273. In the evening of the day on which

The Pulpit in the Greyfriars' Church, Stirling, from which Knox
preached the sermon on the occasion of the Coronation of
James VI., in 1567. (Now in a side-room of the church.)

If we are inclined to think that the Church
might have been more tolerant, and Knox more
conciliatory, it is fair to remember that Scotland
was then passing through an ecclesiastical crisis,
and that the very existence of the Scottish Reformed Church appeared to be at stake.   Continental Catholic powers were laying aside mutual
jealousies, and were prepared to unite in accomplishing the suppression of Protestantism.[1]   The
numerous and powerful Catholics in the northern
English counties were believed to be ready for
co-operation.[2]   Mary had succeeded in driving
from her Court and Council the more zealous Protestant statesmen, and in replacing them with

---

he had preached, Knox was summoned from his bed before
the Privy Council, at royal instigation.   Darnley had come
home " crabbit " (*Diurn. of Occ.*, 81).   The Reformer declared
that "he had spoken nothing but according to his text"
(Knox, *H. of R.*, ii., 497, 498; Laing, *W. of K.*, vi., 230).   In a
marginal gloss, inserted apparently by David Buchanan,
Knox is represented as adding that "as the King (to pleasure
the Queen) had gone to mass, so should God make her an
instrument of his ruin"; whereupon "the Queen being in-
censed fell out in tears."   But Mary does not appear to have
been present; and the gloss is probably an alleged *vati-
cinium post eventum*.   The Reformer was ordered to abstain from preaching so long as their Majesties remained in
Edinburgh; but as they left the city very soon after, the
prohibition was little more than nominal (*Diurn. of Occ.*).

[1] The Catholic League of 1565 was not consummated until
the autumn of that year, but arrangements with a view to it
had already been made (Burton, *H. of Sc.*, iv., 135, 136;
Tytler, *H. of Sc.*, vii., 18).

[2] Burton, *H. of Sc.*, vii., 131.

men not unfavourable to the restoration of Romanism. She had told Knox plainly, long before, that she meant to maintain and defend the Church of Rome [1]; and her private correspondence with continental Courts and potentates reveals that she had been encouraged by others, and herself hoped to inaugurate a Catholic reaction.[2] The marriage with Darnley appeared to Knox not as a mere love match, but as part of an extensive Romanist conspiracy.[3] Even in itself the marriage was objectionable. It was one thing for Scottish Protestants to tolerate a Catholic Queen who was the legitimate heir to the throne; it was another thing to acknowledge as royal Consort one whose presence and high station would enhance the influence of the Court against the Reformation.

III. Few details are known of Knox's life and work between his sermon before Darnley in August, 1565, and the General Assembly which met in the end of that year. But one outstanding fact is recorded. Although the Reformer had no share in the recent insurrection, he appears to have chivalrously stood by those who were at one with him in condemning the Queen's marriage as peril-

---

[1] See above, page 274.

[2] Labanoff, *Lettres de Marie Stuart*, i., 176, 177, 281, 343, 345, 356.

[3] Before Darnley's return, Knox wrote to Randolph, the English ambassador, in reference to the proposed restoration of Lennox and his son: "To be plain with you, that journey and progress I like not."—Laing, *W. of K.*, vi., 541.

ous to the Reformed Church. In his services at St. Giles' he prayed for the banished lords, and spoke of them as "the best part of the nobility." [1] The autumn and early winter of 1565 were among the most "dolorous" periods of Knox's public life. The Queen, emboldened by her success against the nobility and gentry, "began to declare herself in the months of November and December to be a maintainer of Papists." Influential nobles "went to mass openly in her Chapel." Catholics "flocked to Edinburgh for making Court." Friars received permission to preach publicly in the capital. "The faithful in the realm were in great fear, looking for nothing but great trouble and persecution to be shortly." [2]

In these depressing circumstances the General Assembly was convened on the 25th of December. One chief part of the proceedings was to arrange for a solemn Fast, on two successive Sundays, in order to escape "the plagues and scourges of God." Knox and his colleague, Craig, were appointed to "set down the form of exercise to be used." [3] It was the first national Fast since the

---

[1] Some of the Privy Council would have had Knox brought to trial for encouragement of rebellion; but Maitland, who was present at the services, testified that "nothing was spoken whereat any man need to be offended"; and he reminded his fellow Councillors that Scripture bids us "pray for all men."—Knox, *H. of R.* ii., 514.

[2] *Ibid.*, ii., 515, 516.

[3] The Fast was to be on the last Sunday of February and the first Sunday of March. It was to be held from 8 P.M. on

Reformation. Its appointment was grounded partly on the peril of the Reformed Church in Scotland as the outcome of national "sin and ingratitude," "declension and carnal wisdom"; partly on the dark prospect for evangelical truth throughout Christendom. At home, "that idol of the mass is now again in divers places erected." "Some whom God made sometime instruments to suppress that impiety have been the chief to conduct that idol throughout the realm." The Queen had signified "in plain words that the religion in which she had been nourished, and which is mere abomination, she shall maintain and defend." Abroad the outlook was no less gloomy. "The Council of Trent had concluded that all such as are of the new religion shall be utterly exterminated"; "the whisperings whereof are not secret, neither yet the tokens obscure." [1]

It was a critical time, indeed, as we have already seen, at once for the Scottish Reformation and for Protestant Christendom. The eyes of Europe were turned, with hope or with fear, towards the young Queen of Scots who had recently released herself from bondage to Protestant counsellors. If, at this period, Mary Stuart was restrained from taking fully and effectively the part in favour of Rome to which the Catholic League and

---

each Saturday until 5 P.M. on the Sunday; but even at the latter hour food was to be limited to "bread and drink."

[1] Calderw., *H. of K.*, ii., 303–306. The order of the Fast is contained in Laing, *W. of K.*, vi., 381–430.

her own ambitious zeal alike prompted her; if, at this crisis, the Scottish Reformed Church, although depressed, was not suppressed, and the Scottish State was preserved from becoming the tool of continental Romanism against English Protestantism,—the prevention of these issues was mainly due to the stirring power and educative influence of Knox's preaching and policy. The Reformer had created and maintained in Scotland such a force of popular antagonism to Rome as the Queen dared not ignore, much less provoke into conflict.[1] The resolute spirit of the Church under Knox's leadership in this time of trial is illustrated by two commissions given to the Reformer by the General Assembly. On the one hand, a discreditable withholdment of ministerial stipends by the Exchequer having been reported, Knox composed, by order of the Assembly, a pithy pastoral to the "Faithful in the realm," exhorting them to let "the bowels of their mercy be opened," and not to let the "Papists rejoice over us that our niggardliness banished Jesus Christ from us."[2] On the other hand, not

[1] See Moncrieff, "Influence of Knox and the Scottish Reformation on England," pp. 33–36 (*Exeter H. Lectures*, 1859–60).

[2] Knox, *H. of R.*, ii., 518; Laing, *W. of K.*, vi., 431–436. Simultaneously, an address on the subject was presented to the Queen; and the grievance was remedied, although tardily; for at the second Assembly after, in December, 1566, an "assignation of money and victuals" is acknowledged as an instalment of what "justly pertaineth to the patrimony of the Church."—Calderw., *H. of K.*, ii., 329.

content with the maintenance, in such adverse
circumstances, of Reformed congregations already
existing, the Church resolved to "lengthen her
cords" as well as to "strengthen her stakes"; and
Knox was instructed to "visit, preach, and plant
[new] Kirks in the south, where there was not
a superintendent" already intrusted with this
duty.[1] His work, however, there was erelong interrupted by an event which occasioned his recall to Edinburgh,[2] and proved to be the beginning
of the end of the Catholic reaction in Scotland.

IV. The power of Rizzio at Court was obnoxious to almost every party in Scotland; and
men of different views were for a time united in
desiring his downfall. Protestants saw in him
the embodiment of the influences which had led
Mary to depart from her earlier policy of acquiescence in the Reformation settlement, and to
scheme for the toleration and eventual restoration
of Romanism. Even Catholic nobles and gentry,
who sympathised with the incipient Roman reaction, could have no liking for a low-born foreign
favourite by whom they saw themselves superseded at Court. The exiled lords and their friends
at home attributed to Rizzio the threatened for-
feiture of their estates. Darnley himself, whose

---

[1] Calderw., *H. of K.*, ii., 306.

[2] Knox speaks of his being "called back from exile"
(Laing, *W. of K.*, vi. 481). The Assembly which sent Knox
to the south perhaps considered that his life was in danger
at the time in Edinburgh.

dissolute habits had already alienated the Queen's affection, and whose political incompetency deprived him of her confidence, resented keenly his displacement as her adviser, and believed himself (probably without real foundation) supplanted even as a husband.[1] The outcome of all this antipathy was the plot into which Darnley and Lennox entered with Morton, Ruthven, Lyndsay, and other Protestant lords to remove out of the way the hated Italian.[2] The terms of the compact were that Darnley was to receive the Crown Matrimonial; that Moray and other exiles were to be pardoned and restored; and that the Reformed religion was to be maintained and confirmed. It was proposed at first that Rizzio should be tried and sentenced by the nobility; but Darnley objected to this course as "cumbersome"; and the victim was assassinated at Holyrood almost in the presence of the Queen, on the 9th of March, 1566.[3]

What share, if any, had Knox in this crime? Tytler endeavours to prove the Reformer's complicity on the ground of a memorandum of uncertain date but ancient authorship attached to a

[1] Ruthven, *Relation of the Death of Rizzio*, p. 30; Hay Fleming, *Mary Q. of S.*, pp. 125, 398.

[2] Catholic lords who were in Holyrood on the night of the assassination, although they had no share in the plot, appear to have acquiesced in the issue, after receiving assurance of Darnley's complicity (Keith, *Affairs of Ch. and St.*, iii., 270).

[3] Knox, *H. of R.*, ii., 521; Calderw., *H. of K.*, ii., 311–314; Keith, *Affairs of Ch. and St.*, iii., 202–208.

genuine and contemporary letter from the ambassador Randolph to Secretary Cecil.[1] The memorandum enumerates sixteen persons as consenting to Rizzio's death, and among the sixteen are both Knox and Craig. Even, however, if this document be reliable, it may involve the two preachers in no more than what the Protestant conspirators at first designed, viz., not Rizzio's assassination, but his trial and execution on the charge of treason. There are strong reasons, however, for discrediting the trustworthiness of this anonymous memorandum. The document to which the list of conspirators is attached, and a subsequent letter of Randolph, dated 27th March, both contain lists from which the names of Knox and Craig are absent. In an extant letter from Morton and Ruthven, the writers expressly refer to the assertion of "some Papists" that the murder had been instigated by the ministers, and they declare upon their "honour that none of them were art and part in this deed." Finally, at a meeting of the Privy Council, held by the Queen soon after the assassination, it was resolved to summon seventy-one persons to answer the charge of complicity; yet even in this extended list of suspected accomplices, Knox and Craig, notwithstanding the Queen's desire to be revenged on the former, do not appear.[2] While

---

[1] Tytler, *H. of Sc.*, vii., 427–438.

[2] McCrie, *Sketches of Scottish Church History*, App., Note A; Hume Brown, *Life of Knox*, ii., 304–310.

Knox, however, had, in all probability, nothing to
do with Rizzio's actual assassination, he certainly
afterwards gave his approval to the "just act"
of the conspirators "most worthy of all praise."
He regarded the killing of Rizzio very much as,
twenty years before, he had regarded the murder
of Beaton. Rizzio, in his view, was a "great
abuser of the Commonwealth," whom the Queen
and her Government not only tolerated but favoured. It was necessary, for the sake of Church
and State, to put an end to his power of mis-
chief [1]; and when those to whom God had
committed the administration of justice failed to
perform an obvious duty, those who stood next
to the throne—the nobles of the realm—were entitled to intervene, to see that justice was executed and the nation delivered from peril. Knox's
religious patriotism, which saw in Rizzio a "vile
knave, justly punished," [2] blinded him to the fact

[1] It appears to have been intended, at the Parliament
summoned for March, 1566, not only to accomplish the
attainder of Moray and his fellow-exiles, but to restore
the Spiritual Estate, and to take the first steps "anent
restoring the old religion" (letter of Mary Stuart in Labanoff, i., 343). The writer of the Fifth Book of Knox's *History of the Reformation* (using, probably, materials left by
Knox) states that "if the Parliament had taken effect, it
was thought by all men of the best judgment, that the true
Protestant religion should have been wrecked and Popery
erected." He adds that twelve altars were found in Holyrood Chapel ready to be "erected in St. Giles' Church" (*H.
of R.*, ii., 524).

[2] Knox, *H. of R.*, i., 235.

that unless intermeddlers with justice, unauthorised by men, can vindicate, by evidence, a claim
to divine authority, his principles must issue in
perpetual revolution and anarchy.

The decision of Knox, however, to stand by the
friends who, in his absence, had been guilty of
assassination, was accompanied by painful heart-
searching and severe depression. A pathetic
prayer has come down to us, entitled "John Knox
with deliberate mind to his God," composed by
the Reformer in Edinburgh three days after the
tragedy, and probably on the night of his arrival
in the city. He who never quailed before men
humbles himself in the dust before God, on account of "manifold sins, chiefly those whereof the
world is not able to accuse me." "In youth and
age, and now after many battles, I find nothing in
me but vanity and corruption." "Pride and ambition assail me, on the one part; covetousness
and malice trouble me on the other." While he
gives thanks to God for "using my tongue to set
forth Thy glory, against idolatry, errors, and false
doctrine," he "would repose in" God's "mercy
alone," and "in the obedience and death of our
Lord Jesus Christ." But the burden of life and
work in a troublous time, and his failure to find
"justice and truth amongst the sons of men"
drive him, like Elijah, to seek "an end to this my
miserable life." "To Thee, therefore, O Lord,"
he cries, "I commend my Spirit; for I thirst to

be resolved [released] from this body of sin"; and then, after a brief intercession for "the Kirk within this Realm" and for his "desolate" wife and "dear children," he closes with these words "tending to desperation," "Now Lord put an end to my misery."[1]

V. On the death of Rizzio, Moray, who had not been directly concerned in the plot, returned from exile, and was even received "pleasantly" by the Queen[2]; while Knox, as we have seen, was recalled by the Church to Edinburgh in order to give his counsel as to the "duty of the faithful" in a troublous time.[3] The baneful influence of Rizzio having been removed, and the King, being now pledged to support the Protestant cause, it was hoped, doubtless, that the statesmen favourable to the Reformed Church would again come into authority. But assassination is a dangerous pathway to power: and the Queen, for the time at least, skilfully circumvented the conspirators. Dissembling her wrath against Darnley, she affected to believe that he was merely a tool in the hands of others; and she persuaded her worthless husband virtually to renounce his recent compact, and actually to co-operate with Huntly, Bothwell, and others in antagonism to his former allies.[4]

[1] Laing, *W. of K.*, vi., 483, 484.

[2] Keith, iii., 274.

[3] Laing, *W. of K.*, vi., 481.

[4] Tytler, *H. of Sc.*, vii., 41-44.

As the outcome of this unique transformation, Morton, Ruthven, and other leading conspirators against Rizzio fled across the Border; Moray found himself tolerated but impotent; Knox retired to Kyle in Ayrshire to resume his interrupted "visitation," [1] and to occupy his comparative leisure with the completion of his *History*. His feelings at this time are expressed in the Preface to the Fourth Book of that work, written in May, 1566. He mourns over the "miserable dispersion of God's people within this realm" when "good men are banished," while "such as are known unworthy" bear the whole "regiment"; and he attributes the unfortunate issue to that policy of unworthy compromise (as he considered it) which the Protestant statesmen had adopted after Mary's return to Scotland. "The most part of us," he writes, "declined from the purity of God's Word, and began to follow the world; and so again to shake hands with the Devil and idolatry. . . . From this fountain hath all our misery proceeded." [2]

---

[1] The *Diurnal of Occurrents* for 17th of March, 1566, states that on "this day John Knox departed from the said burgh [Edinburgh] with a great mourning of the godly."

[2] Knox, *H. of R.*, ii., 265–267. The Reformer's visit to Ayrshire at this time was signalised by at least one gleam of comfort amid many grounds of depression. The Earl of Cassilis, through the persuasion of his Protestant wife, and also, perhaps, in part, through Knox's influence, renounced Romanism and became an earnest propagator of the Reformed Faith (*ibid.*, ii., 533). He afterwards, however, went

Transliteration of Extract from MS. of Knox's
Historie in the Library of Edinburgh University.
The marginal note is in Knox's handwriting.

[So assemblit at Linlythqw, the said Cardinall, the Erlis Ergyle,] Huntely,
Bothwell, the Bischoppis and thare bandis; and thairefter thei passed to
Striveling, and took with thame bayth the Quenis, the Mother and the
Dowghter, and threatned the depositioun of the said Governour, as in-
obedient to thare Haly Mother the Kirk, (so terme thei that harlott of
Babilon, Rome.) The inconstant man, not throwgtlie grounded upoun
God, left in his awin default destitut of all good counsall, and having the
wicked ever blawing in his earis, "what will ye do! Ye will destroy
yourself and your house for ever: "—The unhappy man, (we say) beaten
with these tentations, randered himself to the appetites of the wicked;
for he qwyetlie stall away from the Lordis that war wyth him in the Palice

*The Governour
violated his faith,
refused God, and
took absolution
of the Dewill.*

of Halyrudhouse, past to Stirling, subjected himself to
the Cardinall and to his counsall, receaved absolutioun,
renunced the professioun of Christ Jesus his holy
Evangell, and violated his oath that befoir he had maid,
[for observatioun of the contract and league with
England.]

Facsimile of part of a page of MS. of Knox's *Historie* in the library of Edinburgh University; the marginal note is in Knox's handwriting.

VI. During the summer of 1566 Knox appears
to have remained in comparative retirement and
security among the Protestants of Ayrshire.[1]   He
was absent from the General Assembly held in
June, and his place as senior minister of St. Giles'
was temporarily supplied.[2]   In the early autumn,
however, he emerged from obscurity.   By that
time, in spite of the birth of their son, the future
James VI., on the 19th of June, the estrangement
of the Queen from Darnley had become complete,
and Bothwell's malign influence over Mary had
been established.   Knox could hardly, at this
stage, have retained any respect for Bothwell;
but the Earl professed to be a Protestant and had
formerly received from Knox a double service.[3]
The Reformer, accordingly, may have trusted that
this nobleman's influence at Court would save him
(Knox) from royal interference.   We find him at
St. Andrews in the beginning of September,[4] and

over to the Queen's party, and fought for her at Langside
(Keith, ii., 816).

[1] The Queen on one occasion wrote to a nobleman with
whom Knox was residing, requesting the banishment of
Knox from the house; but apparently without result.   See
Letter of Bishop Parkhurst to Bullinger in Burnet, *Hist. of
Ref. in E.*, iii., 473).

[2] Calderw., *H. of R.*, ii., 321; Keith, iii., 141, 142.

[3] Knox, *H. of R.*, ii., 324, 325, 328. Knox, in 1561, had
first reconciled Bothwell with the Earl of Arran, and had
afterwards persuaded Moray and others that Arran's subsequent charge of treason against Bothwell was the outcome of
"phrenzied fancy."

[4] Laing, *W. of K.*, vi., 548; Edin. T. C. Records, 25 Sept.,
1566 (quoted by Hume Brown, *Life of J. K.*, ii., 231).
21

in Edinburgh before the close of that month. In the former city he procured a gathering of over forty ministers and professors, to consider a request, conveyed through him from Beza of Geneva, for an approval of the Second Helvetic Confession. The approval was cordially given to a document which is described as "resting altogether upon the Holy Scriptures" and as expounding "most faithfully, holily, piously, and indeed divinely," "whatever we have been constantly teaching these eight years." A characteristic *caveat*, however, is appended, "with regard to what is written in the Confession concerning the festivals of our Lord's Nativity, Circumcision, Passion, Resurrection, Ascension, and Sending of the Holy Ghost." "These festivals," it is declared, "obtain no place among us: for we dare not religiously celebrate any other feast day than what the divine oracles have prescribed." The procedure of the St. Andrews Convention was ratified by the subsequent General Assembly.[1]

No record remains of Knox's life and work in Edinburgh during the autumn of 1566; but at the General Assembly which met, as usual, on Christmas Day of that year, the Reformer is the leading actor. Under his guidance the Assembly protested strongly, in a "Supplication" to the Privy Council, against a serious interference

---

[1] Laing, *W. of K.*, vi., 544–548; Calderw., *H. of K.*, ii., 331–332.

by the Queen with the Reformation settlement, at Bothwell's instigation, viz., the reinstatement of that "conjured enemy to Christ" and "cruel murderer of our dear brethren," the ex-Archbishop of St. Andrews, in his ancient disciplinary jurisdiction. The issue showed that this restoration of the Primate was designed, not expressly as an encroachment on the Reformed Church, but as a means of enabling the archbishop first to declare nullity of marriage, owing to consanguinity, between Bothwell and his Countess, and thereafter to pronounce sentence of divorce. This was a necessary preliminary to that subsequent marriage of Bothwell and the Queen which was even then in contemplation; Mary hoping at this time to procure simultaneously a divorce from Darnley. To Knox, however, and to the General Assembly, the Primate's reinstature naturally appeared to be the first step in the "setting up again of that Roman Antichrist within this realm." [1]

VII. Another notable proceeding of this General Assembly bears still more conspicuously the marks of the Reformer's intervention. It was twelve years since he had ceased to be a minister of the Church of England; but the zeal which he had manifested in former days for Puritan usages within that Church was not dead, but only

---

[1] Continuation of Knox, *H. of R.*, ii., 539–548; Keith, iii., 152–156; Calderw., ii., 326, 335–340.

dormant. It was now reawakened by the "dolorous bruit" that many of her clergy, including
"some of the best learned," had been punished
with deprival [1] for refusing to wear "such gar-
ments as idolaters in time of greatest darkness
did use, in their superstitious and idolatrous service." At his own suggestion, we may assume,
Knox was requested to prepare a letter of remonstrance to the "Bishops and Pastors of God's
Church in England." The letter is characteristic
of the writer. It blends a broad spirit of ecclesiastical fellowship and a fine appeal to Christian
charity, with some plain speaking which was not
calculated to win concession. He recognises cordially the Church of England as a sister communion, "professing with us in Scotland the truth
of Christ"; and he "commits heartily" her bishops and clergy to the "mighty protection of the
Lord Jesus." Nothing, moreover, could be more
becoming than his reminder, "what tenderness is
in a scrupulous conscience"; his "crave that
Christian charity may so prevail with you that
ye do to one another as ye desire others to do to
you"; and his personal appeal to his readers "not

[1] Among the deprived were several of Knox's personal
friends, including Miles Coverdale, the translator of the
Bible, Foxe, the martyrologist, and Sampson, Dean of Christ-
church, Oxford. The special occasion of the deprival was
nonconformity to the "Advertisements" of 1564,—a series
of strict injunctions regarding vestments and ceremonies.
The Advertisements were enforced by the bishops under
royal pressure (Marsden, *Early Puritans*, pp. 46–52).

to refuse the earnest request of us your brethren."
But when he proceeds to apply to the question
the Apostle's words, "What hath Christ to do
with Belial?" and to denounce "surplice, corner
cap, and tippet" as "Romish rags, and dregs of
that odious Romish beast," it is to be feared that
most of the prelates addressed would be rather
irritated than persuaded.[1]

Knox himself was probably the bearer of this
communication to the English clergy; for on the
same day on which the letter was approved he
received permission from the Assembly to "pass
to the realm of England to visit his children, and
to do his other business." Nathanael and Eleazer
were by this time ten and nine years of age, and
had been sent to live with their grandmother,[2] or
some other of their maternal relatives, with a
view to their education. The permission of the
Church to Knox was accompanied by the condition that he should return to Edinburgh before

[1] Continuation of Knox, *H. of R.*, ii., 544–547; Keith, iii.,
148–152; Calderw., *H. of K.*, 332–335. In spite of his strong
language, however, to the bishops, Knox did his best to
dissuade deprived clergy from secession and schism at this
time. A letter is extant, written to Knox in 1568 by one of
the Puritans who *did* secede, thanking the Reformer for a
"gentle letter" which he had addressed to the seceders, but
adding: "it is not in all points liked," and indicating that
Knox had expressed himself "not well contented" with their
procedure. See Lorimer, *John Knox and the Church of England*, 229–235, 298–300.

[2] Mrs. Bowes survived until a short time before Knox's
own death (Laing, *W. of K.*, vi., 513).

the ensuing General Assembly (25th June, 1567), and by a warm tribute to his "inculpable life," "pure doctrine," and "fruitful use of the talent granted to him by the Eternal for the propagation of the Kingdom of Jesus Christ." [1] Of the six months or less spent by Knox in England at this time no record remains. His headquarters would naturally be Berwick or its neighbourhood, the abode of his wife's kindred. We cannot tell whether the voice, which had been so effective in the pulpit of Berwick parish church in former years, was again heard in the same place; but many old friendships with those who had been his fellow-workers in the town and throughout the county would be revived. That he would endeavour to follow up, by personal interviews with leading churchmen, the General Assembly's plea for those Puritans who were partly his own spiritual offspring, is what might be expected from his strong convictions, ardent aspirations, and dutiful self-assertion.

VIII. During Knox's absence in England occurred that tragic event which (whatever may have been Mary's relation to it) issued in her own life's tragedy—the murder of Darnley at Kirk of Field, Edinburgh, on the 10th of February, 1567. The mock trial and acquittal of Bothwell on the 12th of April; the marriage of the infatuated Queen to the reputed murderer, on the 15th of

---

[1] *Universal Kirk*, 85; Keith, iii., 148, 149.

May, confirming the widespread belief in her connivance; the outbreak of civil war, when an army
composed of Catholics as well as Protestants was
raised as a national protest against misgovern-
ment and toleration of crime; and the encounter
between the Queen's supporters and opponents at
Carberry Hill in Midlothian, issuing in the flight
of Bothwell, the surrender of Mary, and her con-
finement in Lochleven Castle—such was the series
of events which took place in Scotland while
Knox was still residing in England.

On the 25th of June, nine days after the Queen
became a prisoner, the regular meeting of the General Assembly was held. Knox, according to agreement, had already returned to Edinburgh. He
found the great mass of nobles and gentry hostile
to Bothwell, but divided in opinion as to what was
to be done with Mary.[1] On the one side were the
Earls of Morton, Mar, and Glencairn; Lords Lyndsay, Ruthven, and Ochiltree, Kirckaldy of Grange,
and many others who would be satisfied with nothing less than the deposition of Mary, the coronation of the infant Prince, and the establishment
of a regency. On the other side were the Duke of
Châtelherault, the Earls of Huntly, Argyle, and
Crawford, Lords Boyd and Herries, Maitland of
Lethington, and a numerous following, who were
willing to restore the Queen to her position, if

[1] Calderw., *H. of K.*, ii., 371; Contin. of Knox, *H. of R.*, ii.,
563; Laing, *W. of K.*, vi., 552; Froude, *H. of E.*, chap. xlix.

security were obtained that her connexion with Bothwell would cease. Moray was absent in France. It depended largely on the attitude of the Church which party in the State would prove the stronger; and the importance of the procedure of the approaching General Assembly was enhanced by the fact that, owing to the circumstances of the Queen, there could be no constitutional meeting of Parliament. It lay with the supreme court of the Church to voice the national will.

Knox, as the acknowledged leader of the Assembly, was practically master of the situation, and he had no difficulty in coming to a decision. At once as a patriot and as a Reformer, he saw in the continued rule of Mary, apart from her alleged criminality (in which he believed) regarding Darnley's murder, the gravest danger both to Church and to State.[1] Bothwell, moreover, was still at large: if the Queen were restored to power he might be eventually reinstated; and it was known that he harboured murderous designs against the infant son of his victim. For Knox, the only alternatives as regards Mary could be imprisonment and compulsory abdication, or trial for complicity in her husband's assassination, involving, if her guilt was proved, a sentence of death.[2] From the

---

[1] Letter in Laing, *W. of K.*, vi., 566; Knox's Prayer after the Regent's murder, in Calderwood, ii., 515.

[2] Laing, *W. of K.*, vi., 553, 554; Tytler, vii., 164, 165.

ecclesiastical point of view, Knox, who knew
the men on both sides, had much more to hope
for the Reformed Church from the Confederate
Lords, as they were called, who had imprisoned
the Queen, than from the party, headed by
Châtelherault, who were, for the most part,
lukewarm Protestants or acknowledged Catholics.
The Reformer allied himself with the Confederate party. At his suggestion, probably, the
Assembly was adjourned from the 25th June to
the 20th July, with a view to a more effective
declaration of the Church's policy. A missive,
signed by Knox and five other ministers, was sent
to Protestant nobles and gentry of the Queen's
party, who had absented themselves from the Assembly, urging them "in God's name" to give
their "presence, labours, and concurrence" with
a view to the removal of "impediments" which
had "stayed the Reformation."[1] A public Fast was
appointed to be held on Sunday, the 13th of July,
in order to bring home more impressively to the
people the gravity of the situation. From his
pulpit in St. Giles's, Knox denounced day after
day the conduct of the Queen, as well as of Bothwell, and prepared the public mind for the drastic
policy which the Confederate Lords had already
resolved to pursue.[2] When the Assembly met
again on the 20th of July, a conference was

---

[1] Calderw., ii., 368–370; Keith, iii., 164–168.

[2] Keith, iii., 171; Laing, *W. of K.*, vi., 554.

arranged between representatives of the nobility and delegates of the clergy. Articles were
adopted and signed by over sixty lords, by commissioners of the burghs, and by representatives of
the ministers. The signatories bound themselves
to "further the punishment of the horrible murder of the King . . . upon all and whomsoever
persons shall be found guilty"; and also to defend the Prince against those that would do him
injury. It was the prelude to the intended deposition of the mother, and acknowledgment of
the son as king. Thus the Church supported the
politicians; the politicians also undertook to support the Church. The signatories engaged, "in
the first Parliament that shall be holden," to
ratify and complete the establishment of the
Reformed Kirk; to make more adequate provision for the ministry; and to "root out" all
remaining "monuments of idolatry." [1]

While the General Assembly was still in session,
Mary was constrained to abdicate her throne in
favour of her infant, James, and to sanction the
appointment of Moray as Regent. A few days
after the Assembly had been dissolved, the young
King was crowned in the Greyfriars' Church, Stirling, by the Earl of Atholl; the Earl of Morton
and Lord Home took an oath, on behalf of the
infant Sovereign, that he would maintain the Protestant religion; the Bishop of Orkney, who had

---

[1] Calderw., ii., 378–383.

St. Giles' Cathedral, Edinburgh. (From the west.)

embraced the Protestant faith, anointed the
newly crowned child according to ancient usage;
and Knox preached what George Buchanan eulogises as an "excellent sermon" from a pulpit
still preserved, taking as an appropriate text the
passage in II Kings which records the coronation of Joash.   Within a month a commission of
regency was granted to the Earl of Moray, who
had returned to Scotland early in August.[1]   The
great majority of the nobility, including many
who had favoured less drastic measures, now accepted, or at least acquiesced in, the situation.[2]
There remained, indeed, a party, including the
Hamilton faction, able and ready, as will be seen,
when opportunity arrived, to give serious trouble.
But the support of Knox and the Church, backed
apparently by the majority of the people, rendered the new Regent's party the strongest in the
State; and the Parliament which assembled in
December, 1567, reflected the national mind when
it confirmed the Regency, as well as the policy, on
the whole, of the Confederate Lords.

Moray did not fail to recognise that to the
Church, under Knox's leadership, he owed largely
the position which he held; and the compact of

[1] Throgmorton to Elizabeth in Laing, W. of K., vi., 556;
Contin. of Knox, H. of R., ii., 565; Calderwood, ii., 384.
According to Calderwood, Knox "repined" at the ceremony
of anointing, but his objection was either not persisted in or
was overruled.

[2] Tytler, vii., 193.

July between the General Assembly and Confederate Lords was fairly kept. The Parliament of December, 1567, accordingly, marks an epoch in Scottish Church history. Among its enactments was the ratification of the Acts against Romanism and in favour of Protestantism, passed by that Convention of 1560 which had virtually been a Parliament, but from which Mary Stuart had significantly withheld her *imprimatur*. The Reformed Church became thus constitutionally as well as practically established. Other statutes followed. In all schools, colleges, and universities there was presented to teachers the alternative of conformity to the Reformed faith or of deprivation. A more effective security was provided for the due payment of ministers' stipends as a first charge upon the "thirds" of the ecclesiastical revenues; while some prospect was held out of the ultimate restoration of the teinds, as the Church's "proper patrimony," to ecclesiastical use.[1] The provision for the Protestantism of the Sovereign, which formed so important a feature in the revised constitution of England at the Revolution of 1689, was anticipated, as regards Scotland, by the enactment that "all kings, princes, or magistrates occupying their place, shall at the time of their coronation take their great oath, in the

---

[1] According to Spottiswoode (ii., 83) "the Regent did what he could to have the Church possessed with the patrimony," but "it could not be obtained."

presence of God, that they shall maintain the true
religion now received, [and] shall abolish and withstand all false religion contrary to the same." [1]
So fully satisfied was John Knox at this time
with the secure and hopeful position of the
Reformed Church that, in February, 1568, prematurely old through constant toil and frequent
trouble, he thought of spending the evening of
his life among the remnant of his congregation
at Geneva, "if they stood in need of [his] labours"; "seeing it hath pleased God's Majesty,
above all men's expectation, to prosper the work
for the performing whereof I left that company." [2]
For the Reformer, however, there was to be no
quiet eventide.   His life-work was not yet completed; and unforeseen "dolours" were in store
for the Scottish Church and State.

[1] Calderw., ii., 388–390; Tytler, vii., 196–200.

[2] Knox to John Wood.   Laing, *W. of K.*, vi., 559.

CHAPTER XIII

1568–1572

THE closing years of Knox's life were for the
Reformer himself, for the Church, and for
the country a period of trouble.

I. The virtual deposition of Queen Mary was
not followed by any effective foreign intervention
in her favour. In the eyes of Catholics abroad,
Mary, personally, had come under a cloud through
her marriage with Bothwell and its attendant
circumstances. France, moreover, at this period,
was distracted by intestine warfare between Romanists and Huguenots; Spain was occupied with
the suppression of rebellion in her Flemish dominions; the interference of England went little
beyond remonstrances of doubtful sincerity. But
trouble arose at home. First came the escape
of the Queen from Lochleven in May, 1568, when
a large proportion of the Scottish nobility, Protestants as well as Catholics, including many who

had acquiesced in Moray's regency, rallied to her standard at Hamilton. The defeat of the Queen's army at Langside and her flight into England lessened the strain, but did not remove the peril. The Hamiltons, Huntly, Argyle, and others occupied several strongholds, and gave serious trouble in the north and in the west. At this crisis the staunch adherence of the General Assembly, which guided Protestant opinion and itself received direction from Knox, was a valuable aid to the Regent's Government. The Assembly of February, 1569, appointed a Commission to use "all means possible" to bring the nobles to an "acknowledgment of his authority." A letter composed by Knox was directed to the Protestant Lords who had "made defection," charging them with "most treasonable" opposition to the "authority most lawfully established," and exhorting them "speedily to return to obedience." [1] In November, 1569, a brief rebellion broke out in the north of England. The Earls of Northumberland and Westmoreland hoped, with the help of Scottish allies, political and religious, to restore Mary to liberty and power, and to re-establish the Catholic Faith in both realms. When the rebel leaders, after defeat, had fled into Scotland, the Regent offered to deliver the Earl of Northumberland to Elizabeth, on condition that Mary was surrendered to himself, under a guarantee that her life

[1] Calderw., *H. of R.*, ii., 481–484.

would be spared.[1]   In no other way, it appeared,
could Catholic intrigues be suppressed.   Knox
supported the policy of Moray and sent a private
letter to Cecil by the Regent's envoy, warning the
English statesman that "if ye strike not at the
root, the branches that appear to be broken will
bud again." [2]

The negotiations regarding the removal of the
Queen to Scotland were interrupted by the gravest trouble which at this period darkened Knox's
life—the assassination of the Regent at Linlithgow on the 23rd of January, by James Hamilton,
of Bothwellhaugh, a nephew of the ex-Primate.
How great Knox's anxiety for Scotland was at
the time of this tragic death is shown by the
prayer which he offered up on the following day:

"Seeing that we are now left as a flock without a
pastor in civil policy, and as a ship without a rudder
in the midst of the storm, let Thy presence, Lord,
watch and defend us in these dangerous days, that
the wicked of the world may see that as well without
the help of man as with it, Thou art able to rule,
maintain, and guide the little flock that dependeth
upon Thee." [3]

---

[1] Tytler, *H. of Sc.*, vii., 299.

[2] Laing, *W. of K.*, vi., 568.   It is held by many that these
words point to Mary being executed in England; but in view
of the occasion of the letter, they seem rather to suggest the
impolicy of withholding Mary from the control of the Regent's
Government.

[3] Calderw., ii., 513; Laing, *W. of K.*, vi., 568.

To Knox the death of Moray was a heavy personal bereavement as well as public calamity. Their friendship had begun while the future Regent was a youth; to Knox's influence his religious convictions were largely due; and the letter of the Reformer to the statesman at the time of their estrangement, amid severe reflections on Moray's policy of concession and compromise, contains evidence that the affection of the writer was only repressed, not extinguished. If the Regent in his dealings with others was sometimes tortuous, he acted towards Knox a straightforward as well as friendly part. During the years which followed their reconciliation, the personal friendship appears to have been unclouded, and the ecclesiastical co-operation complete. At the funeral sermon, unfortunately not preserved, which Knox preached in St. Giles' from the significant text, "Blessed are the dead which die in the Lord," the voice which was wont from that pulpit to rouse men like a trumpet-call to conflict, moved, by its words and tones of pathos, a vast congregation to tears. The scene was doubly memorable. It revealed that within the Reformer's rough exterior there was a tender heart; and it expressed the popular sentiment, attested afterwards by two historians of very different ecclesiastical standpoint, for whom the impression created by the tragedy of Linlithgow must have been one of the earliest

22

memories of their childhood. "He moved three thousand persons to shed tears," writes Calderwood, "for the loss of such a good and godly governor." "Loved as their father whilst he lived," records Spottiswoode, "mourned grievously at his death," and "to this day honoured with the title of the 'Good Regent.'" [1]

II. To political trouble was added ecclesiastical anxiety.

1. The coalition of Catholics and Protestants who aimed at Mary's restoration was naturally strengthened by the removal of the head of the opposite party who were responsible for her enforced abdication. The Earl of Lennox (now a professed Protestant) and the Earl of Mar (Lord Erskine), who successively held the regency between Moray's assassination and Knox's own death, had neither the sagacity nor the influence of their predecessor; and the Earl of Morton, who mainly guided the policy of the party, while a man of high ability and a steadfast although self-seeking Protestant, did not possess and did not deserve the full confidence either of Church or of nation. After Moray's death, moreover, the "King's party" was weakened, and the Queen's party correspondingly reinforced by a considerable number of secessions from the former to the latter. Maitland, who under Moray's rule had been a secret adversary of the Regent, now openly joined the

[1] Calderw., ii., 525, 526; Spottisw., ii., 121.

other side, and was followed by Kirkcaldy of
Grange, to whom Moray had intrusted Edinburgh
Castle.[1]   To Knox the secession of Kirkcaldy was
a source of special sorrow.   Both had been dis-
ciples of George Wishart.   They had shared the
perils of the siege of St. Andrews' Castle, the hardships of the French bondage, the toil of the Reformation conflict; and the Reformer never forgot
his former friend's "early courage and constancy
in the cause of the Lord."[2]

The partisans of Queen Mary, including as
they did a numerous and influential Protestant
section, were careful not to alienate popular
sympathy by giving their countenance to an
ecclesiastical counter-revolution.   Soon after Moray's death they "purged themselves of any intention to alter religion," and declared that they
"preferred the advancement" of the established
religion "to their lands and lives."[3]   At their so-
called Parliament in June, 1571, they expressly
ordained that none should "innovate, change, or
pervert the form of religion and ministration of
the sacraments publicly professed within this
realm."[4]   But Knox was too clear-sighted and
far-seeing not to discern that along with the
Queen's restoration, if accomplished, would be renewed erelong those Protestant concessions and

[1] Calderw., ii., 488, 555, 558.

[2] Laing, *W. of K.*, vi., 657.

[3] Calderw., *H. of K.*, ii., 551, 552.

[4] Spottisw., ii., 161.

Roman aggressions which had almost issued, a few years before, in the restoration of the Catholic Church.

2. On the other hand, the policy of the definitely Protestant King's party, which loyally acknowledged the successive regencies and disowned the Queen's authority, was to Knox and the General Assembly only a little less obnoxious than that of their political rivals. The Reformed Church was wounded in the house of her professed friends. Knox complains of "unworthy men who had been thrust [by patronage] into the ministry of the Kirk," and of " merciless devourers of her patrimony." He describes both factions as "fighting against God," and declares that his own political party "as little repented the troubling and oppressing the poor Kirk of God as ever they [their adversaries] did." "For if," he continues, "they can have the Kirk lands annexed to their houses, they appear to take no more care of the instruction of the ignorant, and of the feeding of the flock of Jesus Christ, than ever did the Papists." [1] That these were not outbursts of individual resentment on Knox's part appears from a strongly worded letter of remonstrance by the "mild" Erskine of Dun to Regent Mar against "unrighteous usurpation" and "spoil of the Kirk" by the civil authority [2]; and also from various

---

[1] Laing, W. of K., vi., 603; Calderw., iii., 113–114.
[2] Ibid., iii., 156–162.

Statue of John Knox, which is about to be erected in St. Giles's. (By kind permission of the sculptor, Pittendrigh MacGillivray, Esq., R.S.A.)

records of the General Assemblies held in the
years 1570 and 1571. These Assemblies protest
against simoniacal presentations and the appointment of minors, laymen, or otherwise unqualified
persons to pastoral charges. They protest, further, against the unlawful assignations to laymen from the Church's share of the "thirds,"
and against the illegal withholdment from ministers of their lawful stipends. Against persistent
offenders in such matters the General Assembly
issued what was then the stern threat of excommunication.[1] The remonstrance and petition of
the Church, however, although they received the
personal approval of the Regent Lennox, were
treated with contempt by the Estates through the
influence of Morton, who "ruled all." The Commissioners of the General Assembly were stigmatised as "proud knaves," and Morton declared "he
should lay their pride, and put order to them." [2]

It is greatly to the credit of Knox and other
leaders of the General Assembly, that the Church
never allowed herself to be provoked by inconsiderate treatment endured from the King's party
into any negotiations with the opposite faction.

---

[1] *Universal Kirk*, pp. 122, 127; Calderw., iii., 5, 7, 38.

[2] *Ibid.*, iii., 137, 138; Bannatyne, *Mem.*, p. 186. This
meeting of the Estates was held at Stirling in the end of
August, 1571, a few days before the slaughter of the Regent.
It was on this occasion that the young King—a child of five—
noticing an aperture in the roof of the hall, remarked, with
unconscious prescience, "There is a hole in this Parliament."

The partisans of the Queen, at this period, would readily have conceded, for the time, almost any ecclesiastical demands, in order to secure the valuable support of the leaders of the Reformation. The loyalty of the Church, under Knox's leadership, contributed largely to save the State from a successful political revolution, such as would have resulted primarily in the restoration of Mary, and might have issued eventually in the triumph of Romanism in both realms[1]

III. In the case of Knox, troubles in Church and State were accompanied by private trials. In the autumn of 1570 he had a stroke of apoplexy which affected his speech; and although he speedily recovered sufficiently to resume his preaching, his activity thenceforth was curtailed, infirmity began to manifest itself, and pulpit work was limited to Sunday ministrations.[2] In December of the same year, he came into personal controversy with his former friend, Kirkcaldy, the Governor of the Castle, who had broken into the city prison and rescued a man charged with manslaughter. Knox denounced this conduct from the pulpit; Kirkcaldy, to whom an exaggerated report of the sermon had been given, brought the matter before the Kirk Session of Edinburgh, and demanded an apology, which Knox refused to give. When a report spread that the Governor

---

[1] Cook, *H. of Church*, i., 101, 159
[2] Bannatyne, *Memorials*, p. 62.

had "sworn himself enemy to John Knox and will slay him," a remarkable communication was sent to Kirkcaldy by thirteen noblemen and gentlemen of the south-west, emphasising the "great care that we have of the personage of that man," and "protesting that the life of our said brother is to us so precious and dear as our own lives." [1] In the following March (1571) the Reformer was troubled with anonymous libels thrown into the meeting-place, or affixed to the door, of the General Assembly. The chief charges against him were his alleged defamation of the Queen in his sermons as an "idolatress, murderer, and adulteress," and his omission of her name from his intercessory prayers. The General Assembly refrained from any formal endorsement of the Reformer's language, but "all said they would bear their part of the same burden with him." Some of his friends entreated him to "pass over such [anonymous] accusations with silence." But Knox regarded the libel as requiring a public answer. Mary Stuart, although a prisoner in England, was at this very time, as her correspondence proves, conspiring with Catholics at home and abroad for her own restoration and the advancement of the Catholic cause.[2] The Castle of Edinburgh was in the hands of her adherents; at least one-half of the nobility were on her side; at any

---

[1] Bannatyne, *Memorials*, pp. 72–82.

[2] Labanoff, iii., 222, 231.

moment she might become a power in the realm.
At the close of his sermon, accordingly, on the
Sunday after the delivery of the libels, Knox re-
asserted his charges against Mary, although he
denied that he had ever spoken of her as a "repro-
bate" who "cannot repent." He vindicated his
refusal to pray for her as sovereign; "for sovereign to me she is not"; and ended by challenging
his anonymous assailants to accuse him "face to
face at the next General Assembly." [1]

IV. Towards the end of April, 1571, Edinburgh became the scene of conflict between the
two political parties—conflict which continued,
with periods of intermission or truce, until after
Knox's death, and was dignified with the title of
"the wars between Leith and Edinburgh." [2] The
Regent's forces, from their headquarters in Leith,
threatened the Castle; the garrison of the Castle
warned citizens who were not on their side to
leave the town. The leaders of the Queen's party
had no desire to injure Knox personally, but they
declined to guarantee his safety at the hands of
fanatical followers who regarded him as the chief
enemy of their Queen.[3] The incident of a "bullet
shot in at the window [of his house] of purpose
to kill," and a plain intimation from Kirkcaldy
that Knox must either take refuge in the Castle

---

[1] Bannatyne, *Mem.*, pp. 91–100.
[2] Calderw., iii., 71.
[3] *Ibid.*, iii., 72.

or leave the city,[1] were used by the Reformer's
friends, including his colleague, Craig, as a means
of constraining him to leave Edinburgh for a time.
Knox at first refused, till they said that if he
stayed, it would be the " occasion of the shedding
of their blood for his defence."[2]   This consideration moved him; and so, after joining in a last attempt, at a private conference in the Castle,[3] to
convince the leaders of the Queen's faction of
their errors, Knox, on the 5th of May, left Edinburgh for St. Andrews.[4]   After a visit to Abbots-
hall,[5] on the way, he arrived early in July, with
his wife and their three children,[6] in the city
where "God had first opened his mouth."   He
took up his abode in the Novum Hospitium of
the Priory; it was to be his home for fully a year.[7]

Knox's ecclesiastical and academic environment was partly congenial, partly the reverse.
On the one hand, the College of St. Leonard's—a
"well" of evangelical teaching from Gavin Logie's
time—was in full sympathy with the Reformer.
Patrick Adamson, who had recently succeeded
George Buchanan as Principal of the College, had
not yet shown any of that subservience to the

---

1 Calderw., iii., p. 242.

2 Bannatyne, *Mem.*, p. 118.

3 *Ibid.*, pp. 125–132.

4 Calderw., iii., 73.

5 Bannatyne, *Mem.*, p. 119.

6 James Melville's *Diary*, p. 26.

7 Bannatyne, *Mem.*, p. 255.

civil power which was afterwards rewarded with an archbishopric; and among the academic "regents" was John Davidson, afterwards minister of Prestonpans, whose *Breif Commendation of Uprichtness*, published in 1573, is mainly a lamentation over the death of Knox,

> " That fervent faithful servant of the Lord,
> A most true preacher of the Lordis word." [1]

St. Leonard's "yaid" was Knox's favorite resort in leisure hours. There " he would call us scholars unto him and bless us"—so an alumnus of that time testifies—"and exhort us to know God and His work in our country; to stand by the good cause; and to learn the good instructions of our masters." [2] He publicly vindicated the St. Leonard's students, because he knew their conduct to be "upright and just," when a serious charge was made against them by the head of the rival College of St. Salvator.[3] If he was wont to give the young men solemn counsel, he was also ready to share in their innocent recreations; and one catches a glimpse of the broad sympathies of the Puritan Reformer, when we read how John Davidson "made a play at the marriage of Mr. John Colvin," a fellow-regent, "which," writes Melville, "I saw played [by the students] in Mr.

---

[1] McCrie, *Life of Knox* (ed. 1855), p. 451.

[2] Melville's *Diary*, p. 75.

[3] Bannatyne, *Mem.*, p. 258.

Knox's presence." [1] On the other hand, there
were in St. Andrews at that time men in high
position who were lukewarm Protestants, favoured the Queen's party, and bore no good will
to Knox as a steadfast supporter of the Regency.
Robert Hamilton, one of the ministers of the city,
accused the Reformer of being privy to Darnley's
murder, but had to disavow the calumny. [2] Archibald Hamilton, a regent of St. Salvator's College,
who eventually renounced Protestantism and became a bitter Romanist, began even at this time
to defame Knox, whom after the latter's death
he grossly maligned. [3] The Provost of St. Salvator's, John Rutherfurd, while professing his "good
opinion of Knox," discloses in correspondence and
otherwise a scarcely friendly disposition [4]; and
the relations of the Reformer even with his old
colleague, John Douglas, the Rector of the University, could not at this time have been very
cordial, in view of the latter's readiness, as we
shall see, to become a "tulchan" archbishop.

In his correspondence with friends, Knox gives
a somewhat doleful account of his physical condition at St. Andrews. He describes the "daily
decay of his natural strength" and forebodes his
"sudden departure from the miseries of this life."
He is "weary of the world"; and at the close of

[1] Melville, p. 25.

[2] Bannatyne, p. 260.

[3] *Ibid.*, 262, 263; Archibald Hamilton, *De Conf. Calv. Sect.*

[4] Bannatyne, pp. 257, 258; Calderw., iii., 207.

one of his letters refers to himself as "lying in St. Andrews half dead." [1] But this "half-dead" man was far from being either torpid or idle. His "infirmity of the flesh" did not prevent him from preaching regularly in the parish church, and James Melville's memorable description of his pulpit efforts during this year supplies graphic testimony to his continued effectiveness as a preacher:

"I heard him teach the Prophecy of Daniel that summer [1571] and the winter following. I had my pen and my little book, and took away such things as I could comprehend. In the opening up of his text, he was moderate, the space of half an hour: but when he entered to application he made me so to grew [thrill] and tremble, that I could not hold a pen to write. . . . I saw him every day of his doctrine go hulie and fear [slow and wary] with a furring of martricks about his neck, a staff in one hand, and good godly Richard Bannatyne, his servant, holding up the other oxter, from the Abbey to the parish kirk; and by the said Richard and another servant lifted up to the pulpit, where be behoved to lean, on his first entry. But ere he had done with his sermon, he was so active and vigorous that he was like to ding that pulpit in blads, and flee out of it." [2]

---

[1] Laing, *W. of K.*, vi., 605, 616.

[2] Melville, p. 75; comp. John Davidson in his *Breif Commend. of Uprichtness*, referring specially to this period of Knox's ministry:

"For weill I wait [wot] that Scotland never bare
  In Scottish leid [language] ane man mair eloquent."

Preparation for the pulpit was not the only literary work which occupied Knox's time at St. Andrew's. From his extant correspondence it appears that he was engaged in collecting copies of important documents bearing on the four books of his *History*, already composed, as well as in arranging materials for a continuation of the work.[1] He also prepared for the press an elaborate answer to a controversial letter addressed by James Tyrie, Professor of Theology in the Jesuit College at Paris, to his Protestant brother, David Tyrie, of Drumkilbo, Perthshire. The letter had been received about six years before, and had been forwarded at the time to Knox, with a request for a refutation which was hastily supplied but not published. In the interval, however, other Jesuits had been "stirred up to trouble godly hearts" with similar arguments, and Knox now printed and issued Tyrie's letter along with his own reply. The Jesuit professor had endeavoured to discredit the Reformed Church as being "no Kirk," on account of its being "new found," not "Catholic," "invisible," and devoid of "apostolic succession." Knox replies that the Church of the Reformers has in reality the "same antiquity as that of the Apostles"; that Catholicity is no test of righteousness, otherwise "sin," being

[1] Laing, *W. of K.*, vi., 608–612. These materials were afterwards used by David Buchanan in the composition of what is called Book V. of the *History of the Reformation in Scotland*.

universal, "should have been good"; that the Reformed Scottish Kirk is visible in the same sense as the Churches of Corinth and Philippi; although the Church of Christ is also invisible in so far as it is not confined to any special building, place, or outward organisation, but exists wherever Christ truly is; and finally, that the Reformed Church possesses what the Church of Rome lacks, genuine apostolical succession, inasmuch as "in our kirks we admit neither doctrine, rite, nor ceremony which by the Apostles' writings we find not authorised." [1]

V. During Knox's residence at St. Andrews, and under his own eyes in that city, an ecclesiastical policy was inaugurated which, for over a century, under four Stuart kings, became the fruitful source of discord, despotism, and persecution; issuing in schism, rebellion, and revolution. A modified episcopacy was introduced into the Reformed Church of Scotland.

After the Reformation, the bishops (as well as the abbots and priors) of the Roman Church, although deprived otherwise of ecclesiastical status, continued not only to receive two-thirds of their emoluments, but also to exercise parliamentary functions as the Spiritual Estate of the realm. In the eleven years, however, that had intervened, many of these prelates had died; and if the Spiritual Estate were allowed to become

---

[1] Laing, *W. of K.*, vi., 471–512.

Edinburgh Castle, as it was before the siege of 1573.

extinct, the validity of parliamentary proceedings, in which one branch of the legislature was wholly unrepresented, might be subsequently challenged —so it was believed—by any party desirous of effecting an ecclesiastical counter-revolution. Additional considerations, public and private, induced the Government of the Regent, under Morton's influence, to revive the office of bishop in the Reformed Church. The King's party looked forward to the "union of the kingdoms" under James, at Elizabeth's death: and it was considered prudent to bring the Scottish Church, by anticipation, into conformity so far with the Church of England.[1] The Government, further, lacked the money required to maintain its position effectively against the Queen's party, which received financial support from France. To annex for secular purposes the entire episcopal revenues would have provoked the combined opposition of the Church party and of the Marian faction; whereas the appointment of bishops content to retain only a part of the revenues would render practicable an arrangement through which the larger portion of the emoluments would be transferred to the State. Members of the nobility, moreover, including Morton himself, had been invested, temporarily at least, with the possession of episcopal or abbatial revenues, as the reward of past or prospective services; and it was

[1] Melville, *Diary*, pp. 47, 48.

obviously their interest to promote any enactment by which their perpetual tenure of the
greater portion of the spoil might be legalised.

Among the Reformed clergy there was from the
first a party who had no prejudice against an
episcopate; and the ministry, along with the
Church as a whole, while by no means enamoured
of episcopacy, were not committed at this time
to any belief in its inherent unlawfulness. The
Presbytery, as a court possessing ecclesiastical
jurisdiction, had not yet come into existence; it
was as yet nothing more than a gathering of clergy
for mutual edification. In the circumstances then
existing, several considerations of expediency
united to render the leaders of the Church willing
to acquiesce in the appointment of Protestant
bishops without the obnoxious powers of an
ecclesiastical hierarchy. The proposal afforded
some prospect of the Church recovering a further
portion of her ancient patrimony. The organisation of superintendents, moreover, had never been
completed. Owing mainly to the lack of sufficient emoluments, only five out of the ten ecclesiastical provinces, into which Scotland was
divided by the Book of Discipline, had been provided with these officials: their place was inade-
quately supplied by commissioners of the General
Assembly. The substitution of bishops for superintendents, with substantially similar authority,
would remove the financial difficulty, and also

restore to the Church direct parliamentary influence. Finally, the Regent's party, which inaugurated the new policy, although aggressive and illiberal (since Moray's death) in its relations with the Church, was less objectionable to steadfast Protestants than the Queen's faction, the triumph of which might eventually involve the disestablishment and disendowment of the Reformed Church altogether. At once, therefore, to recover ecclesiastical revenue and to secure civil protection, the Church of that period was prepared to accept the restoration of the episcopate in a modified form.[1]

The outcome of negotiations between representatives of Church and of State was the Concordat of Leith early in 1572: an agreement between the Privy Council, whose action was confirmed by the ensuing Parliament, and an ecclesiastical Convention, whose proceedings were ratified by a subsequent General Assembly. The main provision of this Concordat was the restoration (at least until the King should reach his majority) of the offices, dioceses, and emoluments of bishop and archbishop, with the important proviso that the members of this revived episcopate should be subordinate, spiritually, to the General Assembly as the supreme depositary of ecclesiastical jurisdiction. The Concordat was ratified in August, 1572, by the Assembly at Perth, in terms which

[1] Cook, *Hist. of the Ch.*, i., 163–173.

indicate that the Church regarded the episcopate, not as ecclesiastically indispensable, or even as theoretically desirable, but as, on the whole, in existing circumstances, an expedient "interim" arrangement "until further and more perfect order be obtained." [1]

VI. What was Knox's attitude towards the Concordat and the policy which it embodied? He was present neither at the Leith Convention nor at the Perth Assembly: but from his watch-tower at St. Andrews he was an interested onlooker; his mind and pen were occupied with the question, and an opportunity occurred of giving his practical testimony. The Reformer made no protest against episcopacy in itself. For five years he had ministered in the episcopal Church of England; and he had never, in subsequent days, condemned the office of bishop, under proper conditions, as unscriptural. There is no recognition of the Presbytery in the Book of Discipline as an ecclesiastical court; and the institution of the superintendentship implies the lawfulness of one minister being set over others. With Knox, apparently, it was a secondary matter whether the subordinate executive of the Church were vested in presbyter or in bishop, so long as the supreme jurisdiction remained in the hands of a non-hierarchical General Assembly composed of laymen as well as clergy. In a communication,

---

[1] Calderw., iii., 168–172.

accordingly, addressed to the Perth Assembly in August, 1572, he assumes, without protest, that the procedure of the Leith Convention will be confirmed.[1] Nevertheless, he had grave misgivings as to the outcome of the Concordat, withheld from it any positive approval, and warned the Church of the ecclesiastical abuses to which it might lead. Beza appears to have been consulted by him on the subject; for in April Knox received a strongly worded letter from that Reformer, declaring that "bishops brought forth the papacy," and warning his friend not "to admit again that plague in Scotland."[2]

Early in February the Earl of Morton had nominated John Douglas, Rector of St. Andrews University, to the archbishopric—prematurely, for the proceedings of the Convention had not yet been ratified either by Parliament or by General Assembly. Apart from this irregularity, it was generally believed that a simoniacal compact as to the emoluments had been made between the Earl and the episcopal presentee. Knox declined to take part in the ceremonial of installation, although he preached in Morton's presence the sermon which preceded it.[3] His feeling towards Douglas was chiefly one of "pity"; the new dignity, he declared, "will wrack him and disgrace

---

[1] Letter of Knox to Perth Assembly, with Articles, in Laing, *W. of K.*, vi., 619–621.

[2] Laing, *W. of K.*, vi., 614.

[3] Bannatyne, *Mem.*, p. 223.

him." [1]   None the less (if Calderwood's testimony can be trusted), Knox, in "open audience of many denounced anathema to the giver, anathema to the receiver." [2]   At a meeting of the General Assembly, held in March at St. Andrews (probably for the Reformer's convenience), "he opposed himself"—so James Melville reports [3]—"directly and zealously" to the making of bishops after the manner, at least, of the recent appointment; and in his communication to the Perth Assembly in August, when the question was formally discussed and determined, he urged strongly the adoption of certain provisions (in addition to the safeguard of the bishops being subordinate to the General Assembly) in order to avoid ecclesiastical abuses. The main objects of Knox were, on the one hand, to prevent prolonged vacancies, and the appointment of laymen or otherwise unqualified persons to bishoprics; on the other hand to "ordain all bishops to give account of their whole rents and intromissions therewith once in the year." [4]   The last provision was designed to protect ecclesiastical property from simoniacal alienation by subservient bishops and "greedy patrons."   The Assembly pronounced Knox's safeguards to be "both reasonable and godly."   "We have taken like order as we could," they declare, "for the

[1] Melville, *Diary*, p. 31.

[2] Calderw., *H. of R.*, iii., 206.

[3] Melville, *Diary*, p. 31.

[4] Laing, *W. of K.*, vi., 620, 621.

furtherance thereof "; and in subsequent years
we read of bishops undergoing trial by the
General Assembly for "simoniacal paction" and
"dilapidation of patrimony." [1] But these ecclesiastical trials do not appear to have been effective;
and the popular nickname of "tulchan" bishops,
during this period, was fully justified. "For the
Lords got the benefices, presented such a man as
would be content with the least commodity, and
set the rest in feus, tacks, and pensions to them
or theirs." [2] The *bon-mot* of Patrick Adamson, of
St. Leonard's College, on the occasion of the installation of Archbishop Douglas, was none the
less witty and trenchant because, by a grim irony
of history, Adamson himself eventually became
"tulchan" Primate.

"There are three sorts of bishops," he is reported
to have said, "the Lord's bishop, my lord bishop,
and my lord's bishop. 'The Lord's bishop' is the
true minister of the Gospel; 'my lord bishop' was in
the time of the papistry; 'my lord's bishop' is now,
when my lord getteth the benefice, and the bishop
serveth for a portion out of the benefice, to make my
lord's title sure." [3]

---

[1] Calderw., iii., 330, 347, 361.

[2] *Ibid.*, iii., 208. The tulchan was a stuffed calfskin
placed before a cow in order to induce her to give milk more
readily. The tulchan bishop facilitated the process of drawing
ecclesiastical revenues, of which much the greater part, by
a private compact, was appropriated by the lay patron.

[3] *Ibid.*, iii., 206.

ADDITIONAL NOTE TO CHAPTER XIII

Catholic Calumniators of Knox

Archibald Hamilton (*De Confus. Calv. Sect.*, 1577;
Demonstratio, 1581), James Laing (*De Vita et Moribus
Heret.*, 1581), and Nicol Burne (*Disputation*, 1581),
after waiting till Knox was dead, accused him of
numerous gross immoralities, including repeated
adultery and incest.   The vileness of the charges and
the virulence of the writers deprive them of credi-
bility in the absence of any real evidence.   A fourth
detractor, Alexander Baillie (in his *True Information*,
1628), represents Knox as *defending* incestuous
adultery.   Similar charges, without substantial foundation, were brought against Luther, Calvin, Beza,
and other Reformers, by Laing, Bolzec, and others.
The calumnies against Knox appear to have taken
their rise from: (1) the ill-natured reflections of some
Catholic members of the Bowes family on Knox's
pastoral intimacy (of which they disapproved) with
his future mother-in-law (see p. 103); (2) a vile accusation made against Knox in 1563, by one Euphe-
mia Dundas.   From the Town Council Records of
Edinburgh, for 18th June of that year, it appears that
this woman, on being cited to give evidence, took
refuge in a denial that she had said what was attributed to her.   Hamilton's earlier work was
answered by Principal Smeton of Glasgow, in his *Ad
Virulentum Archib. Ham. Dial. Responsio*, 1579.   See
Notes F F F and G G G in McCrie, *Life of John
Knox*.

CHAPTER XIV

KNOX'S LAST DAYS—HIS DEATH—CHARACTER AND
INFLUENCE

1572

EARLY in August, 1572, commissioners arrived
at St. Andrews from Knox's congregation in
Edinburgh. They brought a letter to the Reformer, craving his return to the city and to his
ministry. A truce had been arranged in the end
of July between the Regent's party and the
Queen's faction, whose conflicts in the capital had
led to Knox's departure in the previous year. He
would no longer be exposed either to peril of life
or to interference in work. A coolness, moreover,
between Craig and the congregation, arising out
of the former's too friendly relations (as was
thought) with the garrison of the Castle, had
resulted in his translation from St. Giles' to
Montrose. In their "destitution" accordingly,
the brethren desired "most earnestly" that if
Knox's "person might sustain travel, his voice
might once again be heard among them." [1]

Knox agreed to return to Edinburgh on the

[1] Bannat., *Mem.*, p. 254.

characteristic condition that he should not be expected "in any sort to temper his tongue, or cease to speak against the treasonable dealings of the Castle." He left St. Andrews on the 17th August, "not without dolour of the godly in that town, but to the great joy of the rest," especially of the "Hamiltons and their faction," who smarted under his invectives for "their murder of the Regent." On the 23rd of the month he reached Leith by boat; on the following Sunday he occupied once more his pulpit in St. Giles'. His voice, however, proved to be now too weak "to be heard of the whole multitude that convened"; and he preached thenceforth in what was called the Tolbooth—a portion of the nave of the cathedral curtained off from the rest of the building, and otherwise used for Council meetings. Meanwhile steps had been taken to secure a new colleague for the Reformer, and his own choice, as well as that of the congregation, had fallen upon James Lawson, sub-Principal of Aberdeen University. "Beloved brother,"—so Knox wrote to him on the 7th of September,—"seeing . . . that I look not for a long continuance of my battle, I would gladly discharge my conscience into your bosom"; and the touching postcript is added, "Haste, lest ye come too late." The summons met with no tardy response: within nine days Lawson arrived.[2]

---

[1] Bannat., *Mem.*, p. 255.

[2] *Ibid.*, pp. 263, 264; Cameron Lees, *St. Giles'*, p. 157.

II. Knox, however, was not the man to discontinue prematurely his pulpit ministry because relief was now within reach. The English Ambassador, Henry Killigrew, records on the 6th of October that the Reformer, although "now so feeble as scarce can he stand alone, yet doth he every Sunday cause himself to be carried" to the church, "and preacheth with the same vehemence and zeal that ever he did." [1] Two memorable pulpit functions were yet to be discharged before the voice which had stirred thousands of hearers was stilled. The first occasion was when tidings reached Scotland of the Massacre of St. Bartholomew. That massacre had begun on the 24th of August; but a declaration had been issued, in the name of the King of France, to the effect that the slaughter of Huguenots had been accomplished in order to "prevent the execution of a detestable conspiracy"; and some weeks elapsed before reliable reports of the nature and magnitude of the carnage reached Edinburgh. When at length the truth became known, Church and State in Scotland joined in the reprobation of the bloody crime, which was widely expected to inaugurate a general uprising of Catholics against Protestants throughout Christendom. The Privy Council summoned a national convention on the 3rd of October to devise means of "defence from the furious rage of the bloody papists."

[1] Laing, *W. of K.*, vi., 633.

The General Assembly responded with the appointment of a "public humiliation," and with a demand that the Acts of Parliament against "Papists" be put in force. The ministers of Edinburgh "did most vehemently inveigh against this most beastly and more than treasonable fact." Knox, feeble in body but strong in spirit, hurled his anathema from the pulpit in the white heat of righteous indignation; and "bade declare to the French Ambassador to tell his master, that murderer the King of France, that God's vengeance shall not depart from him, nor from his house, and that none who come from his loins shall enjoy that kingdom in peace, unless repentance prevent God's judgments." [1]

The other and last notable appearance of Knox in the pulpit was on the 9th of November, when Lawson was formally inducted in St. Giles' as his colleague and successor. The Reformer himself conducted the service, and "made the marriage, in a manner"—to use Bannatyne's words—"between Mr. James Lawson and the folk." "He declared to the whole assembly the duty of a minister, and also their duty to him"; "praised God," who had given to the congregation one in his own room; and prayed fervently that any gifts which he (Knox) had possessed might be bestowed on his successor "a thousand fold." But his "weak voice was heard" only by "a

[1] Bannat., pp. 271-273, 276.

few"; and he went home that day leaning on his staff and attended by his flock, from pulpit to death-bed.[1]

III. The details of the last fortnight of Knox's life have been graphically recorded by his devoted secretary, Richard Bannatyne, and have also been described by another witness, "who sat by Knox during his sickness until his latest breath." [2] On the Tuesday after Lawson's induction, the Reformer's mortal illness began. He "was stricken with a great hoast," which so enfeebled him that by Thursday he was obliged to discontinue his "ordinary reading of the Bible." Thenceforth he listened while his wife or his secretary read to him daily portions selected by himself, including the 53rd chapter of Isaiah, the 17th of St. John, and some portion of the Book of Psalms. On that Thursday he felt that his end was approaching;

---

[1] Bannat., 280–281; Laing, *W. of K.*, vi., 648, 654. See Additional Note to this Chapter, on "John Knox's House."

[2] Bannat., *Mem.*, pp. 281–289, also the anonymous *Eximii Viri J. K. vera extremæ vitæ et obitus Historia*, appended to Smeton's Reply to Archib. Hamilton's *De Conf. Calv. Sect.*, and included in Laing, vi., 649–660 (translated). Calderwood ascribed it to Smeton himself (iii., 238); but Laing attributes its composition, with greater probability to Lawson (Laing, vi., 648). Where the two accounts differ (as to minor details) Bannatyne has been followed. The simplicity of the latter's work, and its apparent composition in the form of a diary, commend it as more likely to be accurate in details than the rather verbose narrative in Latin of the anonymous writer.

for when he was paying Martinmas wages to his servant, James Campbell, he added twenty shillings to the usual amount, saying, "Thou wilt never get more of me in this life." On Friday his mind was sometimes confused: for he "thought it was Sunday," and insisted on rising to "go to the kirk and preach," he said, "upon the resurrection of Christ," in continuation of a sermon on Christ's death delivered on the previous Lord's Day. On the Saturday two friends came to see him—Archibald Stewart, and John Durie, exhorter at Leith. He made an effort to "come to the [dinner] table, which was the last time that ever he sat at any"; and one realises how far this "chief priest of Puritanism" was from gloomy asceticism, when we read how he "caused pierce a hogshead of wine" for the use of his guests, and with mingled gravity and playfulness bade "the said Archibald send for the same so long as it lasted, for he [Knox] would never tarry until it were drunken." [1]

On Monday, the 17th, he summoned to his bedside the elders and deacons of St. Giles', to "bid them his last good-night." The interview recalls the memorable farewell of the dying Calvin to the dignitaries of Geneva eight years before. Amid repeated acknowledgments of "unworthiness and vileness," he declared that "he had taught nothing

---

[1] Bannat., pp. 283, 285; *Vera Historia*, in Laing, vi., 654, 655.

but true and sound doctrine, and that howsoever
he had been against any one, it was never for
hatred of the person, but for discharge of his conscience before God." He had "never made merchandise of the Word; in respect whereof (albeit
he was weak, and an unworthy creature, and a
fearful man) he feared not the faces of men":
"therefore he exhorted them [his elders and dea-
cons] to stand constant unto that doctrine which
they had heard of his mouth." "And thou, Lawson," he added, turning to his colleague, in the
spirit of St. Paul addressing Timothy, "fight
the good fight of faith, and perform the work of
the Lord joyfully and resolutely." Shortly before
this interview, a letter had been read to him from
Maitland to the Kirk Session, complaining of Knox
having slandered him as "an atheist and enemy
to all religion," and craving redress. Knox was
too infirm to prepare a formal answer: but he
explained to the brethren that he had charged
Maitland with doing "works" which were a "sufficient declaration that he denied that there was
any God to punish wickedness"; referring to the
ex-Secretary's recent maintenance of the Queen's
faction. Yet he did not fail to remember his
fellow-Reformer in his prayers; although, as he
sorrowfully declared, "he had no warrant that
ever he [Maitland] would be well." At the close
of the meeting Knox commended his office-bearers
solemnly to God; and after the "prayer read for

the sick" (from his own *Book of Common Order*), "they departed," we are told, "in tears." [1]

The exertion of addressing his Kirk Session aggravated Knox's malady. "After this speaking he was the worse"; and he "never spake almost but with great pain"; yet, with a brave determination to "die in harness," he continued to see any friends to whom "some exhortation and admonition might be of service." Among other visitors was Lord Boyd, who had joined the party of the deposed Queen: he acknowledged that he had "offended" Knox "in many things." "I am come now," he said, "to crave your pardon." [2]

Lawson, his colleague, and Lyndsay, minister of Leith, were much with him and enjoyed his full confidence. Robert Campbell of Kinyeancleuch, a staunch adherent of long standing, received from the dying man the charge of his wife and children. Specially memorable were Knox's words to Morton, whom, as head of the King's party, he supported but did not love, and his farewell message to Kirkcaldy, the leader of the Queen's faction, whom he loved but strenuously opposed. Long afterwards, when Morton was about to be executed, nominally for alleged complicity in the murder of Darnley, he told the story of his interview. The Reformer pointedly

[1] Bannat., pp. 282–285; *Vera Historia*, in Laing, vi., 656; Calderw., iii., 234.

[2] Bannat., p. 285.

asked the statesman whether he was really privy
to the murder; and after receiving an assurance
to the contrary he charged Morton, who was on
the eve of becoming Regent, to use the many
benefits which he had received from Heaven,
"first to God's glory, to the furtherance of the
Evangel, and to the maintenance of the Kirk of
God and His ministry; next for the welfare of the
King's realm and true subjects." "If so ye shall
do," said the dying man, "God shall bless you
and honour you. But if ye do it not, God shall
spoil you of those benefits, and your end shall be
ignominy." Morton neglected the counsel; and,
after ten years of power, came to an evil end.
Before his death, amid penitent testimony, he
declared, regarding Knox's forewarning, "I have
found it true." [1]

Kirkcaldy was at the time in the Castle, but
kept away from Knox: the Reformer, however,
was mindful of his former friend. "The man's
soul is dear to me," he declared; "I would not
have it perish, if I could save it." He was "earnest with God anent" him; and he bade Lawson
and Lyndsay "go tell him, in my name, that unless he is yet brought to repentance, he shall die
miserably"; that he "shall be hung on a gallows
in the face of the sun, unless he speedily amend
his life, and flee to the mercy of God." [2] The

[1] Calderw., iii., 569.

[2] *Vera Historia*, Laing, vi., 657.

Governor was then under Maitland's baneful influence, and the message at the time was fruitless; yet Knox, after earnest intercession on Kirkcaldy's behalf, declared, "God assureth me that there is mercy for his soul." This assurance of the Reformer was afterwards reported to Kirkcaldy and moved him profoundly. A few months later, when the Castle had been surrendered, and when the ex-Governor, as Knox had foretold, was led out to be hanged, he confessed to David Lyndsay that he now perceived well that Knox was the Lord's "true servant"; and the memory of the past encouraged him to meet his doom not with despair, but with penitent faith and hope in the divine mercy, "according to the speech of that man of God." [1]

Illustrations have been given of the relations of mutual sympathy and helpfulness which subsisted between Knox and various women. We are not surprised to find among visitors to his death-bed "several pious women of high descent and education." One of these, wishing to comfort the dying Reformer, "began to praise him" for the great work which he had accomplished. "Tongue, lady, tongue," was the prompt interruption, "flesh of itself is over proud, and needs no means to esteem itself." [2]   "I have been tempted of Satan," he said to another friend; "he tempted

---

[1] Calderw., iii., 234, 284.

[2] Bannat., 286; *Vera Historia*, Laing, vi., 658.

me to trust and rejoice in myself; but I repulsed
him with this sentence, 'What hast thou which
thou hast not received?' 'Not I, but the grace of
God in me'"; and he protested often that he did
"only claim to the free mercy of God showed to
mankind in the blood of his dear Son, Jesus
Christ."[1]

On Sunday the 23rd of November, the day before he died, Knox passed the time chiefly in the
"delectable land" of silent meditation; but every
now and then, "when he would be lying in a
sleep," writes Bannatyne, "he burst forth in
such words as these: 'Live in Christ, and let
never flesh fear death'; 'I have been in heaven
and have possession'; 'I have tasted of these
heavenly joys where presently I am.'" To the
last, however, the care of Church and country
rested on his spirit.

"I have been in meditation of the troubled Kirk
of God, the spouse of Jesus Christ. . . . I have
called to God for her, and I have committed her to
her Head, Jesus Christ. . . . Lord grant true pastors to Thy Kirk, that purity of doctrine may be
retained; and restore again peace to this commonwealth, with godly rulers and magistrates. . . .
Come, Lord Jesus, into Thy hands I commend my
spirit."[2]

On the following day—his last upon earth—he

[1] Bannat., p. 288; Laing, vi., 660.

[2] Bannat., p. 287; Laing, vi., 658.

24

sat in his chair for half an hour in the forenoon, but the end was visibly drawing near. There were present in his chamber only a little company, including his wife and his physician, Dr. Preston; his secretary, Bannatyne, and his old friend, Campbell of Kinyeancleuch; probably, also, his colleague Lawson. In the afternoon he asked the 15th of 1 Corinthians to be read. "Is not that a comfortable chapter?" he declared. By and by came a request to his wife, "Read where I cast my first anchor." Mrs. Knox understood well what he meant: it was his favourite 17th chapter of the Gospel of St. John, to which he appears to have ascribed his earliest realisation of the Christian hope. Between seven and ten o'clock he lay, for the most part, still. Thereafter the group of watchers "went to ordinary prayers." "Heard ye the prayers?" whispered Preston to his patient. To the dying man the gate of Heaven appeared to have been already opened, and the sounds of earthly devotion had been transmuted into celestial voices. "I would to God that ye and all men heard them as I have heard them. I praise God of that heavenly sound." "Now it is come," he added soon afterwards. These were his last words; but when asked to make some sign that he "remembered upon the comfortable promises which he had taught to others," he raised his hand as if in response to the appeal. "Incontinent thereafter, he rendered the spirit, and slept away without any pain." [1]

The Reformer was buried on the following Wednesday, 26th November, in what was then the churchyard of St. Giles', at or near the spot afterwards indicated by his initials between the church and Parliament House. The concourse of people who followed his remains to their resting-place was preceded by a procession of nobility headed by Morton, who had been appointed Regent on the very day of Knox's death. "He was conveyed," writes Bannatyne, "with many a soreful heart." In his contemporary diary, James Melville records that after Knox's death the Regent gave him an honourable testimony that he neither feared nor flattered any flesh; and when the remains had been laid in the grave "without external ceremony," doubtless, as the Book of Discipline enjoined, but not without many a heart being uplifted in silent invocation, Morton repeated his disinterested witness in the often-quoted words, "Here lieth a man who in his life never feared the face of man." [2]

IV. The leading features of Knox's character reveal themselves prominently in the story of his life.

1. Morton's panegyric at his grave indicates

---

[1] Bannat., 288, 289.

[2] Melville, *Diary*, 60; Bannat., 290; *Vera Historia*, Laing, vi., 660; Calderw., iii., 242.

what most impressed his contemporaries. The man who began his career as a Reformer by standing, sword in hand, beside his "Master Wishart" amid peril, and accepted afterwards the pastorate of a besieged congregation which included Wishart's avengers; the man who denounced before King Edward's Court the intrigues of royal councillors; who taught publicly, for several months, Reformed doctrine under Mary Tudor, and who preached to the Protestants of Dieppe, not as they had been preached to before under the veil of night, but in the light of day; the man who, in 1556, boldly faced the prosecution of the Scottish hierarchy; who hastened, on his return to Scotland in 1559, to the "brunt of the battle" in support of his fellow-preachers; and who himself entered the pulpits of Perth, St. Andrews, and Edinburgh, in defiance of interdicts from the heads of Church and State; the man who, in the days of Mary Stuart's power, told her plainly that when princes "exceed their bounds" they are to be resisted by force, and who denounced publicly not only "pestilent Papists" but unfaithful Protestants who pandered to the Queen, plundered the Church, or betrayed the cause—such a man certainly merited a testimony to his fearlessness from one who himself had recently endured the Reformer's anathema.

2. Beneath Knox's courage towards men was his steadfast faith in God, in his own call to be

God's servant, and in the ultimate triumph of
what he firmly believed to be the divine cause.
He had, like other men, indeed, hours of depression, but none of complete despair; and his prevailing mood was devout and heroic confidence;
confidence not only in God but in himself, yet in
himself only as an instrument in the divine hands;
for he repelled all self-complacent thoughts as
temptations of the devil.[1]   The ground of his self-
reliance was the conviction that the mind of God
had been revealed to him; that he was a man
with a mission which he dared not neglect, and
with a message which he dared not withhold.
His memorable utterance at his trial in 1563,
has been accepted by posterity as the motto of his
life: "I am demanded of conscience to speak the
truth; and therefore the truth I speak, impugn it
who so list." [2]   With this confidence in God and
in himself as God's prophet, he was able himself
to rise above the anxiety caused by temporary
disaster, and also to impart somewhat of his own
faith to others.   The galley-man knew that he
would again preach God's truth in St. Andrews;
the exile on the Continent inspired his brethren
at home with the trust in God and zeal for truth
which produced the First Covenant: the defeated
and depressed host of Protestants who retired
from Edinburgh to Stirling in the autumn of 1559

[1] See p. 368.

[2] Knox, *H. of R.*, ii., 408.

were raised to fresh hope and effort by his assurance that God was on their side; and in the dark days of the Roman reaction under Mary, amid "the miserable dispersion of God's people," he was able to recall for his own and others' comfort the divine promise, "They that wait on the Lord shall renew their strength." [1]

3. The very strength of Knox's faith in the Reformation movement as the cause of God imbued him with an intolerance towards Romanists, as well as towards Romanism, with which it is impossible for us, amid altered circumstances, to sympathise, and in which many even of his Protestant contemporaries did not share. For his uncharitable judgments, on some occasions, regarding the actions and motives of opponents the best apology is that when a man is fighting for what is dearer than life it is not easy for him to keep his brain cool. His condonation of Beaton's and of Rizzio's assassinations, however unjustifiable, had as its foundation the firm belief that these men were enemies of God and of the people, enemies whom "the powers that be" persisted in supporting. Regarding his intolerance of the "Papistry," we must remember the great difference between the Roman Church of Scotland in the sixteenth century and the same Church in the twentieth. In the eyes of Knox, Romanism was the incurable embodiment not

[1] Knox, *H. of R.*, ii., 263.

only of idolatry and superstition, but of shameless immorality. The Church had for him become the "Synagogue of Satan"; and the testimony, previously adduced, of contemporary Romanists, like Ninian Winzet, shows the foundation on which the belief was based. Moreover, Knox's intolerant zeal was kindled and sustained by the fear that tolerance of Romanism would issue in the reascendency of Rome. The event proved that his anxiety was far from needless; for, as we have seen, humanly speaking, during the critical years 1565–66, it was, in great measure, Mary's unforeseen folly that saved the Reformed Church. Had the government of the country in the sixteenth century been in the hands of representatives of the people, Knox could have afforded to be tolerant. But with a Catholic Queen on the throne, with a considerable portion of the nobility and people still Romanist in sympathy, and with France and Spain ready to embrace any favourable opportunity of intervention, there seemed to be no effective security against the restoration of Romanism except its legal suppression.

4. Knox was undoubtedly a stern man, when conscience demanded severity: even the misfortunes of the Queen of Scots did not prevent him from censuring as "foolish pity" the omission of Moray to bring his sister to trial for the murder of her husband. But he was not all sternness. There was a vein of tenderness and sympathy in

the Reformer, of which lifelong conflict did not
deprive him. One catches a glimpse of his domestic tenderness in the almost intolerable pain
which he felt when compelled to chastise his children, and in his pathetic recall, after nearly twelve
years, of the benediction bequeathed to his two
sons "by their dearest mother of blessed memory." [1]   There must also have been many tokens
of sympathy, and some amiable features of character in a man who was repeatedly called in to
reconcile husband with wife and friend with
friend [2]; whom women consulted trustfully in
their difficulties, undeterred by the severe things
he had spoken of their sex in his *Monstrous Regiment;* and whom a young and high-born maiden
accepted as a husband when he was thrice her
age. Even in Knox's intercourse with Mary, as
we have seen, the uniform hardness of attitude
which he felt constrained to adopt is tempered
by an occasional kindliness not to be repressed.
Between the lines of his letter to Moray, when
their quarrel took place, one can discern the yearn-
ings of a wounded yet affectionate spirit [3];   and
the solicitude which he manifested on his death-
bed for the repentance and salvation of his former friend but eventual antagonist, Kirkcaldy, is
surpassed by nothing in Christian biography.

[1] Laing, *W. of K.*, vi., p. lvi.
[2] Knox, *H. of R.*, ii., 376, 324.
[3] *Ibid.*, ii., 382.

Ruins of the Cathedral of St. Andrew's.

5. Knox's unreserved self-dedication—at once devout and patriotic—to the Scottish Reformation stands out in fine relief, as compared with the self-seeking, or defective patriotism, which characterised not a few fellow-labourers in the cause. Protestant nobles reaped spoil from the Church's patrimony; Knox lived and died comparatively a poor man.[1] He never made "merchandise of the Word." Scottish churchmen with Protestant convictions left Scotland and failed to return when the cause of Reform had need of them; Knox was always in his own land when his presence was of real service; even in exile he ministered to the "faithful" at home through epistles of comfort or of admonition; and thrice over he left the quiet haven and congenial society of Geneva for the toil and conflict of a ministry in his native land. His incessant labours after his final return to Scotland, notwithstanding "a weak and fragile body "[2]; his fearless maintenance of divine truth, by voice and pen, before high and low; and his heroic faith, through which the faith of others was sustained, in the ultimate triumph of

---

[1] See his Will. Laing, *W. of K.*, vi., p. liii. Apart from over 800 pounds Scots due to Knox chiefly by his father-in-law, the Reformer's "inventory " after death amounted to less than 100 pounds Scots; and this sum included 100 merks sterling received through his first wife, " which [he says] I of my poverty extended to five hundred pounds Scots, to the utility and profit of my two sons."

[2] Smeton, *Responsio*, p. 115.

what he believed to be God's cause—justify the
judgment of a modern English historian, that "in
the entire history of the Reformation in this
island . . . no grander figure can be found than
that of Knox." [1]

V. The influence of Knox upon Scotland has
been signal and enduring. His assertion—bold in
that age—of the lawfulness of opposing and even
deposing rulers who transgress the laws or op-
press the people, fostered among his countrymen
that opposition to royal despotism which culminated in rebellion—rebellion which history has
vindicated and posterity has ratified. To Knox's
ministry, also, was largely due the growth of an
intelligent and earnest-minded middle class,
whom his preaching and writings educated and
enlightened; inspiring them with strong religious
convictions, and imbuing them with a sense of
national responsibility. Under his training the
smaller landowners, along with the merchants
and upper tradesmen—the most loyal and zealous
supporters of the Reformation—began to occupy
a distinct place in the national life and councils. [2]

To the educational sagacity of Knox Scotland
owes, further, in great measure, that parochial-
school organisation which during subsequent generations, when most other countries lagged behind
in this regard, provided for the poorest in the

[1] Froude, *H. of E.*, x., 193.
[2] *Ibid.*, 194.

land a sound religious and secular education. We
have only now, moreover, begun to realise some of
the Reformer's educational ideals.[1]

Knox was an ardent disciple of Calvin, and he
propagated in Scotland that grand, although one-
sided, recognition of the absolute sovereignty of
God, which is the chief basis of Calvinism. It
was the realisation of this great truth which afterwards sustained the Scottish Covenanters, as it
had already upheld the Huguenots of France and
the burghers of the Netherlands, in protracted
struggles against oppression. For, to those who
lived under a deep and devout sense of the Divine
Sovereignty, earthly rulers were but fellow-vas-
sals, to be served and obeyed only in so far as
they were faithful subjects and vicegerents of the
King of kings. It was a moderate Calvinism,
however, as we have seen, which Knox and his colleagues formally imposed, by authority of the
Estates, on the Scottish Church, through the original Reformed Confession, subsequently displaced
by that of the Westminster divines. The older
document is an embodiment of the more flexible
theology which, but for the influence of English
Puritanism, might have characterised the Scottish
Church of later days. It remains as the possible
starting-point from which a less rigid standard
of doctrine might be formulated for the present
time.

---

[1] See p. 246.

Scotland owes to Knox not its existing Presbyterian government,—this was the subsequent work of Andrew Melville,—but that which is the chief feature and main strength of Presbyterianism, viz., the full recognition (lacking in Episcopacy) of the Christian laity in the administration of the Church, combined with that orderly subordination (which Congregationalism fails to secure) of the whole Church to one representative and supreme authority. It is owing to Knox and his fellow-Reformers that the Scottish Church avoids the danger both of hierarchy and of anarchy; all its courts consisting of ministers and laymen, and its supreme executive, being not a court of clergy, whether bishops, superintendents, or moderators, but a General Assembly of ordained ministers associated on equal terms with lay elders representing the Christian people. In the sphere of congregational worship, it must be admitted that in one important particular Knox has impoverished the Scottish Church. In his anxiety to escape from temporary abuses, he removed from Scottish Christendom what it is now only beginning to recover, the stated and united commemoration of the fundamental facts and truths of Christianity,—a commemoration which is at once helpful to the Christian life, and a wholesome preservative against the obscuration of vital Christian doctrine, or its supersession with a cold and semi-pagan morality.

Not to John Knox, however, and other founders
of the Reformed Scottish Church, but to the later
Puritanism of the seventeenth century, provoked
by the offensive ecclesiastical policy of Charles I.,
is due the discontinuance in Presbyterian churches
of that happy combination of "Common Prayer"
and (within certain limits) "Free Prayer," which
was exemplified in the Reformer's *Book of Common
Order*.

2. The influence of Knox has notoriously extended to other countries than his own: to England, to Ireland, and to all those lands, within
and beyond the British Empire, which Scotsmen
have helped to people. The English and Irish
Presbyterian Churches claim the Scottish Reformer as their virtual founder; and even English
Protestantism, as a whole, may recognise Knox
as in some measure, at a critical period, its pre-
server. No biassed Scot, but the English historian, Froude, has declared that "but for Knox,
Mary Stuart would have bent Scotland to her
purpose, and Scotland would have been the lever
with which France and Spain would have worked
upon England" until Elizabeth had either been
"hurled from her throne," or been constrained to
go "back into the Egypt" of Romanism.[1]   It was
the descendants, moreover, of men taught by
Knox to withstand "the divine right of kings to
do wrong," who set the example to England of

[1] Froude, *H. of E.*, x., 195.

effective resistance to the Stuarts—resistance
issuing eventually in the establishment of a constitutional monarchy. "Thirty thousand armed
Covenanters, sitting down on Duns Law" in
1639, became, as Carlyle has epigrammatically
expressed it, "the signal for all England rising
up." [1]

Nowhere is the influence of Knox, more fully
recognised than in the United States and in the
Dominion of Canada. The Scottish Presbyterians
whom persecution drove, or colonising enterprise
drew, to North America in the seventeenth century, carried with them the sturdy spirit of civil and
religious independence which they had inherited
from Knox and his successors; and the Presbyterian churches which they founded—comprising
a population now more than double that of the
Presbyterians in the United Kingdom—hold the
foremost place alike in the past historical development and in the present theological activity of
American Christendom. [2] In the political sphere it
has been amply attested that during the period of
struggle which issued in American independence,
the earliest and most strenuous opponents of
British despotism were, for the most part, descendants of Scotsmen bred in the Church which

---

[1] *Inaugural Address to the Students of Edinburgh*, p. 63.

[2] *Influence of the Scottish Church in Christendom* (by the
present writer), 140–143, 261, 272; Hodge, *Presbyter. Ch.*,
i., 214; Webster, *Presbyter. Ch. in Amer.*, 66, 68.

Knox had moulded.[1] It is not without significance that a man whom Americans have specially
honoured as a foremost champion in their great
national conflict—John Witherspoon, President
of Princeton College—belonged to a family which
claimed kinship with Knox.[2] If, in the year
when the Reformer and his work are specially
commemorated, America is taking her full share
in the veneration of his memory, this is not merely
because she recognises him as one of the "heroes
of the Reformation," but also because her own
free institutions, educational achievements, and
religious zeal can be traced in great measure,
through acknowledged channels, to influence exerted by John Knox on Scottish Christendom.

ADDITIONAL NOTES TO CHAPTER XIV

I

Did John Knox live in "John Knox's House"?

Fully eleven years of Knox's life, after his final
return to Scotland, were spent in Edinburgh; but for
only one existing building in the city is the claim
made that it was (substantially) a house in which
the Reformer lived. This is the well-known house in
the Netherbow, near the junction of High Street
and Canongate, visited every year by thousands of

---

[1] *Infl. of Sc. Ch.*, 190, 282; Hodge, ii., 398; Briggs, *Amer.
Presbyterianism*, 347–351; R. E. Thompson, *Presb. Ch. in
U. S.*, 56, 57.

[2] Rogers, *Genealog. Memoirs of Knox*, pp. 162–164.

pilgrims from all quarters of the world. The house
is of considerable size, having four storeys, besides
a sunk floor and a garret. The outside stair is a
comparatively modern addition; but the motto:
"LVFE · GOD · ABOVE · AL · AND YI NICHT-
BOUR · AS · YI · SELF" is ancient. On the first
floor above the ground is the "Audience Chamber."
The second floor contains a panelled room used presumably for sitting and dining; a bedroom in which,
according to tradition, the Reformer died; and a
small apartment formed in the wooden casing of the
house, and supposed to be his study. The claim of
the building to have been Knox's home was discussed
in papers read before the Society of Scottish Antiquaries in session, 1898–99 [1] by two learned members
of that body, the late Mr. Robert Miller, Lord Dean of
Guild, who regards the alleged connexion of the house
with Knox as legendary, and Mr. Charles Guthrie,
Q.C., who vindicates its claim to be one of the houses
in which the Reformer lived. The case for and
against the house in Netherbow stands thus:

1. It was certainly not the abode of Knox, during
the greater part of his Edinburgh ministry. (a)
There is evidence of his having lived in another house
from September, 1560 (soon after his permanent
location in Edinburgh), until September 1566, and
probably until later.[2] This house, for which rent
was paid to Robert Mowbray, on Knox's behalf, by
the City Council, up to the latter date, was situated

---

[1] *Proceedings of Soc. of Ant. of Sc.*, xxxiii.

[2] Robert Miller, *John Knox and the Town Council of
Edinburgh* (in which the writer's contributions to the Society
are embodied, with additions), p. 74.

"John Knox's House," High Street, Edinburgh.

near the top of Warriston's Close in High Street. In
the seventeenth century a new tenement was erected
on the site which is now occupied by the City Council
Chambers; while the ground, attached to the house
as a garden in Knox's time, now forms part of the site
of the Cockburn Hotel.[1] It was in this house that
Marjorie Bowes, the Reformer's first wife, died, near
the close of the year 1560. To this house, also, his
second wife, Margaret Stewart, was brought home in
1564. It was in this building that in 1561 the Town
Council gave orders "with all diligence to make a
warm study of deals to the minister, John Knox,
within his lodging above the hall of the same."[2] (b)
There is evidence, further, that in 1568 and 1569,
Knox occupied a house belonging to one "John
Adamson and Bessie Otterburn, his spouse," whom a
minute of Council, in Nov., 1568, ordained to "cause
mend and repair the necessaries of John Knox's
dwelling-house." There is evidence, also, of rent
having been paid for this house in Nov., 1569. The
property may have been any one of three buildings
which belonged to this couple, two of which were on
sites now occupied by the modern St. Giles' Street;
while the third was situated on the north side of
the High Street opposite the corner of the present
Hunter Square.[3]

2. It is probable, in the absence of testimony to
the contrary, that Knox would not have a second
flitting prior to his departure from Edinburgh, in
May, 1571; and that during the interval of a year and

---

[1] *John Knox and the Town Council of Edinburgh*, pp. 80–87.

[2] *Ibid.*, p. 75.

[3] *Ibid.*, pp. 88–107.

25

a half from Nov., 1569, to that date, he remained in
the house repaired for his benefit. With regard to
this interval, however, and also to the three months
between his return to Edinburgh in August, 1572, and
his death in November of that year, there is much
uncertainty; for the Treasurer's accounts show a
blank during the period 1567–1581; and there is no
record of any meeting of Council between 1571 and
1573.[1]

3. It is very improbable that what is called
"John Knox's house" was occupied by him prior to
his departure from Edinburgh in May, 1571. That
house, as it is now admitted, was the property of
James Mosman, goldsmith, and of his wife, from the
year 1556 at latest; and in 1568 it was conveyed by
them to their son John, with reversion to themselves
of life-rent. In Feb., 1571, however, on the occasion
of the father's second marriage, he bought back the
fee from his son, and infeffed himself and his second
wife in the house; apparently with the object of
preventing her from being obliged to leave the family
abode in the event of his pre-decease.[2] It seems all
but certain that after this re-infeftment Mosman
would continue to occupy the house during the three
months which elapsed prior to Knox's departure for
St. Andrews in May of the same year. It is only
reasonable to assume that Mosman bought back the
house from his son because he continued to need it
for himself; and in the extant deeds connected with
the property, there is no specification of the house as

---

[1] *John Knox and the Town Council of Edinburgh*, p. 131.
[2] *Ibid.*, pp. 137, 138.

Room supposed to have been Knox's study in " John Knox's House,"
Edinburgh.

that in which John Knox lived. Such specification was a common, although not invariable usage.[1]

4. There remains the period from August, 1572, when Knox returned to Edinburgh, until his death, in November of that year. Did he re-occupy during this period the Adamsons' house? or did he reside in Mosman's house at the Netherbow? or did he live elsewhere? Certainty in this matter appears, meanwhile, to be unattainable; but we have a moderately old tradition in favour of the Netherbow house being for some time occupied by Knox; and this seems to be the only possible period. In 1796, the Hon. Mrs. S. Murray visited Edinburgh. She describes the house in the Netherbow, incidentally, as the house "whence Knox thundered his addresses to the people"; and she writes, not as if asserting a fact recently discovered, but rather as stating what was generally accepted.[2] Similarly, in a work published in 1806, the author mentions, not in a controversial way, but assuming, evidently, that no one would contradict him, that "among the antiquities of Edinburgh may be mentioned the house of the great Scottish Reformer, John Knox. It stands," he continues, "on the north side of the foot of High Street, projecting into the street."[3] The tradition, accordingly, must have been already of pretty long standing before the close of the eighteenth century. (a) Is there anything which renders the truth of the tradition improbable? (b) Is there any way of reasonably accounting for

---

[1] *John Knox and the Town Council of Edinburgh*, pp. 138–140.

[2] *A Companion and Useful Guide to the Beauties of Scotland*, p. 117.

[3] Stark, *Picture of Edinburgh*, p. 102.

the existence of the tradition except on the assumption of its being true?

(a) We have seen that in February, 1571, Mosman intended to remain in the house and to secure it as a home for his widow. But the times were troublous: the population of Edinburgh was divided into two factions, that of the Queen and that of the Regent. Mosman was a keen partisan of Mary. It is known that some of her adherents took refuge about this time in the Castle, which was held for the Queen by Kirkcaldy, and that at some date prior to 29th of May 1573, when the garrison surrendered, Mosman himself was received within its walls.[1] He had good reason to be afraid; for when the Marian party had been overcome he was executed, along with Kirkcaldy, as a traitor. A truce for two months, indeed, had been arranged on the 31st of July, 1572, and had afterwards been extended to the close of the year; but a goldsmith, who was also a "rotten Papist" and a keen politician, could not afford to run the risk of molestation and even spoliation amid civil war; and it is not unlikely that before the truce was concluded, Mosman had transferred himself, his wife, and his valuables to the safer precincts of the Castle.[2] In these circumstances there was nothing to prevent the Town Council, (who were responsible for Knox's accommodation) putting the Reformer, with

---

[1] See paper of Sir Dan. Wilson in *Proceedings of Soc. of Ant. of Sc.*, xxv., 161.

[2] Miller's argument (*John Knox and the Town Council of Edinburgh*, p. 142) that "as a shrewd business man, Mosman would attend to his goldsmith's booth as long as he could" is not convincing, in the light of the danger which would thus have been incurred.

Mosman's consent, or even without it, as a temporary
tenant into the house from which the owner himself
may by this time have fled.[1]   Although differing
from Knox, both in religion and in politics, he may
have been glad, in such a time, to have his house
safely occupied in his absence by a man whom his
fellow-citizens, as a whole, respected, and whom
Kirkcaldy himself, on account of former friendship,
would be unwilling to molest.   It has been argued,
indeed, not without some force, that both the houses
which Knox certainly received from the town as
residences were in the close neighbourhood of St.
Giles', in accordance with the ancient custom to have
kirk and manse adjacent to each other; and that
this arrangement was particularly necessary in Knox's
weak condition.[2]   But, on the other hand, we are
told that Knox "caused himself to be carried to St.
Giles' "[3]   (410 yards from the Netherbow); moreover, to be close to St. Giles' was also to be near the
guns of the Castle; and the Reformer's friends in
the Council may have preferred to locate him out of
the reach of danger.

(b) As regards the possible origin of the tradition,
on the assumption of its being historically unfounded,
ample evidence, it must be admitted, exists that even
before the Reformer's time, the name of Knox, even
that of *John* Knox, was associated with the Netherbow.   In the immediate vicinity were "Knox's
lands" and "Knox's Close."[4]   But this evidence,

[1] Guthrie, *Proceedings*, etc., xxxiii., 260, 261.

[2] Miller, pp. 146–149.

[3] Laing, *W. of K.*, vi., 633.

[4] Miller, pp. 152–158.

although not to be disregarded, does not point definitely to the particular building known, at least since the eighteenth century, as John Knox's house, being associated with other Knoxes [1]; and while a sufficient reason for the selection of this building (apart from any real connection with *the* John Knox) may exist, and afterwards become known, it is not yet forthcoming.

On the whole, while the belief that this house in the Netherbow was the chief home of Knox must be given up, there is nothing intrinsically improbable in the supposition that the Reformer lived there during the last three months of his life; and while the tradition is not demonstrably old enough to be quite trustworthy, and may any day be contradicted by fresh documentary evidence, it cannot be dismissed as mere legend, and claims consideration as at least possibly, if not probably, true.[2]   Even more interesting, however, to many, although less generally regarded, is the indisputable fact that the chief part of the Municipal buildings in which the magistrates and City Council of Edinburgh conduct their proceedings, occupies the exact site where Knox lived not for three months, but for six or seven years—years, moreover, which included the most influential period of his life.

---

[1] Guthrie, p. 270. " The nearest John Knox to John Knox's house he [Mr. Miller] locates 110 yards away."

[2] *Cf.* Hume Brown, *Life of Knox*, ii., 319 (written, however, before the papers of Mr. Miller and Mr. Guthrie were contributed to the Society of Antiquaries, in Session, 1898–99). " Against the tradition that points to Mosman's house as a residence of Knox no satisfactory evidence has been adduced."

II

Particulars Regarding Knox's Person and Family

1. The Latin epistle sent by Sir Peter Young to Beza in 1579 (along with the portrait reproduced in the *Icones*) contains an interesting description of the Reformer's personal appearance in later years.

His stature was a little under middle height; his limbs were graceful and well proportioned; his shoulders of more than average breadth; his fingers longish; his head of moderate size; his hair black; his complexion darkish; his face not unpleasing in appearance. In his countenance, which was grave and severe, a certain graciousness was united with natural dignity and majesty.

When he was angry, his brow showed a masterful spirit. Beneath a rather narrow forehead, his brows stood out like a ridge; and his cheeks were somewhat full (as well as ruddy), so that his eyes appeared to recede and to lie deep in his head. The colour of his eyes was dark blue [or a dark bluish grey]; and their glance was keen and bright.

His face was longish; his nose beyond the average length; his mouth large; his eyes full, the upper lip being the fuller of the two; his beard was black, with white hairs intermingled; it was a span and a half long, and moderately thick.—(Hume Brown, *Life of Knox*, ii., 323).

2. Knox's widow married, two years after his death, Andrew Ker, of Faldonsyde, near Melrose, and survived till about 1612. Knox's two sons, who had lived in Northumberland for five years or more, matriculated at the University of Cambridge in 1572,

eight days after their father's death, and were admitted to St. John's College at the age of 15½ and 14 respectively. Nathanael died at Cambridge in 1580. Eleazer, after an academic career of considerable distinction, became Vicar of Clacton Magna, in the archdeaconry of Colchester, in 1587, and died four years later. Neither son left issue. Of Knox's three daughters by his second wife, the eldest, Martha, married, in 1584, Alexander Fairlie, of Braid, near Edinburgh, the son of a friend of her father. The second, Margaret, became the wife of Zachary Pont (son of Robert Pont, minister of St. Cuthbert's) eventually appointed Archdeacon of Caithness in 1608. The youngest, Elizabeth, married in 1594, the famous John Welsh, minister of Ayr, who was imprisoned and exiled on account of his opposition to the ecclesiastical policy of James VI. In 1621, when physicians recommended him to visit Scotland on account of his failing health, his wife applied personally to the King for permission. James asked her who her father was. "John Knox," she replied. "Knox and Welsh," exclaimed the King; "the devil never made sic a match as that!" "May be," was the smart rejoinder, "for we never speired his leave." The King said that her husband might return to Scotland if he would submit to the bishops. "Please, your Majesty," replied the high-spirited daughter of Knox, extending her apron, "I would rather kep [catch] his head there."

There appears to be no certainty of any descendant of Knox being now in existence. (Rogers, *Geneal. Memoirs of John Knox*, 137–146; Laing, *W. of K.*, vi., pp. lxiii.–lxxii.)

Stone, in Parliament Square, Edinburgh, marking approximately the place of Knox's grave in what was formerly the Churchyard of St. Giles'.

INDEX

A

Absolution in early Reformed Church, 244–245

Adamson, Patrick, his three kinds of bishop, 357

Alesius, 34, 40, 41, 92

Annand, Dean John, 77

"Appellation" of Knox, 139, 188

Arbuckle, Franciscan Friar, 79

Argyle, fifth Earl of, mediates between Regent, Mary, and Reformers, 200; Protestant leader, 203

Arran, James, second Earl of, appointed Regent, 50; Protestant policy, 51–53; recantation and absolution, 54–56. *See* Châtelherault

Arran, James, third Earl of, aspires to marry Mary Stuart, 259; supports Knox's protest against the Holyrood Mass, 269

Assembly, General, of 1560, first, in 1560, 250; precautions of, before Mary Stuart's return, 262–263; freedom of, demanded, 293; of June, 1565, demands ratification of Reformation, 308; of December, 1565, appoints national fast, 311; of December, 1566, protests against reinstatement of Archibald Hamilton,

323; intercedes for English Puritans, 324; of June and July, 1567, supports Confederate Lords, 329; of February, 1569, supports Regent, 335; of 1572, acquiesces in modified episcopacy, 353

B

Balnaves, Henry, 73; his treatise on *Justification by Faith*, 85

"Band," patriotic, April, 1560, 219

Bannatyne, Richard, memorials of Knox's last days, 363

Bartholomew, Massacre of St., 361; proceedings in Scotland on occasion of, 362

Beaton, David, Cardinal and Primate, 45, 49; arrested and imprisoned, 50; released and triumphant, 55, 56; causes Wishart's martyrdom, 61; assassinated, 68, 69

Beaton, James, Primate, 33, 39

Berwick, Knox's ministry at, 95–99

Beza, Theodore, friend of Knox, 22, 46, 121, 141; includes Knox among his *Icones*, 22, 121; warns Knox against prelacy, 355